A SUDDEN RAI

For Tara Werner

NICHOLAS TARLING

A Sudden Rampage

The Japanese Occupation of
Southeast Asia, 1941-1945

HURST & COMPANY, LONDON

First published in the United Kingdom by
C. Hurst & Co. (Publishers) Ltd.,
38 King Street, London WC2E 8JZ
© Nicholas Tarling, 2001
All rights reserved.
Printed in Malaysia

ISBNs
1-85065-436-0 *casebound*
1-85065-584-7 *paperback*

CONTENTS

PREFACE

This book describes the origins, the methods and the results of Japan's occupation of Southeast Asia in the Second World War. Japanese publicists and policy-makers had recognised that the colonial regimes in that region would not last for ever. They had not envisaged a conquest, but the impact of the European war, and in particular the reaction to it of the United States, seemed to make that necessary. It was possible to prepare military operations that enjoyed brilliant success. It was not possible to prepare occupation policies that had a similar prospect. To a large extent, indeed, they were improvised, often turning to account models derived from the experience of Manchuria or of the homeland itself. For some Japanese, indeed, the invasion was a work of 'liberation', and those who tried to extricate Japan from the war as it became clear that it would be defeated emphasised that rationale. On balance, however, it must be concluded that the peoples of the region 'liberated' themselves, taking advantage of the interregnum. Any sense of obligation to the Japanese was reduced by the violence of their soldiery, which was not directed merely against the defeated Europeans, and the inadequacy of their administration, which was not explained simply by wartime conditions.

The occupation is best seen in the context of Japan's relationship with the outside world over the longer term. Chapter 1 of the book mainly focuses on the period between the Meiji Restoration and the end of the First World War, and Chapter 2 on the interwar period and the outbreak of the Pacific war.

The third chapter offers a short narrative of the course of the conflict, drawing attention also to the attempts to make peace. The fourth chapter discusses the ideology of the Greater East Asia Co-Prosperity Sphere, as it shaped and was shaped by the thoughts and actions of politicians and administrators, diplomats and soldiers.

Chapter 5 outlines the political activities of the Japanese in occupied Southeast Asia. Dealing with them mainly country by country, it places them in the context of previous colonial experience, as well as in the context of the war itself. Chapter 6 focuses on the economic activities of the Japanese in wartime Southeast Asia in general and in each country. Again an attempt is made to relate what they did to prewar experiences as well as to wartime conditions. The final chapter assesses the contribution the occupation made to postwar Southeast Asia in the light of the suffering and destruction it brought.

The book draws on the work of many scholars writing in English or translated into English, to whom the author acknowledges his indebtedness with gratitude. Its title borrows a phrase Matsuoka Yosuke used at the 29th Liaison Conference on 11 June 1941.

New Zealand Asia Institute   Nicholas Tarling
The University of Auckland
March 2001

ABBREVIATIONS AND ACRONYMS

AFPFL	Anti-Fascist People's Freedom League
BB	Binnernlands Bestuur (European civil service)
BDA	Burma Defence Army
BIA	Burma Independence Army
Biba	Bigasang Bayan (National Rice Granary)
FMS	Federated Malay States
GEAPS	Greater East Asia Co-Prosperity Sphere
ICP	Indo-Chinese Communist Party
IIL .	Indian Independence League
IJN	Imperial Japanese Navy
INA	Indian National Army
ISEAS	Institute of Southeast Asian Studies (Singapore)
JMBRAS	*Journal of the Malay(si)an Branch Royal Asiatic Society* (Kuala Lumpur)
JSEAS	*Journal of Southeast Asian Studies* (Singapore)
JSEAH	*Journal Southeast Asian History* (Singapore)
JSS	*Journal of the Siam Society* (Bangkok)
Kalibapi	Kapisanan sa Paglilingkod sa Bagong Pilipinas (Association for Service to the New Philippines)
KMM	(Kesatuan Melayu Muda (Union of Young Malays)
KMT	Kuomintang (Chinese Nationalist Party)
KNIL	(Koninklijk Nederlandsche-Indische Leger) (Royal Netherlands Indies Army)
KRIS	Kekatuan Rakya Istimewa (Special Strength of the People) or Kesatuan Rakyat Indonesia Sememanjung (Union of Peninsular Indonesians)
Makapili	Kalipunang Makabayan ng mga Pilipino (Patriotic League of Filipinos)
MAS	*Modern Asian Studies* (Cambridge)
Masjumi	Madjlis Sjuro Muslimin Indonesia (Consultative Council of Indonesian Muslims)
MCP	Malayan Communist Party
MIAI	Madjlisul Islamil a'laa Indonesia (Greater Islamic Council of Indonesia)
MPAJA	Malayan People's Anti-Japanese Army

NARIC	National Rice and Corn Corporation
NU	Nahdlatul Ulama
OSS	Office of Strategic Services
Parindra	Partai Indonesia Raya (Greater Indonesia Party)
Peta	Pembela Tanah Air (Defender of the Fatherland)
Primco	Prime Commodities Distribution Control Association
Putera	Pusat Tenaga Rakyat (Centre of People's Power)
PSII	Partai Sarekat Islam Indonesia
RICOA	Rice and Corn Administration
SOE	Special Operations Executive
USAFFE	United States Armed Forces in the Far East
VOC	Vereenigde Oost-Indische Compagnie (United East India Company)

MAP

Southeast Asia (1941–5)

N

JAPAN

OKINAWA

TAIWAN
(Formosa)

Manila

PHILIPPINES

Davao

ELEBES
ulawesi)

DUTCH
NEW
GUINEA

PAPUA
NEW
GUINEA

(Port.)

TIMOR

AUSTRALIA

1

EQUALITY AND OPPORTUNITY

Japan, Asia and the West

The Japanese incursion into Southeast Asia in 1941-2 was revolutionary in effect. It was also a revolution in Japan's policy. Yet the connection between the Japanese and what they called the *Nan-yo* dated back at least to the sixteenth and early seventeenth centuries. Then they had taken part in the commercial expansion brought about by the development of China's economy under the Ming dynasty, by the voyages of the European adventurers and by the exploitation of Japan's own silver mines. There were Japanese settlements in several of the port cities of early seventeenth-century Southeast Asia, made up of merchants, persecuted Christians and lordless samurai. Baan yiipun on the outskirts of the Thai capital of Ayudhya had perhaps 1,500 settlers at the height of its prosperity,[1] and there were other settlements at Faifo (Hoi-an) in the southern realm of Vietnam, at Phnom-penh in Cambodia, and in the European capitals, at Manila in the Spanish-held Philippines and at Batavia (Jakarta), the centre of the Asia-wide enterprises of the Dutch East India Company (VOC). Yet, by contrast to European enterprises, the Japanese were not backed by the state.

The state was much more involved in Northeast Asia. Victorious in the long civil wars of the sixteenth century, Toyotomi Hideyoshi had declared in 1590 that 'even if a land be thousands of miles distant, I shall deeply achieve amity and so build with foreign lands the spirit of the four seas as one family'.[2] He sent a letter to Manila, threatening an attack if it did not submit, and the Spaniards there sent emissaries.[3] Northeast Asia's geographical pro-

[1] Yoneo Ishii, ed., *The Junk Trade from Southeast Asia*, Singapore: ISEAS, 1998, p. 1.
[2] Quoted from [hereafter q.] Mary E. Berry, *Hideyoshi*, Cambridge, MA: Harvard Univ. Press, 1982, p. 212.
[3] Rafael H. Soriano, 'Japanese Occupation of the Philippines', Ph.D. thesis, Univ. of Michigan, 1948, p. 29.

1

pinquity gave it a strategic importance, however, that Southeast
Asia entirely lacked.

Hideyoshi invaded Korea in 1592, mobilising some 225,000
soldiers for the purpose. Pusan was taken, then Seoul. When Pyon-
gyang was also taken, the Chinese intervened across the Yalu. A
truce was followed by a new Chinese expedition, and the Japanese
retreated on Pusan. The collapse of peace negotiations was followed by Hideyoshi's second expedition in 1597. A standstill
agreement was facilitated by his death in September 1598. The
reasons for this extraordinary venture are controverted. It is argued
that Hideyoshi 'was inspired by the need of some great undertaking to distract attention from popular grievances, use all available
manpower, and stimulate production', and it is true that the end of
the civil wars had caused unemployment and distress.[4] Several leading merchants, on the other hand, were opposed to conquest, and
'thought legitimate trade more lucrative'.[5] The pride and ambition
of a 'great conqueror' were also involved. His aim, it was said, was
'immortalizing himself with the name and fame of his power'.[6]
'Even China will enter my grip.'[7]

As Shillony reminds us, the five decades of war and expansion,
1895-1945, were exceptional in Japan's history. The abortive Mongol
invasions of the thirteenth century and Hideyoshi's expeditions
contrasted with 'a very long period of peace in which Japan did not
engage in international conflicts, except for the activities of sea
pirates prior to the seventeenth century'.[8] Hideyoshi's successors,
the shoguns of the Tokugawa clan, indeed abandoned his policy,
and adopted quite a different one, that of *sakoku*, the closed country. Korea sent regular embassies, 'received with great ceremony by
the Shogun's government'.[9] The Japanese in Southeast Asia were
'not only abandoned by their home government but ... lost any hope
of repatriation'.[10] Some found their way into intra-regional trade;
others entered the employment of their former rival, the VOC.

[4] G. Sansom, *A History of Japan*, London: Cresset, 1961, II, 361.

[5] Ibid., p. 362.

[6] q. Berry, *Hideyoshi*, p. 213.

[7] q. ibid., p. 207.

[8] In James W. White, Umegaki Michio and Thomas R. Havens, eds, *The Ambivalence of Nationalism*, Lanham, MD: Univ. Press of America, 1990, p. 187.

[9] G. Sansom, *A History of Japan 1615-1867*, London: Cresset, 1964, p. 230.

[10] Ishii, *The Junk Trade*, p. 1.

Japan still sought overseas goods – sappanwood, pepper, deer hides, sharkskin, silk – but they were brought by the Dutch and the Chinese. There were, too, quota limits on the goods, and access was limited to Nagasaki. The VOC supported this policy, which enhanced its monopoly position. The edicts prohibited the entry of Iberian missionaries and the departure of Japanese nationals. The Dutch in effect carried out this edict as far as their main European competitors, the Portuguese, were concerned: they 'did their best to cut foreigners off from Japan'.[11]

When the *sakoku* policy was abandoned, and the Meiji Restoration carried out after 1868, Korea was, not surprisingly, the initial focus of Japan's foreign policy in Asia. Korea was indeed the source of division among the oligarchs who had come to rule Japan. Charles Le Gendre, a French-born American, advised the new foreign office in Tokyo in 1872-3 that Korea was important, not in itself, but as 'a first step towards Japan'. In his *Progressive Japan: A Study of the Political and Social Needs of the Empire* (1878), he wrote of Soejima, a prominent Gaimusho figure: in reference to Korea and Manchuria, 'the possession of these two strategical points to any would-be conqueror of either Japan or China had not escaped his penetration' and, given 'the culpable indifference of China regarding these countries, which in their condition were but abandoned grounds, inviting occupation by any power that would think fit to possess their territory', he felt that 'Japan had a right, if not to annex Corea and aboriginal Formosa, at least to place them under her protecting arm'.[12]

Korea provoked the regime by refusing to recognise it. Some of the oligarchs wanted retaliatory action. The majority preferred to temporise, though imposing the treaty of Kanghwa, and also incorporating the Liuchiu islands as Okinawa. Twenty years later, better prepared and facing a critical Diet, the government went to war with China over Korea. Once the war began, Japan's ambitions expanded. Its aim came to be, the British minister put it, 'to humble China to the dust, and for Japan itself to rise on the ruins of that empire'. 'Why, it is often said, should Japan not conquer and retain China as part of her dominions precisely as England

[11] Bob Tadashi Wakabayashi, *Anti-Foreignism and Western Learning in Early-Modern Japan*, Cambridge, MA: Harvard Univ. Press, 1986, p. 65.
[12] H. Conroy, *The Japanese Seizure of Korea, 1868-1910*, Philadelphia: Univ. of Pensylvania Press, 1960, p. 40.

has done India?'[13] As a result of Japan's success, China recognised the independence of Korea by the treaty of Shimonoseki and ceded the Liaotung peninsula in southern Manchuria. To the latter, however, France, Russia and Germany objected, and in face of the Triple Intervention, Japan backed down.

In 1874 the Japanese had sent an expeditionary force to Formosa, ostensibly to punish aborigines who had murdered castaways. China claimed sovereignty and paid the costs of the expedition.[14] Under the treaty of Shimonoseki Japan acquired Formosa and the Pescadores. Two short-lived republics were proclaimed in opposition to the transfer, and guerrilla opposition continued after the Japanese flag was hoisted. Though Japan made a joint declaration with Spain on their respective spheres of interest,[15] moving further south was not entirely ruled out. The question arose because of the revolt against Spanish rule in the Philippines that began in 1896. The Filipino nationalists were aware of Japan's victory over China. José A. Ramos and Doroteo Cortes went to Japan to solicit its help before the uprising, and contacted the nationalist Oi Kentaro. The revolutionary Katipunan apparently delivered an appeal to the captain of a Japanese training vessel, the *Kongo*, in May 1896, looking for the aid of Japan, as France had once aided the American revolutionaries.[16] While, however, some super-patriots (*shishi*) wanted to go further, and while, indeed some Europeans expected Japanese intervention, the ruling oligarchs, bearing the Triple Intervention in mind, were cautious.

The intervention of the Americans only redoubled that caution. When the *shishi* Sakamoto Shiro suggested occupying Manila while Admiral Dewey was blockading it, the General Staff in Tokyo replied: 'The control of the South Sea is an idea [to be achieved] in Japan's national policy, but today is an inopportune time. You must positively not meddle in the war'.[17] For a while, however, it seemed uncertain whether the United States, when

[13] q. S. Lone, *Japan's Modern War*, Basingstoke: Macmillan, 1994, p. 43.

[14] George H. Kerr, *Formosa: Licensed Revolution and the Home Rule Movement*, Honolulu: Univ. of Hawaii Press, 1974, p. 10.

[15] J.M. Saniel, *Japan and the Philippines*, Quezon City: Univ. of the Philippines, 1962, p. 182.

[16] Usha Mahajani, *Philippine Nationalism*, St Lucia: Queensland Univ. Press, 1971, p. 405.

[17] q. Saniel, *Japan and Philippines*, p. 232.

it defeated Spain, would retain the islands. Okuma Shigenobu, then foreign minister, told the Japanese representative in Washington that the extension of US sovereignty, or a protectorate, would be acceptable. If, however, the Americans did not wish to undertake either, Japan would be willing to join America, singly or with another power, 'to form, subject to proper conditions, suitable government for the territory in questions under the ... protection of the guaranteeing powers'.[18] In the event, the United States assumed sovereignty under the treaty of Paris, though its becoming an 'imperial' power was the subject of deep domestic controversy.

These two periods in Japan's foreign policy, those of Hideyoshi and early Meiji, clearly have similarities as far as Korea and Southeast Asia are concerned. Another perspective suggests continuities that take in the intervening *sakoku* phase as well. Throughout its history, Japan had always been concerned with its great neighbour China, with China's changes of fortune and changes of policy towards its neighbours. The Japanese attitudes varied from an unspoken humility to an outspoken aggression. The policies of Hideyoshi and the Tokugawa were both policies towards China as well as towards Korea and Southeast Asia. One was an aggressive policy that provoked China's intervention; the other was a more realistic policy that accepted China's dominant position in East Asia without undergoing the formula of tribute. It avoided direct political and commercial contacts.

The nineteenth century marked a difference. The Western powers, intervening with force in East Asia, defeated China. It was indeed Britain's success in the first Anglo-China war of 1840-2 that compelled the Japanese to abandon the policy of *sakoku*, hitherto upheld by what had been the leading European maritime state, the Dutch. The approach of the Russians to the Pacific, and their contacts with Japan, had led the Tokugawa to intensify the exclusion edicts. 'Henceforth', the 'no second thought' edict of 1825 declared, 'whenever a foreign ship is sighted approaching any point on our coast, all persons on hand should fire on and drive it off'. It added that it was better to fire on the Dutch ships by mistake than not to fire at all.[19]

---

[18] q. P. Oblas in Chaivat Khamchoo and E.B. Reynolds, eds *Thai-Japanese Relations in Historical Perspective*, Bangkok: Innomedia, 1988, p. 53.

[19] q. Wakabayashi, *Anti-Foreignism*, p. 60.

On 29 August 1842, by contrast, a new edict declared that the shogun wished to 'apply a merciful policy in all things'. '[A] measure leading to firing immediately and without knowing their reasons, at people who are in difficulty, at the mercy of the waves, and who are only coming to ask for food, wood and water, even when they are foreigners, could not be applied anywhere in the world.'[20] The same day China signed the treaty of Nanking, following its defeat by the British. Under it, the first of the 'unequal treaties', the British secured Hong Kong and the grant of extra-territorial jurisdiction in a number of treaty ports.

In 1854 the 'black ships' of the US Commodore Perry were to prompt the shogunate to make the first of Japan's unequal treaties. It was followed by further treaties, including one with the leading power of the day, Great Britain, in 1858. The treaties not only revolutionised the conduct of Japan's foreign policy: they also contributed to the overthrow of the Tokugawa. Seclusion had been designed to assure its dominance after a long period of civil war. Its enemies among the lesser clans made out that ending seclusion would be a national humiliation, however, and used that to gather patriotic opposition. The object was not simply that Japan must survive the change in Asia's politics, but that the Tokugawa should not. A short period of civil war followed more than a decade of struggle, and an oligarchy drawn largely from the western clans overthrew the shogun and ruled in the name of the 'restored' emperor from 1868.

Its caution in the subsequent years can be related to its recognition that Japan had also to undergo a process of modernisation if it was to undo the treaties and take its place as an equal with other nations. That was the aim, as the Meiji emperor told President Grant:

We expect and intend to reform ... so as to stand upon a similar footing with the most enlightened nations and to attain the full development of public right and interest. ... It is our purpose to select from the various institutions prevailing among enlightened nations such as are best suited to our present condition and adopt them, in gradual reform and improvement of our policy and customs, so as to be upon an equality with them.[21]

---

[20] q. P. Akamatsu, *Meiji 1868*, London: Geo. Allen & Unwin, 1972, p. 86.

[21] q. Iwata Masakazu, *Okubo Toshimichi*, Berkeley: Univ. of California Press, 1964, p. 156.

The incursion of the West had not, of course, eliminated China as the essential focus of Japan's policy, but there was now, as it were, a third party, which had, at least for the time being, reduced the power of its great neighbour but had its own role to play. Japan's attitude to the West, it may be suggested, reflected some of the ambivalence it had earlier displayed towards China. It included caution and deference, but also ambition and even aggression. '[W]e now commanded the world's respect', Foreign Minister Mutsu claimed after the Sino-Japanese war, but 'we had also become the object of some envy'.[22] In fact the Japanese had been fighting a regional force rather than a national one. The British would not have allowed them to proceed to Chinese capital, and in fact set limits to their campaign.[23] Even before the Triple Intervention, other powers were imposing limits on Japan.

The role of China itself in this new struggle also varied. Was Japan to support it against the West? Or would it be better to anticipate the West and continue to take advantage of its weakness? The period of seclusion had nurtured dreams still more extreme than those of Hideyoshi. 'With proper spirit and discipline on our part', Sato Nobuhiro had argued, 'China would crumble and fall like a house of sand within five to ten years.'[24] After the first Anglo-China war, the Satsuma *daimyo* argued that even a defensive policy required Japan to have bases in China, in Fukien and Taiwan, for example.[25] The other possibility in what was now a three-cornered struggle was to ally with China against the West. That was the basis of the 'pan-Asian' (*ajia shugi*) approach.

Japan's answer, as Lone suggests, was ambivalent, '[W]e have no leisure', Fukuzawa Yukichi wrote, to await the 'awakening' of China and Korea, 'and together revive Asia'. We must abandon Asia (*datsu-A ron*) and treat Asians 'just as Westerners do'.[26] Others were ambivalent, too. Chinese and Korean leaders might admire Japan's achievements, but were bound to realise that 'any future Japanese development could only be at their expense'. That only made it more difficult for Japan to choose. 'Who could say that China, so vast and unconquerable, would not re-emerge as a major force, and

[22] q. Lone, *Japan's First Modern War*, p. 45.

[23] Ibid., p. 165.

[24] q. W.G. Beasley, *The Meiji Restoration*, Stanford Univ. Press, 1972, p. 80.

[25] Iwata, *Okubu Toshimichi*, p. 190.

[26] q. George Hicks, *Japan's War Memories*, Aldershot: Ashgate, 1997, 1998, p. 8.

then her first target for revenge would be Japan?'[27] Meiji Japan
pursued a policy of expediency, on balance, therefore, 'abandon-
ing' Asia.

In a sense that solved another question. What were the limits of
Japan's objectives? Neither conquest nor seclusion were good
preparations for a modern policy: both encouraged and frustrated
grandiose ideas of Asian expansion. The new policy of independence and 'equality' with Western countries was also open-ended.
What did equality mean? Equality of status was not equality of
power. What measure of independence did the Japanese
envisage? In a world of nations, unequal in power if not also in
status, independence could not be absolute. As the Sino-Japanese
conflict suggested, Japan's objectives were largely defined by
others – fortunately for Japan, in Lone's view: they contained the
war.[28] Its policy was again one of expediency. It was defined by the
opposition it met.

The Meiji Restoration

It was, of course, true that internal factors played a role in the
making of Japan's foreign policy, though they did little to set limits
to its ambitions. Foreign policy had all along been affected by
domestic. The Korean ventures of the 1590s, the initiative of a
conqueror, were also in some way related to the conclusion of the
civil war. The policy of *sakoku*, made feasible by the non-interven-
tion of the Manchus and by the support of the Dutch, was also part
of the Tokugawa shogun's attempt to avoid the renewal of civil
war: its opponents would be constrained not only by an internal
system of checks and balances, but by being cut off from outside
sources of wealth and weaponry.

The Meiji Restoration in part resulted from the change in
Japan's position that Britain's defeat of China brought about. But
it was also the result of a struggle within Japan to determine
whether the Tokugawa clan would continue to dominate, and if it
did not, what would replace it. Foreign and domestic policies were
always closely related. The statesmen and others who were involved,
or thought they should be involved, had to weigh both the external and the internal when they were endeavouring to reach decisions or set priorities.

[27] Lone, *Japan's First Modern War*, p. 172.

[28] Ibid., p. 165.

It is, however, arguable that the Meiji oligarchs set a course in Japan's domestic affairs from which there was little prospect of deviating. At first, indeed, it was not clear that the new government would after all be so different from the old. Fukuzawa thought it might only be 'a collection of fools from the various clans got together to form another archaic anti-foreign government which would probably drive the country to ruin through its blunders'.[29] The attitude of the new rulers was in some measure pragmatic. What, however, they were determined upon was the establishment and maintenance of an effective government. The outcome was a centralised and authoritarian system markedly different from its predecessor. Yet, though its leaders were no 'collection of fools' and did not form an 'archaic anti-foreign government', they inherited something of the past. What they chose from it, and what they chose from other sources, determined the character of the Restoration. In turn that deeply affected what followed.

The central change in modern Japan's history, the Restoration has naturally been the subject of historiographical controversy, itself also prompted by the subsequent course of Japan's domestic and foreign policies. The initial reaction in the West was a mixture of astonishment and admiration. 'The Japanese', wrote Sir Rutherford Alcock, a former British ambassador, in 1872, 'are the only nation in the history of the world that has ever taken five centuries at a stride, and devoured in a decade all the space dividing feudalism and despotism from constitutional government and the other developments, commercial and municipal, of modern life.'[30] 'The political and social revolution which created modern Japan, has been as sudden and complete as a theatrical transformation scene,' Sir Alexander Wedderburn added in 1878.[31]

The transformation attracted the attention of other Asian peoples, not only the Europeans – the Javanese, for example, as well as the Filipinos. Was there 'some kind of abacus', the hero in Pramoedhya's novel *Child of the Nations* asks, to 'use to calculate how many dozens of years it will take the Javanese to reach the same level as the Japanese'?[32] After the Second World War, admira-

---

[29] q. Carmen Blacker, *The Japanese Enlightenment*, Cambridge Univ. Press, 1964, p .27.

[30] q. Yokoyama Toshio, *Japan in the Victorian Mind*, London: Macmillan, 1986, pp. 109-10.

[31] q. ibid., p. 113.

[32] *Child of All Nations*, trans. Max Lane, Melbourne: Penguin, 1982/1991, p. 315.

tion for the Meiji Restoration was renewed. Could it be a model for the transformation of other 'backward' or postcolonial countries into modern states?

The experience of the intervening years had produced rather differing interpretations, renewed in more recent times both within Japan and outside it. Writing at the end of the 1930s, the Canadian E.H. Norman pointed out:

[o]nce the crumbling bastions of the Tokugawa rule had been stormed in the war for the Restoration (1867-8) and after the flank attacks upon the feudal immunities and privileges in the years following had been executed, the new Government set itself as firmly against any demand for further reform on the part of the lower orders as it did against attempts to restore the old regime. Such a policy required a powerful state-machine, a centralized government with a considerable constabulary or military force at its disposal.[33]

More recent writings have suggested that some of the Restoration's success in fact derived from the experience of the Tokugawa phase, in which decentralisation and diversity had fostered innovation and competition, and that such qualities were destroyed by its policies. There were few single-teacher private schools left by the 1880s, a contemporary lamented: 'The world has progressed: our teachers ride to brick-built schools in private rickshaws, students line up for military-style physical training, wear uniforms and caps – every activity is becoming splendidly organized, or regimented, to put it bluntly.'[34] The sense that, with the Restoration, Japan had taken a decisive turn, one that foreclosed other options, also prompted an interest in the protest movements of the time.

In light of the barbarous adventures to be launched in the 1930s in name of the Japanese people and a second 'Restoration'..., we may applaud that they did not go meekly into the new era. But for the very same reasons, we may also lament that the Tengu gangs and the rice cooperative visionaries did not force more fundamental reform with more extreme action.[35]

Creating a strong government was necessary both to perserve Japan's independence in a changing world and to avoid subversion at home. The aim was clear, the method less so, but the Meiji

[33] E.H. Norman, *Japan's Emergence as a Modern State*, New York: IPR, 1940, p. 8.

[34] q. R. Rubinger in Marius B. Jansen and Gilbert Rozman, eds, *Japan in Transition*, Washington, DC: Public Affairs Press, 1986, p. 229.

[35] William W. Kelly, *Defence and Defiance in Nineteenth Century Japan*, Princeton, Univ. Press, 1985, p. 291.

oligarchs knew that finding it was their challenge. Okuma Shigenobu asked Shibusawa Eiichi if he knew the words 'O myriad gods,
aid me according to your divine plan', a Shinto prayer. The *bakufu*
had been overthrown, Okuma went on, and imperial government
restored.

> Our duty is to advance further and build a new Japan. For this reason those
> who are participating in the planning of the new government are the myriad
> gods. The gods have gathered together and are now in the midst of dis-
> cussing how to proceed in building the new Japan. It is not only you who
> does not know where to start. No one does.[36]

The oligarchs found their way towards creating the instruments of
the Meiji state, displacing the feudal structures within which they
had been brought up. At times they differed among themselves,
but there was a fundamental consensus.

That focused on the strength and prosperity of Japan, the guarantee of its future and of its 'equality' with other nations. The
differences were about the means of attaining the goal, and about
the timing or sequencing of the steps to be taken. One faction in
the early Meiji governments emphasised the need for economic
and technological strength (*fukoku*) and the other the need for a
strong army (*kyohei*), and they would at times pull the oligarchy in
contrary directions. Yet

> gravitation of power to these two major groupings ... enabled a cohesive
> official response to internal and external crises. Innocuous elements were
> eased aside and obstreperous elements eliminated. For the most part, com-
> promise and decision by a kind of bureaucratic collegial consent were skil-
> fully practised.[37]

Though the forms of Meiji government were not immediately
established, the oligarchs moved step by step towards a centralised
and authoritarian system. They were influenced in part by their
concern about Japan's future. It must not follow the fate of Poland,
as Kido Takayoshi put it after his visit to Europe:

> If a country is divided among a multitude of petty rulers, ... the lines of
> policy are multiplied, inasmuch as each prince will seek his own advantage
> and devise schemes for his own gain. Under such a system the national
> strength is dissipated and although the fellow rulers may know each other's
> strength, how will they stand in comparison with foreign nations? How

---

[36] q. A. Craig in Jansen and Rozman, *Japan in Transition*, p. 67.
[37] H.J. Jones, *Live Machines*, Vancouver: Univ. of British Columbia Press, 1980,
p. 27.

could they ever withstand a powerful enemy whose forces were harmoniously united?[38]

In the years preceding the Restoration, Japan had become more fragmented, not less, and the military mobilisation of the domains was an argument for their abolition. That carried out in 1871 was, in Yamagata Aritomo's words, 'a second Meiji Restoration'.[39] The resistance to the changes the oligarchs introduced only increased their disposition to strengthen the government. The most substantial challenge was the Satsuma rebellion of 1876-7. But by then the government had created a conscript army, and its success redoubled its authority.

The army occupied a special place in Meiji Japan. Like the centralisation of government, the creation of a national military force was designed to strengthen Japan in a changing world, but also to consolidate its government at home. Indeed, it seems likely that, at least in the case of the army, the latter objective was initially more important than the former. 'The ultimate objective of establishing a conscription system was to provide the nation security in an unfriendly world, but the immediate aim was to devise the most satisfactory method of organizing a national military force loyal to the emperor, which would maintain internal order and solidify the control of the central government.'[40] No foreign power had presented a military threat to Japan. After an initial panic in the 1850s, 'military expansion was spurred by the anticipation of internal rather than external conflict.'[41] Japan's own politics were remilitarised in the renewed internal struggles of the 1860s.

Many of the Meiji leaders were young military leaders who had come to power in their domains in that phase. They were naturally aware of the importance of military power, but also of the need to avoid its dispersal. Characteristically, the 'gods' took radical steps, moving on from the abolition of the domains to the imperial edict on national conscription of December 1872. That condemned the very samurai class from which the leaders were drawn.

After living a life of idleness for generations, the samurai have had their stipends reduced and they have been authorized to take off their swords so

[38] *The Meiji Japan through Contemporary Sources*, Tokyo, 1969-72, p. 102.

[39] q. Umegaki Michio in Jansen and Rozman, *Japan in Transition*, p. 91.

[40] Roger F. Hackett, *Yamagata Aritomo in the Rise of Modern Japan*, Cambridge, MA: Harvard Univ. Press, 1971, p. 60.

[41] D. Eleanor Westney in Jansen and Rozman, *Japan in Transition*, p. 171.

that all strata of the people may finally gain their rights to liberty. ... Neither the samurai nor the common people will have the status to which they were accustomed in the past. Nor will there be any distinction in the service they render to their country, for they will all be alike as subjects of the Empire.[42]

In their reforms the Meiji oligarchs picked up those the Tokugawa had begun, the potential of which had indeed been one reason for the final decision to overthrow it. It had established a training academy for the army in Tokyo, staffed by French army officers, and the new regime continued to look to the French model, even after the defeat of France in 1870-1. At first suspicious of the connection with the Tokugawa, the new regime soon came to employ French officers as the core staff of the military academy. When it was decided to adopt conscription, it was again the French model that was followed. The Japanese force was much smaller – only some 41,000 in 1878 – and, but for political reasons, could have been recruited entirely from the samurai class. As it was, the officer class was predominantly samurai in origin, mainly from the clans of Satsuma, Choshu and Tosa, which had played a large part in the Restoration.

While the suppression of the Satsuma rebellion was a success for the new army, it also revealed deficiencies, and from 1878 the leadership began, under the influence of Katsura Taro, to look more to the German model. The conscription law was modified, and the German system of one year's active training for graduates of the middle and higher schools was introduced. 'Katsura aimed to identify the military's elite, the officer corps, with the village's, the landlord class, and thus increase army prestige and at the same time reinforce both military and village order.'[43]

In France, too, tension had become apparent between the new republic and its elected assembly on the one hand, and the standing army led by professional soldiers on the other. The German monarchy, by contrast, had insulated the army from the Reichstag, and avoided responsible government. Only in 1883, however, did the German general staff free itself from the war minister's jurisdiction and gain direct access to the emperor. Aided by the fluidity of

[42] q. J. Pittau, *Political Thought in Early Meiji Japan*, Cambridge, MA: Harvard Univ. Press, 1967, p. 23.

[43] R. Smethurst, *A Social Basis for Prewar Japanese Militarism*, Berkeley: Univ. of California Press, 1974, p. 7.

Meiji institutions, and the lack of a parliament, the Japanese general staff, created in 1878, gained 'the right of supreme command' before the German. The ultimate object was to guarantee the state against any move away from the imperial system towards a constitutional or republican regime. The *kempeitai* or military police dates back to this period. Founded in 1881, it was a semi-independent branch of the Japanese army, working with Army Intelligence, and commanded by a lieutenant-general responsible to the war minister.[44] Its brief covered subversion.

The navy, for which the Meiji oligarchs looked to British models, grew more slowly than the army. That partly reflected the lack of influence of its leaders, who came from the Tokugawa era, and partly the priority accorded internal security in the 1870s. Only in 1888 was a separate navy general staff created, and only in 1893 did it become formally independent of the navy ministry. That was a departure from the British pattern, though within the navy British traditions were all the more influential for the lack of a countervailing samurai tradition, and until the 1890s the Japanese bought British ships. Only then did production at the Tsukiji and Yokosuka shipyards rise significantly.

In their early years – decisive as they were for the future – the oligarchs put their emphasis on the strengthening of their regime within Japan, carrying through a programme of changes that was at once pragmatic in its approach and yet focused on creating an unprecedented degree of uniformity and centralisation. Two other features – also significant for the future – were also apparent. One was that the oligarchy ruled in the name of the emperor. That helped it to carry out change, since it could meet conservative opposition by appealing to a still older tradition, dubious though its relevance was. The same strategy, moreover, also helped it to oppose change, against which it could invoke past authority. The drawback was that others, too, would be able to invoke higher authority, and claim to act in the name of the emperor, whatever the views of the government of the day. The *shishi* of the late Tokugawa had indeed justified their rebellion in such a way. The emperor they sought to restore still did not rule after 1868. But his counsellors and advisers could be held responsible for what was done in his name, and blamed when it went wrong.

[44] Ma. Felisa A. Syjuco, *The Kempei Tai in the Philippines*, Quezon City: New Day, 1988, p. 6.

The constitutional arrangements were unlikely to offer a way of resolving the problem. Despite their search for effective authority, the arrangements the oligarchs made for its exercise were somewhat incoherent. Their government was 'government by crony'.[45] They did not provide institutions that would help in reaching decisions, selecting options or establishing priorities: they relied on personal contacts. In subsequent decades, the system, if such it may be called, became more diverse and more complex. But that was often the result of improvisation, and did not necessarily enhance coordination.

That was the more significant in as much as Japan's policies increasingly affected other countries besides Japan itself. The revolution had been carried through partly as a result of internal tension, and partly as a result of external insecurity. The latter, it was widely agreed, was an argument for resolving the former. Beyond that measure of agreement, there was plenty of room for disagreement, and faction struggles, both within domains and among them, had been articulated about those disagreements. The same was true after the Restoration. The oligarchs differed about the priority of a Korean expedition. Again that provided a precedent. Political differences within Japan, whatever their domestic origin, tended to focus on its external relations.

Okubo Toshimichi had argued against the expedition on grounds of both domestic and foreign expediency. 'The basis of our government is not yet firmly established.' Relations with Russia and Britain were 'uncertain. ... If we open fire on Korea, Russia will fish out both the clam and the bird and get a fisherman's profit. Thus we should not begin a war in Korea now.' Britain was 'especially powerful' in Asia,

watching with a tiger's eye. Our foreign loans depend on Britain. If there is trouble and we become poor, Britain will surely interfere in our internal affairs on that pretext. Look at India ... observe carefully the process by which India became a colony. We must build our industry, our exports, etc. It is our most urgent business.[46]

The priority in foreign affairs was to revise the unequal treaties. The majority accepted this. But Saigo Takamori disagreed, and was later involved in the Satsuma rebellion. Itagaki Taisuke, a member

[45] P. Duus, *Party Rivalry and Political Change in Taisho Japan*, Cambridge, MA: Harvard Univ. Press, 1968, p. 244.
[46] q. Pittau, *Political Thought*, pp. 29-30.

of the lesser Tosa clan, also resigned. He turned to the 'popular rights' movement.

That was not a movement designed to create a democratic state: of such, indeed, there were then very few examples among other nations. Rather it was a move to limit oligarchy. 'When we humbly reflect upon the quarter in which the governing authority rests', ran Itagaki's petition, 'it rests not with the emperor nor with the people, *but solely with the oligarchical few*. ... The people's access to the government is cut off, and their grievances have no way to reach the government.' What was needed was 'the promotion of public discussion', and, for that, 'the establishment of a national assembly by popular election. ... *Only then will limits be placed upon the power of the oligarchical officials* and will security as well as prosperity be enjoyed by governors and governed alike.'[47]

The majority oligarchs accepted the idea of a constitution. They had other reasons. One was apparent from Ito Hirobumi's observation that there was 'no nation in Europe which does not have a constitutional form of government'.[48] If Japan followed suit, it would better placed to deal with European nations and secure the end of the unequal treaties. The history of those countries, Ito argued, also suggested that none could avoid the impact of the French Revolution of 1789. To avoid disturbances, it was better to accept changes: 'Even as we control the trends, there will be no violence. ... Progress will be orderly and we will set the pace of progress.'[49]

It was, however, essential to centre Japan's institutions on the imperial house. 'If there is no cornerstone, politics will fall into the hands of the uncontrollable masses, the government will become powerless and the country will be ruined.'[50] The German example proved attractive in this, as in the military sphere: it combined an elected Reichstag with an imperial institution. There was a time factor, Ito's colleague, Inoue Kaoru, suggested in 1881. 'To put into effect a Prussian-style constitution is an extremely difficult task..., but at the present time it is possible to carry it out and win over the

---

[47] q. Umegaki Michio, *After the Restoration*, New York University Press, 1988, p. 184.

[48] q. George Akita, *Foundations of Constitutional Government in Modern Japan*, Cambridge, MA: Harvard Univ. Pres, 1967, p. 12.

[49] q. ibid., p. 29.

[50] q. Jansen and Rozman, *Japan in Transition*, p. 21.

majority and thus succeed. This is because the English-style constitution has not become firmly fixed in the minds of the people.'[51] By the end of the decade the Diet had been set up, though the franchise was far narrower than that for the Reichstag: only 460,000 were eligible to vote out of a population of 50 million.

Yet in the early 1890s Diet and oligarchy were at odds. It was only when the government resolved to intervene in Korea – twenty years after the majority of the oligarchs had rejected the idea – that it won parliamentary support. The fact was that the opposition put strength and prosperity ahead of democracy. What the advocates of popular rights

aimed at was not the defence of individual liberties against arbitrary State action, but Government acceptance of the position that the goal of making Japan a rich and strong nation could also be achieved through a representative form of Government. ... Everyone thought ... on the basis of the conviction that national unity and independence should take precedence of all other things. This was as true of the oligarchs as of their opponents. They differed only in respect of the methods to be used in achieving the common goal.

The civil liberties movement 'degenerated into a kind of chauvinism instead of fostering liberal traditions'. Oi Kentaro was a case in point: a popular rights man in 1876; a Korean expansionist in the 1880s.[52] The connection was again significant for the future.

Some found it possible to reconcile the two concepts on the basis of a foreign policy of liberation. One of them was Okuma, who broke with the oligarchs in 1881, joined the popular rights movement, and was also a supporter of a 'pan-Asian' approach to foreign policy. In the event Japanese governments – even that of Okuma when he finally became prime minister – preferred the 'realistic' approach. Any attempt to pursue the 'idealistic' approach, or to combine the two approaches, was undermined by that preference.

Industrialisation

Industrialisation was to link Japan and other parts of the world in yet other ways, sometimes intensifying the traditional mixture of aggression and apprehension, sometimes modifying it. From today's perspective industrialisation appears to be the most significant act of the Meiji oligarchs. That it was their decision is also

[51] q. Pittau, *Political Thought*, p. 166.

[52] P.A. Narasimha Murthy, *The Rise of Modern Nationalism in Japan*, New Delhi, 1973, pp. 119, 131.

significant. In this, as in other fields, foreign expertise was available. It was also necessary to have the determination to use it, the ability to choose the most relevant models, the authority to implement the choices. Those the oligarchs possessed. Like their other revolutionary changes, industrialisation was designed both to strengthen Japan and to entrench their power. Initially the government played a direct role in industrialisation. In subsequent decades government and industry remained closely connected, but their attitudes to the outside world did not always converge.

Given the paucity of its natural resources, the industrialisation of Japan made it dependent on the resources of other parts of the world. The major issue was the means of securing them. Was it best done by forceful or by peaceful means or, if that were conceivable, a mixture of the two? In a sense the decision to industrialise had not made Japan independent: it had made it dependent on the outside world in a new way.

The Meiji government promoted industry, both to reduce dependence on imports and to enhance exports, and also as part of its attempts at social reconstruction. Again, however, the 'gods' did not so much plan as improvise within a generalised set of goals, committed to finding solutions to the problems that emerged 'because they were committed to remaining in power.'[53] The lack of private capital required the input of government finance, but, given Japan's technological backwardness, subsidy was not enough. The government resorted to setting up industries itself. One was the Senju woollen mill. As the Interior Department's petition of 1876 stated

Although it is the natural task of the people to undertake such an enterprise, there is no way to carry out this project except to make it a government affair. How could our people at present carry out such a large and exacting enterprise that requires an enormous investment? It is necessary ... that such an enterprise be first established by the government. Thus the people may be given instruction and guidance.[54]

Later, as the petition envisaged, the industries were made over to private enterprise. One reason was the government's shortage of money: it wished to limit its resort to foreign loans, and relied largely on the land tax to finance its wide-ranging reforms. '[T]he peasant

[53] Thomas C. Smith, *Political Change and Industrial Development in Japan*, Stanford Univ. Press, 1955/65, p. 34.

[54] q. ibid., p. 65.

had to be relentlessly exploited for the modernization of the non-agricultural sector of the economy.'[55]

Concerned to maximise exports, the government wanted to restore the reputation of silk in the overseas market. It set up a model factory at Tomioka, employing four hundred women to learn from French instructors. 'The women employed by the government, after they have been given instruction in expert reeling, will be transferred to the various districts, where they may be used to teach silk reeling.'[56] It was in the private or privatised textile industry that labouring conditions were at their worst: 'The largely female labour force was actually in bonded servitude, employees being indentured by their families.'[57]

Utilising 'under-used' female labour was essential to the transformation. In 1900 'textiles constituted about 40 percent of manufacturing output and 60 percent of the critical export commodities that permitted the import of raw materials and advanced technology'. The textile labour force was 60-80 percent female.[58] By that time, some argue, Japan had achieved industrial 'take-off', though 'competitive economic strength' was achieved only in the First World War, 'when Japan moved from the status of debtor to creditor nation'.[59]

That success did not, however, determine that Japan's relationships with the outside world were to be primarily economic in nature. There were yet other factors, besides the concern about security, the inheritance of expansionist ideas, the ambitions of the popular rights movements and the fact that industrialisation itself depended on access to raw materials on the one hand and to markets on the other. Japan accepted Malthusian doctrines: it was a land of too many people and too little food. Relatively few Japanese were in fact to emigrate, even to countries where their immigration was acceptable. Japan's success in increasing rice yields was remarkable. Even so, population pressure was an argument for expansion, not surprisingly, given the extraordinary migrations of

[55] Ibid., p. 85.

[56] q. ibid., p. 59.

[57] Jones, *Live Machines*, p. 20.

[58] Sharon H. Nolte, *Liberalism in Modern Japan*, Berkeley: Univ. of California Press, 1987, p. 90.

[59] Jones, *Live Machines*, p. 21.

the European peoples in the nineteenth century, those who had colonies of settlement and those who did not as well.

Merely economic expansion had not been enough for Western states either: they offered the example of imperialism, as well as of industrialisation. The Japanese navy used the arguments of Alfred T. Mahan. In 1894, when Japan went to war with China, Tokutomi Soho argued that it was necessary 'to transform Japan, hitherto a contracting nation, into an expansive nation'. It must become a world power, an imperial power, a civilising power.[60] The resources of an empire might make up for Japan's deficiencies, and imperial control might be a way of making sure of them. Yet it is not easy to argue that the Japanese set out with a plan to build an empire, though in the event they built one.

Colonial policy

The striking features of the Meiji achievement are exertion of authority and compliance with it. When they first established a colonial empire the Japanese had their own Meiji model in mind:

> It is not too much to say that Japanese colonialism in its formative stage cannot be understood outside the perimeters of *fukoku kyohei* – that collective exhortation of early Meiji that bound all of Japan's modernizing reforms to the twin goals of a strong and prosperous state. All that Japan undertook in its colonies during the first quarter century of the empire was based upon Meiji experience in domestic reform.[61]

And yet, of course, there were differences. The object of the Meiji oligarchs was to preserve Japan's independence, and that objective was offered as a rationale to those they ruled. Such a backing for the model could not be readily secured in colonial territories. In Korea and Taiwan, indeed, the Japanese imperialists set themselves against nationalism. A rather different line was to be adopted in Manchuria and in Southeast Asia, but remnants of the Meiji approach persisted.

The adoption of such an approach was not, however, an indication that Japan had set out to build an empire. Indeed it may rather signal the reverse. In this field, as in others, it followed a pragmatic approach, though setting it within the broad objectives

---

[60] Iriye Akira, *Pacific Estrangement*, Cambridge, MA: Harvard Univ. Pres, 1972

[61] Ramon H. Myers and Mark R. Peattie, eds, *The Japanese Colonial Empire, 1895-1945*, Princeton Press, 1984, p. 23.

of maintaining Japan's strength and prosperity. Colonial powers commonly applied in their dependencies legal and administrative concepts familiar in the metropolis. Japan was even less concerned than others with their relevance or acceptability:

> Lacking a colonial tradition or colonial expertise, Japan, not surprisingly, in modernizing its newly acquired territories [Taiwan and Korea], set out with vigor, confidence, and determination to apply those strategies, so recently successful in the homeland, to the administration and development of its empire.[62]

Colonial policy was to continue to reflect both that pragmatism and that focus. The Korean independence movement of 1919 was met with a change of style rather than of substance: Governor-General Saito Makoto's administration 'strove to remove the more obnoxious trappings of colonialism while at the same time further entrenching Japanese rule'.[63] Taiwan received its first civilian government in 1919. Under it assimilationist policies were accelerated, while a 'nugatory degree of local autonomy was introduced'.[64]

In the later acquisitions more account was taken of nationalist aspirations. That was evident with the creation of the puppet state of Manchukuo in 1933, and it was again evident in the case of some at least of the territories acquired in Southeast Asia after December 1941. Back in 1917 Tsurumi Yusuke had argued, in his *Travel Sketches of the South Seas*, that 'Democracy, even if progressing slowly, is germinating in the countries of the South Seas. ... It would be Japanese "imperialism" in a true sense for Japan, as an advanced country, to help and lead the progress of those countries.'[65]

Again, however, pragmatism was to be the rule, and the focus was on Japan's strength and prosperity, and indeed survival. The object was not to build an empire, but to acquire resources. Liberating the region from colonial rule was more of an *ex post facto* justification than a purpose. It was also designed as a means of securing a settlement with the Allies.

---

[62] Ibid., p. 24.

[63] Carter J. Eckart *et al.*, *Korea Old and New*, Seoul: Ilchohak, 1990, p. 281.

[64] Simon Long, *Taiwan's Last Frontier*, Basingstoke: Macmillan, 1991, p. 29.

[65] Shimizu Hajime, 'Southeast Asia in Modern Japanese Thought: The Development and Transformation of "Nanshin Ron" ', thesis, Australian National Univ. (ANU), Canberra, 1980, p. 32.

The Russo-Japanese war

The role of Japan in the region and in the world was not, of course, only defined by Japan itself. That was the case in the seclusion phase, and it was true in the post-seclusion phase, too. Japan's policies were not determined simply by its own politics and ideologies, its economic needs, its security imperatives. They were also, perhaps indeed to an unusual degree, determined by the actions and reactions of others. Of those the Japanese were certainly deeply conscious, even though they interpreted them in their own ways. The others now included, as before, the Chinese, the Koreans and the Taiwanese, and they later again included the peoples of Southeast Asia. They also included the Europeans, now far more powerful, the Russians, who had penetrated to the Pacific shores, and the Americans, coming from across the Pacific. It was about the Russian and the Western states that Meiji Japan was, of course, most apprehensive.

The caution of the ruling oligarchs was redoubled by the Triple Intervention. Whatever their opponents' rhetoric, they recognised Japan's relative weakness, not only as a state that had to 'catch up' with the West, but as a state with limited resources that had to be amplified, by one means or another, and used with maximum effectiveness. Their reforms within Japan were carried through with that as well as their own power in mind. Their activities outside Japan again reflected their recognition of reality. Whatever the future might hold as far as access to resources or acquisition of empire were concerned, their initial priority was quite clear: the undoing of the unequal treaties. To that internal reforms contributed, and so did the country's new skills in international diplomacy.

Diplomacy is more effective as a supplement to strength than as a substitute for it, but by the turn of the century Japan could consider itself and be considered as the possible ally of a European state. In 1902 it concluded an alliance with Britain, the leading naval and imperial power. Their common concern was Russia, which was building the trans-Siberian railway, had acquired Port Arthur and failed to withdraw its troops from Manchuria after the powers intervened in the Boxer uprising in China. That was a threat to Japan's security, as well perhaps as a threat to its larger hopes, whatever they might be, on the mainland. Britain was concerned at the threat to the integrity of China, a pillar of a nineteenth-century policy designed also to ensure a commercial 'open door'.

The alliance was not, however, simply a counter to Russia. For Japan it was a kind of recognition: it was a sign that it was among the major powers of the world. For Britain it was, somewhat paradoxically, a sign that its nineteenth-century primacy was passing, and, more particularly, that the rise of Germany was prompting it to concentrate more of its effort in Europe. There were further paradoxes.

The alliance led to the Russo-Japanese war, begun, without declaration, by the Japanese in February 1904. Britain had hoped that the alliance would deter Russia. But the Japanese had taken the alliance as a guarantee that, if they went to war with Russia, there would be no repetition of the Triple Intervention of 1895. No one expected the Japanese to win, as they did: ' "Jap" the Giant Killer', as *Punch* put it.[66] The image yet remained of a power that looked to the opportunities provided by others, and to allies who, if they did not afford support, at least held the ring. In the struggle, indeed, soldiers had been squandered like 'human bullets'.[67]

The victory had been the result of a mighty effort, but the readiness to produce it was too little recognised outside Japan, and nationalists in Japan believed that, thanks to a government that was excessively deferential to foreign powers, the rewards had been quite inadequate. In subsequent years, however, the British renewed the alliance, increasingly with the view to exercising a restraining influence on their partners.

There was yet another paradox. Elsewhere in Asia, the Japanese victory was hailed as an Asian triumph over a European power, and the supposed example inspired nationalist movements in India and, as Pramoedhya's hero ruefully suggests, in Southeast Asia. Not all were ready to recognise what Japanese success involved. The defeat of the Chinese might be received with a certain relish, given the criticism nationalists offered of their economic prominence and their own nationalist aspirations. But Japanese forces had acted with great violence at Port Arthur in 1894, and they had destroyed an admittedly hastily conceived republic in Taiwan and then faced prolonged guerrilla warfare.

[66] James C. Thomson *et al.*, *Sentimental Imperialists*, New York: Harper & Row, 1981, p. 140.
[67] Lone, *Japan's First Modern War*, p. 152.

One outcome of the Russian defeat was the incorporation of Korea into a growing Japanese empire, initially as a protectorate, and then, after the brutal suppression of the rebellion of 1908-10 and the assassination of the resident general, Ito Hirobumi, in 1909, by direct incorporation, the fulfilment, as General Terauchi saw it, of Hideyoshi's dream.[68] 'Japan's victory in its war with Russia is also a great advance for us,' declared the Vietnamese nationalist, Phan Boi Chau, '... our consciousness has been raised'. Phan Chu Trinh had reservations.[69]

Versailles and Washington

The First World War – the 'grace of Heaven' for Japan[70] – helped Japan to become a creditor nation. It also facilitated the expansion of its empire. That was the more feasible because of the aftermath of the Chinese Revolution of 1911. The revolutionaries had sought to strengthen China, the weakness of which had been demonstrated so vividly by recent events; but overthrowing the Manchus was insufficient. The new republic lapsed into instability, civil war and warlordism, an invitation to further foreign intervention. Should Japan take up the pan-Asian cause or continue to take advantage of China's weakness? The latter course remained the more tempting.

Nor, even prewar, were the other powers interested in China so well placed as before to restrain Japan, whatever policy it adopted. Britain was its ally. The terms of the alliance had been modified in 1905, partly perhaps in the hope of exercising some kind of restraining influence on the Japanese. But its focus on Europe, and in particular the reduction of its naval forces to meet the threat from Germany, reduced Britain's capacity to sustain the integrity of China. Japan had come to terms, too, with Britain's entente partners, France and Russia, while the United States – though, like Britain, it endorsed the integrity of China and the Open Door – accepted the outcome of the Russo-Japanese war, Japanese dominance over Korea and south Manchuria.

[68] J.W. Dower, *Empire and Aftermath*, Cambridge, MA: Harvard Univ. Press, 1979, p. 39.

[69] q. Tran My-Van, 'Japan through Vietnamese Eyes (1905-1945)', *Journal of South East Asian Studies, JSEAS*, 30, 1 (March 1999), pp. 128-9, 132-3.

[70] q. Shimazu Naoko, *Japan, Race and Equality*, London and New York: Routledge, 1998, p. 102.

On the outbreak of the world war, it was difficult for Britain to turn aside Japan's offer of help, though following British representations, the foreign minister declared that his country sought no territorial aggrandisement, and gave a limited assurance to the Chinese minister. Japan absorbed the German concession in Shantung, and later in the year it acquired the islands in the Pacific that the Germans had picked up on the dissolution of the Spanish empire.

In 1915, however, it turned back to China, and presented the 21 Demands. 'When there is a fire in the jeweller's shop', the Japanese minister in China explained, 'the neighbours cannot be expected to refrain from helping themselves.'[71] And yet that neighbour now had a government led by Okuma, the old popular rights politician and supporter of pan-Asian policies. Indeed, it was criticised by the military oligarch, Yamagata Aritomo. The 21 Demands were inconsistent with 'the self-protection of Asians and ... the co-existence and co-prosperity of China and Japan'.[72] Okuma told him that the *genro* (elder statesmen) had no responsibility for national affairs, and Kato Takaaki, the foreign minister, regarded their advice as gratuitous.[73]

The demands – which required China's assent to any subsequent arrangement over Shantung – involved strengthening Japan's position in Manchuria, made Fukien a Japanese sphere of influence, prohibited the cession of any port or island to another power, envisaged the use of more Japanese advisers and the granting to Japan of more railway concessions. They were later described by Chiang Kai-shek, a leading nationalist figure, as 'the grand culmination of all the unequal treaties',[74] and the Chinese retaliated with boycotts of Japanese goods.

Absorbed in the war, Britain could do nothing. Not yet in the war, the US decided against intervention: 'It would very likely provoke the jealousy and excite the hostility of Japan', President Wilson thought, 'which would first be manifested against China itself.'[75] When the United States entered the war in 1917, it recog-

---

[71] q. Jerome Chen, *Yuan Shih-kai*, Stanford: Stanford Univ. Press, 1972, p. 156.

[72] q. Tsunoda Ryusaku *et al.*, eds, *Sources of Japanese Tradition*, New York: Columbia Univ. Press, 1964, II, 210.

[73] q. Joyce C. Lebra, *Okuma Shigenobu*, Canberra: ANU Press, 1973, p. 119.

[74] q. Hackett, *Yamagata Aritomo*, p. 285.

[75] q. Chen, *Yuan Shih-Kai*, p. 156.

nised the 'special interests' that Japan derived from its geographical propinquity.

Although China also entered the war, it failed to regain Shantung in the peace negotiations at Versailles. The day, 4 May, when this decision was published became another day of humiliation, but it also gave its name to a new movement to redeem China. The Japanese had been all the more determined to secure Shantung because of their failure to secure the inclusion in the covenant of the new League of Nations of a declaration in favour of racial equality. In such ways, the new principles that Wilson hoped would inform the conduct of international relations were qualified.

Yet there was a change, and the Japanese recognised it. 'Today it is a worldwide trend to honor pacifism and reject oppression,' declared Makino Shinken, the plenipotentiary at the peace conference, 'Everywhere in the world the so-called Americanism is advanced,' and conditions have definitely altered since the days of the old diplomacy.'[76] Japan's policy in Korea did not really change, but its policy in China did.

In some ways the Asian counterpart of the Versailles treaties, the Washington agreements of 1921-2 also represented an extension of the new diplomacy. In a four-power treaty, the United States, Britain, France and Japan agreed to respect each other's rights in insular possessions in the Pacific; to confer on any dispute; and to communicate in the case of threats from other powers. A five-power treaty – also including Italy – prescribed ratios for building capital ships and aircraft carriers, and also prohibited modernising naval fortifications in East Asia. A nine-power treaty, involving also Belgium, the Netherlands, China and Portugal, committed the parties to the integrity of China and the Open Door.

The Anglo-Japanese alliance was brought to an end. The United States had long been opposed to it, it had hardly proved effective as a restraint on Japan and it epitomised the old diplomacy. Britain, now the lesser power, accepted the US view. The two powers had also been anxious to avoid a naval competition, and they were agreed, at least in principle, on the integrity of China and the Open Door.

The reasons Japan accepted the treaties are less obvious. The British alliance had been a pillar of Japan's policy and a sign of its equality with other powers, and now it had to be given up. Yet

[76] q. Iriye, *Pacific Estrangement*, p. 232.

participation in the new diplomacy signified equality as did participation in the old, and while the naval agreements did not allow 'parity', the ratios, and the limits on fortification, ensured Japan's security in East Asian waters. Endorsing the integrity of China and the Open Door was acceptable partly because the Washington powers envisaged only a gradual undoing of the unequal treaties, and partly because the Japanese governments of the early and mid-1920s adopted the so-called 'China friendship' policy associated with the foreign minister, Shidehara Kijuro.

His vision of Japan was a democratic nation, with a developed commerce and industry, seeking and relying upon overseas markets, but not through territorial expansion, which would destroy international cooperation and provoke trade boycotts:

> Like England we must obtain our sustenance abroad and our products must go to overseas markets. China's markets and materials mean to other countries only more trade; to Japan they are vital necessities ... the Open Door and equal opportunity in China mean economy, if not actual salvation, for Japan.[77]

In face of a Chinese nationalism impatient to undo the unequal treaties – whether it was allied to communism, as before 1927, or whether it was at odds with it, as from 1927-8 – that policy was difficult to sustain. Nor was domestic support for Shidehara's approach unequivocal. Kato himself had embraced democratisation, and universal male suffrage was introduced in 1925. But the object was to strengthen the state – had not democratic governments been victorious in the war? – and, if that goal were not achieved, Japan's institutions would have to be worked in a different way. The installation of the Tanaka government in 1927 marked a shift both in domestic and in foreign policy.

The approach of the Northern March of the Chinese nationalists to Manchuria produced a sense of crisis. China as a whole was more important to Japan than it was to other powers. Some 70 per cent of its foreign population in 1931 was Japanese, and Japan took about a quarter of its import and export trade. China absorbed nearly 82 per cent of Japan's foreign investment, less than 6 per cent of Britain's, and less than 1.5 per cent of that of the United States. In regard to Manchuria itself, there was a sense of unfulfilled promise: it had yet to realise Japan's hopes of settling its

[77] q. Yanaga Chitoshi, *Japan since Perry*, New York: McGraw-Hill, 1949, p. 448.

population surplus or supplying its industries with raw materials. Yet Japan's position there rested on treaty rights, acquired by the expenditure of blood and treasure. 'Manchuria and Mongolia are Japan's lifeline,' an official of the Japanese-owned South Manchuria Railway claimed in 1931.

....Every nation has a lifeline that holds the key to its existence. As Gibraltar and Malta are to Great Britain and the Caribbean Sea to America, there definitely is an important point from which it is impossible to retreat if the nation expects to exist.[78]

The economic depression after 1929 added decisively to the crisis. With some backing from the military at home, the local Kwantung army seized control in September 1931, fanning out from the railway zone. The cabinet at home was unable to check it. Saionji Kinmochi, the last of the oligarchs, conveyed the Showa emperor's views to the new prime minister: 'The meddling of the army in domestic and foreign affairs is something which, for the welfare of the nation, must be viewed with apprehension.'[79] Inukai Ki wanted to negotiate a settlement with the Chinese government that would preserve at least a fiction of Chinese sovereignty in Manchuria, while protecting Japan's interests : 'If the situation develops towards the formation of an independent country, we shall have serious trouble with the Nine Power Treaty Nations. For this reason, I am actively trying to achieve our national purpose in Manchuria within the existing forms of political power.'[80] But he failed.

In March his cabinet authorised the creation of a separate Manchurian government with Pu Yi, the claimant to the throne in China, as head of state. Inukai Ki's successor, Admiral Saito Makoto, recognised the new state of Manchukuo in August, the foreign minister, Uchida Yasuya, telling the Diet that it was his 'fervent hope that the day is not far distant when Japan, Manchukuo, and China, as three independent Powers closely linked by a bond of cultural and racial affinities, will come to cooperate hand in hand for the maintenance and advancement of the peace and prosperity of the Far East.'[81]

[78] q. C. Thorne, *The Limits of Foreign Policy*, London: Hamilton, 1972, p. 35.

[79] q. J.B. Crowley, *Japan's Quest for Autonomy*, Princeton Univ. Press, 1966, p. 150.

[80] q. ibid., p. 158.

[81] q. ibid., pp. 182-3.

These moves were not only a break with the policies of Shidehara. They represented a broader reconception of Japan's regional relationships. Unlike Taiwan and Korea, Manchuria was not to be subjected to a merely colonial relationship. A somewhat more subtle approach was designed to evoke and utilise a Manchurian nationalism, even as Korean nationalism was decisively rejected. In a sense, that amounted to countering the other Washington powers with their own principles of nationality and self-determination.

Manchukuo was the first of what came to be called puppet governments, and it was indeed hard to give such governments sufficient power for them to function and win support, while yet retaining the control Japan wished to assert. The rhetoric of co-operation and cultural affinity was designed to help. The new policy also meant countering Chinese nationalism by sponsoring a rival nationalism in an outlying part of the old empire. At the same time, however, Japan still looked to China's collaboration, the rhetoric in this context evoking the pan-Asian spirit espoused by some earlier expansionists and recalled by Yamagata in 1915.

The Washington treaties had not been accompanied by provisions for enforcement should a participant breach them. Nor, given the depression and their naval weakness, were the Western powers in a position forcefully to intervene. 'Neither our obligations to China, nor own interest, nor our dignity require us to go to war over these questions,' President Hoover declared.[82] The British could not risk acting alone, and in any case there was considerable sympathy for Japan. The Japanese, according to Sir John Pratt of the British Foreign Office, had 'a great deal of right on their side'.[83] The strengthening of the Soviet position in the Far East – both cause and effect of the Japanese actions – did not reduce that sympathy.

If, however, the other powers did not act, they did disapprove, and they put that disapproval in the severe form, proposed by the US Secretary of State Stimson, of declining to recognise any agreement impairing the integrity of China or the Open Door or brought about by means contrary to the Kellogg Pact outlawing war. That was not simply intended as a moral position: it was in-

---

[82] q. Thorne, *Limits of Foreign Policy*, p. 162.

[83] q. W.R. Louis, *British Strategy in the Far East*, Oxford: Clarendon Press, 1971, p. 187.

tended to add to the difficulties that the Western powers thought must bring Japan's adventure to an end. Japan had 'bitten off more then she can chew', wrote Lord Lytton, who headed the League of Nations inquiry, 'and if left alone circumstances will be too strong for her ... liberal opinion ... will begin to assert itself and the military party will be criticised for the mess they have got the country into'.[84] It was an over-optimistic view, and its chances were worsened by non-recognition, not improved.

In 1914-15 it was perhaps with some relief, as well as some reluctance, that Britain had witnessed Japan's concentration on China. In the 1930s its new adventure again seemed likely to absorb its attention. China was, somewhat paradoxically, to find the entrenchment of Western powers under the unequal treaties of some help in resisting the encroachments of the Japanese. At the same time, the Western powers increasingly saw China's resistance to the Japanese as a defence of the *status quo* in Southeast Asia.

Colonial Southeast Asia

Most of Southeast Asia had come under the control of Western powers during the period of Japanese seclusion. Stage by stage the Dutch had acquired territorial control over Java in the later seventeenth and eighteenth centuries, consolidating it by their victory in the Java war of 1825-30. Supported by an understanding with the British, the treaty of 1824, they had been able to lay claim to most of the rest of the archipelago, and by the 1890s they had established control over almost all of it, though that control was in places still fragile or contested.

The British themselves had secured Penang in 1786, acquired Melaka (Malacca) from the Dutch and occupied Singapore in 1819. Based on these Straits Settlements they had built up relationships with the Malay rulers of the peninsula, installing 'Residents' in a number of the tin-bearing west coast states in the 1870s and creating the Federated Malay States in 1895. In northern Borneo they rather reluctantly maintained a colony at Labuan, and in 1888 they established protectorates over the three disparate territories that had emerged: the raj of Sarawak, ruled by the Brooke family; the state of North Borneo, ruled by a chartered company; and the remnant of the Sultanate of Brunei, where they installed a resident in 1905.

---

[84] q. Thorne, *Limits of Foreign Policy*, p. 281.

Burma the British had acquired stage by stage as a result of three conflicts with a monarchy that refused to accept the limitations on its independence that the rulers of India believed they had to impose: in the 1820s they occupied Arakan and Tenasserim, in the 1850s Pegu, and in 1885-6 they took over the rest of kingdom, subsequently establishing their authority over the Shan states and the mountainous fringes of the old kingdom.

The French established themselves stage by stage in what they came to call French Indo-China, creating a colony of Cochinchina, making protectorates of the rest of Vietnam, Annam and Tonkin, and of Laos and Cambodia, and drawing all the territories into a federation, formalised in 1897. The Thai kingdom of Siam made concessions, territorial and otherwise, to both the British and the French, but the core of the kingdom retained its independence between the two European empires.

Spain had created the Philippines, though without successfully incorporating the Muslim or 'Moro' areas to the south. At the end of the century, Spain's was the first colonial regime to be challenged by a nationalist movement.

In the ensuing rebellion the Spaniards and the Filipinos at first reached a truce. The conflict was renewed in the context of the Spanish-American war of 1898. The revolutionaries proclaimed a republic in June, but it received neither international support nor recognition. Early in 1899 a struggle with the Americans began, to be followed by a long guerrilla war. Only when the revolutionaries' resistance had been largely terminated did Americans turn their attention to the Moros. They had not joined in the struggle against the United States, which had seen fit to make a separate treaty with the sultan of Sulu in 1899. In 1904 it abrogated the treaty, but the attempt to establish its authority met violent resistance, subdued only after the massacres at Bud Dajo in 1906 and Bud Bagsak in 1913.

The changes in China and in Northeast Asia at the turn of the century were a sign that the primacy of the British – which had been created by their security in Europe after 1815, their naval predominance, their empire in India, but above all their pre-eminence in the industrial revolution – was now under challenge: they were inactive in the war of 1894-5, despite its challenge to the integrity of China, and they made an alliance with Japan in 1902, despite its equivocal attitude to the *status quo*.

The colonial structures in Southeast Asia had been established under the aegis of the British: they had favoured the preservation of the Dutch and Spanish empires; they had themselves acquired Burma and Singapore and put parts of Malaya and northern Borneo under their protection; they had not opposed the French venture, but had been anxious to preserve Siam as a buffer state. In the Philippines crisis, their preference was for the continuance of Spanish control. If that were, as it proved, impracticable, the next best answer was the establishment of American control.

Under growing pressure in Europe, Britain in general began to look to the United States as its successor. It accepted its dominance in the Caribbean, for example. Acquisition of the Philippines, by contrast, recruited the US to the ranks of the colonial powers and shored up the *status quo* in Southeast Asia.

There was, however, some equivocation. Imperialism was contested in the United States, and in the Philippines itself peace was secured, not merely by a level of violence at least on a par with that of other colonial powers, if not with Japan itself, but also by offering the prospect of self-government to an elite that had boldly sought independence. That was a source of some concern to other colonial powers. It was not only, nor even primarily, that by offering the Filipinos self-government, if not independence, the Americans might be setting a course which would stimulate their own subjects to seek the same. It might also indicate that the United States, having become a colonial power amid controversy, might cease to be one. On a copy of President Taft's statement of 1911 that 'we are likely to remain in the Philippines for a considerable time', an unidentified official in the Dutch Foreign Office wrote: '*hoera!*'[85] The Japanese were in his mind, as they were indeed in the minds of Manuel Quezon and the new generation of Filipino leaders.

If the United States was a colonial power with a difference, Japan was an independent Asian state with a difference. It had 'modernised' and it aspired to be treated equally. Yet there was also a sense of insecurity, which suggested the need to take further steps, without setting a clear goal or a measure of the their extent. And there was also a legacy of expansionist ideas, reinterpreted by *shishi* extremists and popular rights activists, who thought that the cautious opportunism of the oligarchs was an unworthy

[85] q. N.A. Bootsma, *Buren in de koloniale tijd*, Dordrecht: Foris, 1986, p. 23.

answer to the problem, and the deferential attitude to other powers an undignified one. It was possible, too, to point to the sympathy that Japan's successes seemed to evoke elsewhere in Asia, particularly where it focused on its apparent success against the dominant West rather than on the prospect that Japan's dominance would replace it.

The colonial powers were at once somewhat fearful of Japan and, noting its caution and deference, somewhat inclined to depreciate it. But there were clear advantages for the status quo in Southeast Asia in treating its desire for equality at face value. On 10 June 1907 Britain's ally Japan and its new entente partner France signed a treaty that involved a mutual recognition of each other's situation and territorial rights on the continent of Asia and mutual assistance in maintaining order and security in the neighbouring regions of China.

'The strength of Japan has been felt in the Northwest, all the way to the Ch'ing and to the Russians', the Vietnamese nationalist Phan Boi Chau had written to Okuma in 1905. 'Why then had Japan allowed the French to trample over Vietnam without trying to help us?'[86] In 1909, however, he was deported.

The passage of the Russian fleet through their islands – on its way out to be sunk by the Japanese at Tsushima – caused the Dutch some anxious moments, and the following years were filled with spy scares. Somewhat apprehensive, too, of the alliance between Japan and their nineteenth-century guarantor, the British, the Dutch sought to fit it into the normal pattern in which, like Britain, other powers gained an open door for their commerce in the Indies while accepting the political predominance of the Netherlands. The 1912 Netherlands-Japan commercial treaty was on a most-favoured-nation basis. The increasing use of oil as a fuel, and the discovery of oil in eastern Borneo and southern Sumatra, however, increased the apprehensions of the Dutch. For the Japanese had none of their own.

In the First World War those apprehensions increased. In the hope that the Dutch might join in against the Germans, the British foreign secretary, Sir Edward Grey, suggested that he might secure from the Japanese 'a guarantee ... to respect the possession

---

[86] q. D. Marr, *Vietnamese Anticolonialism*, Berkeley: Univ. of California Press, 1971, p. 113.

by the Netherlands of their East Indian colonies'.[87] The Dutch had, however, received an assurance from the Germans that their independence would be respected, unlike that of the Belgians, and thought it essential to preserve complete neutrality. Their continued concern about the East Indies was kept alive by spies, by the movements of Japanese warships – the British insisted that they were undertaken in accordance with arrangements for pursuing German marauders – and by the pronouncements of Japanese extremists. Takekoshi Yosaburo, journalist and historian, suggested, for example, that a weak state, unable to maintain neutrality, might be a source of anxiety, and that Japan should secure the Straits of Sunda and rescue the Malays from Western dominance.[88]

In 1916 the British consul-general in Batavia, W.E. Beckett, suggested a change of policy. 'The native is tired of his Dutch masters, and is making every effort to get rid of them by revolution or otherwise.' The Dutch interpreted neutrality so that it favoured Germany. They should be asked whether they would continue to 'coquet with Germany' and throw in their lot with that power, or place the 'destinies' in the hands of the allies. In the former case,

an arrangement with Japan would settle Japanese ambitions as indicated by Mr Takekoshi in a manner consonant with our Imperial interests. In the latter case, in return for a guarantee of protection and in view of the proven inability of the Dutch to control so large an area as that now represented by the Netherlands East Indies, that area would be curtailed in such a manner as to leave Java and the islands to the East to Holland and the possession of Sumatra Borneo and Celebes decided by consultation between Great Britain and Japan.

The notion received no support in London. The object of the alliance was after all to restrain Japan, not encourage it. 'If the Netherlands Indies are not too friendly', minuted W.L. Langley, 'they are harmless. It would be quite another matter if the islands were in the hands of the Japanese.'[89]

By contrast the British did what they could to preserve friendly relations between the Dutch and the Japanese. The Dutch minister

---

[87] Conversation, 7 August 1914. FO 371/2163 [37384/30342], Public Record Office, London.

[88] N. Tarling, ' "A Vital British Interest" ... ', *JSEAS*, 9, 2 (September 1978), p. 186.

[89] Beckett to Grey, 14 October 1916, 277, and minute. FO 371/2691 [23543/31466].

in Tokyo was suspicious even of Japan's increased commercial interest in the islands, and referred to 'a secret society for the penetration of the South Sea Islands'. The Japanese were 'spying out the land', as Lyons put it at the British Foreign Office, but he doubted if they had decided the direction of their expansion. 'China undoubtedly [comes] first on the list.'[90] At the suggestion of the British ambassador, Van Asbeck sought renewed assurances from the Japanese government, and they were given. But his suspicions remained.

With the end of the war, the Dutch renewed their encouragement of Japanese trade, 'partly', as Frank Ashton-Gwatkin of the British Foreign Office put it, 'to balance British and American interests in the islands, and prevent any one country getting a predominant share'.[91] Anxiety had not, however, entirely disappeared. The Dutch were concerned that the Washington four-power treaty covered the insular possessions only of the signatories. Their foreign minister suggested supplementing it by 'the simultaneous but independent presentation at The Hague of an identic note by America, Great Britain, France, and Japan, declaring their intention of respecting the island possessions of Holland in the region of the Pacific'. Though the British thought such a procedure 'embarrassingly superfluous', they agreed to follow it.[92]

The Manchuria crisis revived apprehensions about Japan, particularly when it left the League of Nations in 1933, while the mutiny on the *De Zeven Provincien* demonstrated Dutch weakness. Asked 'whether, in the event of conflict breaking out in the Pacific, Japan might not be compelled to seize the oil supplies in the Pacific', the Japanese ambassador in The Hague naturally denied any such intention.[93] Matsuoka Yosuke, leader of the delegation at Geneva, included an oil clause in the non-aggression pact he suggested, though nothing came of it.

The Japanese, Ashton-Gwatkin had written in 1921, were interested in the oil of the East Indies and in its trade. They appeared to have no definite political ambitions in this region. But they are obsessed by the idea that their country is one day destined to be mistress of the

[90] Minute. FO 371/2691 [264948/31466].
[91] Memorandum, 8 September 1921. FO 371/6696 [F3600/901/23].
[92] q. Tarling, ' "A Vital British Interest" ...', p. 192.
[93] Ibid., p. 192.

Pacific and of its islands. They regard Holland as a very weak Power, and
her colonial empire as doomed to disruption. Japan must have a say in the
disposal of this rich empire. So she is steadily increasing her knowledge of
the country, her vested interests therein, and the numbers of her merchants and colonists

and keeping an eye on the native movement.[94] The analysis coin-
cides with Shimizu Hajime's interpretation of Taisho *nanshin-ron*:
it 'stressed trade and industrial development for Japan's sake.
... The only things that Japan really tried to do on behalf of the
political liberation of Southeast Asia were trying to understand its
nationalism and giving passive support to independence from its
Western masters.'[95]

After the Manchuria crisis, Consul-General Fitzmaurice offered
an appraisal that allowed for the possibility of a more aggressive
approach. Some of the Dutch officials thought that the adviser for
Far Eastern affairs, Mouw, underestimated the threat. His view
was that there was, 'at any rate for the present, no ground to fear
sinister intentions on Japan's part': except in the commercial
sphere, it would 'be fully occupied for many years to come with
her own internal affairs and those of the Manchukuo State'.
Fitzmaurice thought its activities might be 'largely consistent with
a policy of gradual economic expansion only, but seem more consistent with a longer view on the part of Japan – with a vision
perhaps of the possibility that in a near or distant future she may
wish to take more active measures to increase her influence'.[96]

The Depression, furthermore, seemed likely to add to the risk.
Japan competed very successfully with Western importers, and the
colonial powers were tempted to put up economic barriers against
it. That might produce in turn a stronger Japanese reaction. In the
Indies the Dutch introduced a Crisis Import Ordinance in 1933,
and negotiations with the Japanese followed. They claimed the
right to share in the development of the Indies as an Asiatic land:
that 'sounds so much like Manchuria', said Ashton-Gwatkin.[97] The
Dutch rejected it.

[94] As note 91.
[95] Shimizu Hajime, ' "Nanshin-ron": its Turning Point in World War I', *The
Developing Economies*, 25, 4 (December 1987), p. 396.
[96] Fitzmaurice/Foreign Secretary, 29 June 1933, 77. FO 371/17407 [W9005/
663/29].
[97] q. N. Tarling, *Britain, Southeast Asia and the Onset of the Pacific War*, Cambridge
Univ. Press, 1996, p. 23.

The talks brought home to the Japanese, J.W. Meyer Ranneft thought, 'the thought that it is impossible for them ... to propose to "help" us in a "friendly" way to develop the Indies. The Netherlands sovereignty is a hindrance to the materialisation of the Japanese ideal which they hope to achieve by peaceful means.'[98] The Dutch, Howard Dick argues, were unduly suspicious.[99] Their reaction to what Van Gelderen called 'semi-political penetration'[100] might indeed only prompt the Japanese to abandon peaceful penetration for a less peaceful alternative.

Nor did the nationalists encourage the Japanese cause. Back in 1929, Sukarno had seen Japan as a menace to China, and forecast that, '[i]n the coming gigantic struggle between the imperialistic powers of England and the United States, Japan herself will take a part and become a menace to the freedom and welfare of the countries of the Pacific Ocean'.[101] Manchuria had a bad press. Hatta saw the incident as imperialist aggression. 'Japan's Asianism is being tainted by the influence of Japanese fascism, which dreams of becoming Asia's leader.'[102]

Yet the long-term prospects of the decolonisation of Southeast Asia were still sufficiently encouraging. Neither the reaction to Manchuria, nor the 1934 negotiations, prompted the Japanese to change their policy. Discreet contacts with the nationalists, and with the Thais, were still worthwhile. Above all, it seemed likely that the United States would cease to be one of the colonial powers in Southeast Asia. It had recruited itself to their ranks, but under the five-power treaty, it could not build a modern naval base in the Philippines. It had also indicated that it would grant the Philippines independence when it was fit, though it did not set a precise date till the creation of the Commonwealth in 1935.

The other main maritime power had been permitted to build the naval base at Singapore, but it had been slow to do so. Even

[98] q. Bob de Graaf in P. Lowe and H. Moeshart, eds, *Western Interactions with Japan*, Folkestone: Japan Library, 1990, p. 72.

[99] Howard Dick, 'Japan's Economic Expansion in the Netherlands Indies...', *JSEAS*, 20, 2 (September 1989), p. 266.

[100] q. Anne Booth, *The Indonesian Economy in the Nineteenth and Twentieth Centuries*, Canberra: ANU/Macmillan, 1998, p. 221.

[101] q. George S. Kanahele, 'The Japanese Occupation of Indonesia', Ph.D. thesis, Cornell Univ. 1967, p. 14.

[102] q. Goto Ken'ichi, *'Returning to Asia': Japan-Indonesia Relations, 1930s-1942*, Tokyo: Ryukei Shyosha, 1997, p. 314.

that was to be the base, not for a permanent Pacific navy, but for the use of a one-ocean navy when it was needed in Asia. The prospect that it would be needed in Europe was increasing as Germany rearmed. Nor could colonial powers boost themselves by creating national armies: their Southeast Asian forces were essentially constabularies.

If it was possible to argue that Japan would be kept too busy in China to act elsewhere, it was also possible to suggest that frustration in China might prompt it to turn to Southeast Asia. Such frustration was, however, unlikely on its own to lead to a full-scale invasion. The prospects in Southeast Asia made that superfluous. Cutting those off would be another matter.

2

DIPLOMACY AND FORCE

Expansionism

Those who argued that China would absorb the energies of the Japanese were in one way borne out in the 1930s. In another sense they were entirely mistaken. They expected the opposition of the Chinese and the pressure on Japan's resources, coupled with Western disapproval, to bring expansionism to a halt. Yet the striking feature of Japan's policy was the continued expansion of its objectives. Those did not, however, come to envisage the conquest of Southeast Asia. In 1934 Amo Eiji enunciated a kind of Monroe doctrine, but its focus was on East Asia. The rhetoric of 1936 was more pan-Asian in form, taking up the talk of 'co-prosperity and co-existence', but they were the words Yamagata had employed in 1915 to define the proper relationship with China. The focus was still on China, and though that had implications for Southeast Asia, they were limited. The Japanese hoped still to make gains in Southeast Asia without the military activity to which they had resorted in China. Indeed, while the growing conflict with the Russians in the north focused the army's concern, the situation in Europe suggested that the colonial powers were open to diplomatic pressure in the south. It was a matter of selectively speeding up a long-term change.

What began as an attempt to defend Japan's privileges in Manchuria expanded into an ambitious venture designed to bring about a compliant China. Once begun, the venture was indeed difficult to terminate. One reason was, of course, the resistance of the Chinese. That, indeed, the Japanese found it difficult to understand, for the Kuomintang (KMT) government was weak. They failed to recognise the strength of Chinese nationalism, which made it difficult, if not impossible, for Chiang Kai-shek to compromise. Pressing him to do so only made it easier for his communist opponents to identify with the nationalist cause, even though the Japanese claimed to be saving the mainland from communism. Their misinterpretation also led them to over-emphasise the extent to which Chinese resistance was sustained by support from the Western powers.

A second reason for the continuance of the conflict was the failure of the Japanese to define their objectives. Since Meiji, they had spoken of strength and prosperity and of equality with other nations. Such goals were inspiring, but also open-ended. There was a gap between them and the tactics that the oligarchs and their diplomats had followed. There were no intermediate strategies. Japan's foreign policy had been defined by a combination of its own opportunism with the opportunity offered by others.

The nature of the governmental structure that the oligarchs had created led the same way. Meiji Japan was not a monolithic state, but, as Duus puts it, a 'truncated Leviathan'.[1] The Privy Council, high command, bureaucracy, House of Peers, all were held together by the governing clique, more or less institutionalised as the *genro* or elder statesmen. Though they played a role in setting them up, their hold was weakened by the rise of the parties, as Yamagata's position in 1915 shows. The constitution was not changed in the 1920s, but run in a different way. Yet the chances that the parties could effect the coordination that the cronies had once effected were slim. That was particularly evident in the case of foreign policy. The governments to which Shidehara belonged were exposed to attack from the opposition in the Diet on the ground that they were humiliating Japan rather than securing its national objectives.

It was in an attempt to secure a more moderate foreign policy that the last of the oligarchs, Saionji Kinmochi, moved away from party government, and recommended the appointment of men like Inukai. Japan began to run its institutions in another way. Yet the bureaucratic governments of the 1930s did not pursue moderate foreign policies. They tended to act, not surprisingly, in what may be called a bureaucratic way: accommodating the interests of the organisations they represented by cumulating rather than prioritising them; and making up policies by reaching agreement about formulae. The process was sure to have an expansionary effect: the cabinet would agree on something for everyone. Indeed policies might be developed in search of resources rather than vice-versa.

---

[1] Duus, *Party Rivalry*, p. 244

The institutions that were improvised were suggestive of the process: the inner cabinet, the liaison conference between the leading civilian ministers and the high commands, and the imperial conference, where conclusions were ratified, rather than contested, in the emperor's presence. The processes by which decisions were thus reached were preceded by negotiations among subordinates, often influenced by ad hoc committees including officers, bureaucrats, businessmen, interest groups and academics. But, even after they had been reached, their interpretation could still be contested, and their implementation varied, expedited or delayed. That was the more likely because of the legacy of the *shishi* past, and also because of more recent developments in the armed forces.

Those who made policy in Japan made it – as under the shogunate, so too under its successors – in the name of the emperor. The extent to which he could actually determine policy was, however, limited. Certainly Saionji believed it essential to avoid using a theoretical power, lest its practice proved that it did not exist. 'Should the Emperor express himself and the army disobey, it would seriously damage the Imperial character'.[2]

Yet, as the *shishi* had found in the years before the Restoration, it was possible to act in the name of the emperor in defiance of his current counsellors, and allege that they were misleading him. That idea, for example, lay behind the army mutiny of February 1936. But it could also be adduced on other occasions, often affording an argument to those who wanted to implement an extreme version of a given policy formula. A special 'imperial' messenger might be needed to restrain them.

The army itself had undergone changes since it had been created in the years after 1868. Not at first large, it had of course grown in size, as Japan's capacity and its ambition had grown, though it was still under 300,000 before 1937. As a result of its expansion its officer class was no longer so aristocratic as it had been. Many of the mid-level officers of the late 1920s and 1930s came from social groups much affected by the economic storms of the period, and tending to welcome the propaganda of the nationalist societies of the day, extreme as it often was. They were impatient not only with the caution of the government, but also with their own top brass.

[2] q. S. Ogata, *Defiance in Manchuria*, Berkeley: Univ. of California Press, 1964, p. 152.

Carrying out a military policy ultimately depended on the soldiery itself. In the war in Southeast Asia when it came, the Europeans were to be horrified by its violence, baffled by its determination,
impressed by its dedication.

A soldier who accepted captivity was deemed to have brought eternal
shame to Emperor, homeland, community, and family. Universal aban-
donment and rejection, engendered by military inculcation and societal
psychology, were the price of ignominious survival. The prisoner was morally
'dead'; he might as well be physically dead too.[3]

Such attitudes were not simply the legacy of the past, still less an
intrinsic part of a national character. Japanese leaders of the 1930s
had what they considered good reasons for encouraging them.

After the Imperial Army had been severely mauled by the Red
Army at Nomonhan in the summer of 1939, its study groups had
recognised the importance of firepower, mobility and *matériel*. 'But
so far as combat was concerned, there seemed to be no practical
way to bridge the quantitative and technological gap imposed by
first-class adversaries ..., except by exploiting Japan's "cheapest"
available commodity: Men.'[4] 'Although we can fabricate equipment that resembles that of the Russians, we cannot be expected to
exceed a capacity of 80% or so. The only method of making up for
the missing 20% is to draw upon spiritual strength.'[5] Japan was
engaged on an endeavour beyond its physical capacity.

'A have-not and outnumbered country simply could not afford
a national military establishment with assets distributed equally
among competing land, sea, and air forces in support of an overextended imperial policy.'[6] One option was to set bounds to that
policy. That the Japanese found impossible. That only made it
more difficult to decide, given that 'assets' could not be distributed
'equally', how they should be distributed. The struggle to secure
resources became intense, but the results were often compromises
that conduced to further expansion.

Konoe Fumimaro

The process by which the policy had become 'overextended' by
1939 itself illustrates the paradoxes in Japan's policy-making,

[3] Alvin Coox, *Nomonhan*, Stanford Univ. Press, 1985, p. 929.

[4] Ibid., p. 1091.

[5] q. ibid.

[6] Ibid.

though it also shows up the role of Konoe Fumimaro. To secure the objectives that had by the mid-1930s come to define the search for strength, prosperity and equality, it was necessary, as the army general staff emphasised, to carry out a policy of total mobilisation, programming the intensive use of the resources of Japan, Korea and Manchuria, so that what strength Japan could muster was applied with maximum effectiveness, and meanwhile avoiding further 'incidents'. Konoe's approach was different. He needed to secure support for that policy at home, and that required a gamble in foreign policy. The policies were at odds. And he did not succeed.

In 1935 the KMT government in China had sought a friendship agreement with Japan. Chiang Kai-shek was ready to offer *de facto* recognition of Manchukuo, but that was not enough for an inner cabinet influenced by the war ministry and the field armies. The following year, however, the army became committed to consolidation rather than expansion, its concern focused on the Soviet build-up in the Far East. The navy accepted the need for a moderate policy in China, but wanted peaceful penetration of the South Seas, above all with oil in mind. Moderation in China, coupled with the threatening situation in Europe, it was argued, would lead the British to recognise Manchukuo and support that penetration. With oil from the East Indies, Japan could meet the risk that the US fleet in the Pacific would cut off the normal source of supply.

These considerations led to the negotiated compilation of the Fundamental Principles of National Policy of August 1936. They aimed at the 'frustration of Soviet aggression in East Asia' and the 'acquisition of naval power sufficient to secure command of the Western Pacific'.[7] The restrictions on naval building had already been rejected, Japan withdrawing from the second London naval conference in January, and the navy, advantaged by the setback the mutiny had given the army, had begun a programme of expansion. Now the cabinet envisaged 'footsteps' in the southern seas, taken discreetly lest they caused apprehension among the powers concerned.

The actions that resulted were novel, but moderate, and indeed, in their opportunism, not without a precedent. The army expanded its Kwantung forces. The navy organised ostensibly private busi-

[7] q. Crowley, *Japan's Quest*, pp. 295-6.

ness organisations to promote investment in the south seas. The foreign ministry concluded the Anti-Comintern Pact with Nazi Germany. That was not an alliance, although its secret clauses provided that if one party were attacked by the Soviet Union, the other would not assist the Soviet Union but would consult on measures to preserve the common interests of the two parties. It was a diplomatic thrust, designed to reduce the Soviet threat in the Far East, and to make Britain and France more worried and so more amenable in Southeast Asia, and Britain's client, the Netherlands, more compliant.

Within a year Japan's policy had been transformed. An incident at the Marco Polo Bridge not far from Peking on 7 July escalated into the 'undeclared war' between Japan and China. That escalation was not in keeping with the desire of the military to avoid incidents while Japan engaged in its long-term build-up. In part, indeed, it resulted from the reaction of Chiang Kai-shek: he could not accept another Manchuria. But increasingly it was Prime Minister Konoe who escalated the conflict. His cabinet made more stringent the terms under which Japan would conclude the struggle and when, after an attack on his capital, Nanking, that was to remain notorious for its violence, Chiang sued for a settlement, the price was put higher. Indeed the terms of 11 January 1938 were designed to be unacceptable. Japan, said Konoe, would deal only with 'a new Chinese regime'.[8]

Installing bureaucratic cabinets had not moderated Japan's foreign policy, as Saionji hoped. Konoe was a politician, not a bureaucrat, and was even less moderate. He had indeed a political mission. Total mobilisation required another transformation in the way Japan's institutions were operated. It also required the full-hearted collaboration of the great industrial combines, the *zaibatsu*. So far that had not been forthcoming. Their trade in China had been threatened by the boycotts that military expansionism provoked, and their leaders were among the victims of the extremists. In Manchuria the army found it necessary to create more cooperative 'new *zaibatsu*'. It was to win *zaibatsu* support, to overcome the remaining opposition in the Diet and to outwit the general staff that Konoe turned the China incident into a great patriotic endeavour. Cabinet approved the National Mobilisation Bill in February and the Diet passed it on 16 March.

[8] q. ibid., p. 375.

'The government takes the view that we should utilise the China Incident as an opportunity to make another decisive stride in Japan's industry and economy', the commerce and industry minister had declared in December 1937.[9] Konoe's 'electrifying declaration' the following month 'was as much an instrument to obtain approval for sweeping reform legislation ... as it was an indication of the end of patience with Chiang Kai-shek'.[10] Success at home was bought at an excessive cost. Konoe hoped also to bring the war to a prompt end. Indeed his contribution to the total mobilisation programme would otherwise make no sense: it would in fact be counter-productive. In that, however, he failed. The result was that he had committed Japan to an even more encompassing endeavour in China, rather than providing it with the means to deal with the Soviet threat.

The failure to bring the China war to an end led Konoe to interest himself in negotiations. His interest was short-lived. Instead, in November, he redefined Japan's aims in a yet more ambitious way, though still one that did not explicitly include Southeast Asia. 'It is the establishment of a new order that will enable us to maintain [the] permanent peace of East Asia that the Empire seeks. This is really the ultimate object of the present expedition.'[11] 'Is it possible', the emperor asked, 'to put into effect a plan which calls simultaneously for long-term hostilities in China, military preparations against the Soviet Union, and the expansion of the navy?'[12]

The European crisis

In this situation Japan once more tried to turn international relations to its advantage. That proved impossible. Italy, one of the Washington signatories, had joined the Anti-Comintern Pact, and it had recognised Manchukuo late in 1937. After the failure of mediation in the undeclared war in December, Hitler had cast aside Germany's long connection with the KMT regime, and also recognised Manchukuo. Now the imperial army wanted a closer

---

[9] q. Gordon M. Berger, *Parties out of Power*, Princeton Univ. Press, 1977, p. 145.

[10] q. M. Barnhart, *Japan Prepares for Total War*, Ithaca, NY: Cornell Univ. Press, 1987, p. 105.

[11] q. J.B. Crowley in J.W. Morley, ed., *Japan's Foreign Policy*, New York: Columbia Univ. Press, 1974, p. 78.

[12] q. Crowley, *Japan's Quest*, p. 378.

connection with Nazi Germany. That would diminish the threat of the Soviet army, which gave a fair account of itself in July-August 1938 in the Changkufeng clash on the Manchukuo-Russian border.

Hitler's price for a closer relationship was, however, a more definite pledge of action against the maritime powers than that in the Anti-Comintern Pact, since he wished to prevent the British from obstructing his reconstruction of Europe, and the US from supporting them. Such a pledge the imperial navy opposed. The diplomatic position illustrated the over-commitment of the Japanese: it could not redeem it.

Early in 1939, the navy somewhat shifted its ground. In a struggle with the Soviet Union, Britain and France might join Russia. A larger alliance would, moreover, give the navy a larger share of the budget. It was thus agreed that, while the United States would be excluded from the application of a Germany-Japan alliance, Japan would consider aiding Germany and Italy if they were involved in a war with Britain and France. That was still not enough for the Germans. A meeting of the five ministers tried again in June. Under its new formula, Japan might intervene if Germany and Italy were involved in a war with a power other than the Soviet Union, though the treaty should be regarded as an extension of the Anti-Comintern Pact, and it would operate only after a date to be determined by Japan.

The army made one more effort after Nomonhan, but in vain. No new pact was made. Hitler adopted a different strategy. He determined to facilitate changing the map of Europe, not by a closer connection with the Japanese, but by something that would alarm them, a deal with the Soviet Union. The Non-Aggression Pact of 22 August was, however, to precipitate war in Europe early in September.

Japan's policy had continued to be shaped not only by the Russian threat it had conjured up but also by the opportunities the West gave it and the limits it imposed. Over China the Western powers were not entirely in agreement. The British would have welcomed a deal with Japan, even at the cost of recognising some of Japan's gains. The US stuck by the non-recognition line. Indeed, in reaction to the Marco Polo Bridge incident Secretary of State Hull generalised the Stimson principles:

We advocate abstinence by all nations from use of force in pursuit of policy and from interference in the internal affairs of other nations. ... Upholding the principle of the sanctity of treaties, we believe in the modification of provisions of treaties, when need therefor arises, by orderly processes carried out in a spirit of mutual helpfulness and accommodation.[13]

China's resistance to Japan was supported by words, though not by force. That ruled out any British attempt at a deal that would sacrifice China, lest it sacrifice the relationship with the United States that Britain had on wider grounds to preserve.

With that, and the aggression of the Japanese, American and British policies to China came still closer. China, it was believed, would continue to resist. Indeed Japan was 'getting bogged down on the Asian mainland',[14] and conciliating it would only encourage it to look south. 'We must leave the Chinese to fight their battles – or ours for us – and give them such assistance as we can.'[15] That was not much, though it was enough to convince the Japanese that China would be more compliant but for the West. The American words indeed helped those in the KMT government who opposed compromise. So did steps like the completion of the Burma Road in December 1938.

The German threat in Europe could, however, be used to undermine this connection. The Munich crisis was followed by the Japanese attack on Canton, taken on 21 October 1938, the call for a new order following a fortnight later. In February 1939 the Japanese occupied Hainan and in March the Spratly islands. Those were further moves in the war that the Japanese had now carried to southern China.

They had other implications, too. They were also moves that gave the navy a role in the China struggle. At the same time, like the expansion into southern China itself, they brought Southeast Asia into a closer focus. The army aimed to cut off the aid that reached the KMT forces overland along the Burma Road or through French Indo-China. The navy could see its advances, not only as a means of constraining China, but also as a means of adding to the pressure on colonial Southeast Asia. Acquiring Hainan did not, however, mean that an attack had been decided on, whatever

[13] q. Tarling, *Pacific War*, p. 14.
[14] Bradford A. Lee, *Britain and the Sino-Japanese War*, Stanford Univ. Press, 1973, p. 111.
[15] q. Tarling, *Pacific War*, p. 20.

extremists might hope. Successful pressure might avoid the need for it.

The phoney war and the fall of France

Germany's change of strategy was a shock to the Japanese. 'Our foreign policy is our biggest failure since the beginning of our history,' Saionji complained.[16] In the north Zhukov had just begun a destructive counter-attack at Nomonhan. The border differences now had to be patched up on terms advantageous to the Soviet Union. At least, however, the Western powers could be subjected to more pressure. Already in July Japan had been able to settle a dispute with the British at Tientsin to its advantage, and now the Abe cabinet invited the belligerent nations to withdraw their remaining troops from China. Britain more or less did so, but the United States was less accommodating. During the Tientsin dispute, it had given six months' notice of its intention to terminate its commercial treaty with Japan. Now, on 19 October, the US ambassador in Tokyo, Joseph C. Grew, declared that the American people were opposed to the effort 'to establish control, in Japan's own interest, of large areas on the continent of Asia and to impose upon those areas a system of closed economy'.[17]

In Southeast Asia the Japanese remained cautious during the 'phoney war'. A discussion in the House of Peers in December made Esler Dening of the British Foreign Office apprehensive about 'trouble over the NEI [Netherlands East Indies], if Germany invades the Netherlands'. His colleague, Ashley Clarke, was, however, 'still inclined to think that so long as things are not going too badly for us in the West Japan will be wary of embroiling herself with the United States and ourselves'.[18] The replacement of the Abe government by the Yonai government on 14 January did not appear to portend a change of Japanese policy. The *Asama Maru* incident was settled by a compromise, and final settlement of the Tientsin dispute was advanced.

The phoney war ended with the German attack on Denmark and Norway in early April. That was followed by attacks on the Low Countries on 10 May. Those events shifted Japanese policy,

[16] q. R. Storry, *The Double Patriots*, London: Chatto & Windus, 1957, p. 256.

[17] q. David J. Lu, *From the Marco Polo Bridge to Pearl Harbor*, Washington, DC: Public Affairs Press, 1961, p. 65.

[18] q. Tarling, *Pacific War*, p. 82.

but it remained cautious, its object being to keep the East Indies out of the hands of a major power and to secure access to their resources. The surrender of France followed in June. That was far more surprising than the overrunning of the smaller states, and it produced a major reaction among the other powers.

The British did not give in, though they had only hopes of American support, rather than promises. Apprehensive that they might give in, or be forced to do so, the United States indeed focused for a time on hemisphere defence. On 20 July President Roosevelt signed the bill authorising the building of a two-ocean navy, a recognition of the fact that the security of the United States and of Latin America had depended substantially on the independence of the British and the presence of the navy in the Atlantic. When, by August, Roosevelt became more persuaded that Britain would survive, he renewed and increased the support the United States offered. The most obvious outcome was the destroyers-for-bases agreement. Keeping Britain's resistance alive in Europe also meant that it must continue to have access to the resources of its empire in India, Australasia and Southeast Asia.

The policies, though related to the unexpected catastrophe in Europe, had implications for Japan. The termination of the commercial treaty had been part of a series of American actions, termed a 'moral embargo', designed to discourage the creation of a new order in East Asia. On 2 July 1940 the National Defense Act empowered the president to place embargoes on arms and munitions, and some categories of oil and scrap iron were later added to the restricted list.

The object was to restrain Japan, but not to provoke it. The policies were indeed predicated on a traditional appraisal of Japan: it was cautious in respect of the major powers, and it had bitten off more than it could chew. That endured despite the ambitious cast Konoe had given to Japan's policy, perhaps in a sense because of it.

The American moves that followed the collapse of France were, however, far from traditional: they altered US policy in Asia. The creation of a two-ocean navy undid the basic calculations on which the Japanese had constructed their naval policy since Washington. Japan's security had in part been provided by the fact that the other major signatories, the United States and Britain, had to meet worldwide commitments, unlike Japan. When Japan abandoned the agreement in search of parity in 1934, the United States had

been to slow to build. But if it were now to employ its vast resources in a major navy programme, the days of Japan's predominance even in the Asian region were numbered.

The growing American interest in the fate of the Southeast
Asian colonies – another result of the shift in the balance of power
in Europe in Germany's favour – also concerned the Japanese. It
renewed US commitment to the area at a time when, since the
establishment of the Commonwealth in the Philippines, it had
seemed clear that the imperialist adventure of the Americans was
only temporary. The prospect that Japan could expand at the expense of the colonial powers without a conflict was reduced.

At the same time the Japanese began to feel a greater sense of
urgency about the transformation of Southeast Asia. In its ultimate
fate they had long had a strong interest, and they were convinced
that its future lay more with them than with the colonialists. Now
it seemed that other powers were lengthening the timetable. Their
wish, on the other hand, was to shorten it. Again that arose in part
because of the steps taken by others. Oil was a focus of this shift,
rather than idealism. If the United States were going to embargo
oil, it would have to be obtained elsewhere, and Netherlands
India was the obvious source.

So far oil had been a concern of the navy rather than the army,
and it had been the navy that had advocated footsteps in the south.
During 1940 the army began to attach more importance to the
issue. Without oil, it argued, the military machine would come to
a halt. Remaining nervous about the Soviet Union in the north, it
nevertheless became more interested in the south. Other powers
were imposing a priority among the wide-ranging objectives of
the Japanese. But it was a priority that might lead to a conflict with
the Western powers such as Japan had so far avoided, though they
thought it would still avoid it.

At first it seemed possible that a diplomatic approach, applied
more forcefully, might yet succeed. Japan indeed enjoyed some
success at the cost of defeated France in 1940, though that related
more to the war with China than the resources of Southeast Asia.
And then Konoe made his second attempt to solve Japan's problems at a blow. The Tripartite Pact of September – concluded
despite new American embargoes – did not, however, achieve the
objectives he had optimistically set.

The first move on Indo-China

The possessions of the French, unlike those of the Dutch, bordered China. They had as a result no wish for a strong Chinese government. The extension of the undeclared war to southern China was also, however, a menace. Even in September 1936 there had been rumours of an attack on Hainan, which 'commands the Gulf of Tonkin, our ports of Haiphong and Tourane, and the Singapore – Hong Kong route'.[19] When the undeclared war began the French banned the transit of arms across Tonkin into China. In return they hoped the Japanese would preserve the status quo in the Gulf of Tonkin. In fact, in December 1937 they raised the idea of sending a Japanese officer to whom the French could offer proof that they had closed the border, and in 1938 they occupied the Spratlys and the Paracels.

When they landed troops on Hainan in February 1939, the French foreign minister, Georges Bonnet, reiterated that 'the measures taken to prevent the transit of war material across Indochina ... constitute ... from the French point of view, the counterpart of Japanese abstention in the Gulf of Tonkin in general and at Hainan in particular'.[20] The negative response of the Japanese led the French informally to relax their ban.

Indo-China was, however, virtually defenceless, as conversations with the British in Singapore in June 1939 emphasised. Those considered two possibilities: a European war in which Japan intervened, and a European war in which it did not. In the latter case it must be deterred by reinforcement and diplomacy. In the former the two allies must act defensively until reinforced. Either way, the officers agreed on the importance of Indo-China 'as an advanced position in the defence of Singapore and Allied possessions in the Indian Ocean'. They also agreed on 'the present inadequacy of the Allied Naval and Air Forces in the Far East'.[21]

The opening of the war in Europe revived the notion of a deal with the Japanese, but it was quickly ruled out. In the phoney war phase, as Governor-General Georges Catroux put it, France would, in order not to 'jeopardize Indo-China ... follow a policy of purely

---

[19] q. John F. Laffey, 'French Far Eastern Policy in the 1930s', *MAS*, 23, 1(1989), p. 131.

[20] q. ibid., p. 142.

[21] q. Tarling, *Pacific War*, p. 47.

political expediency'.[22] The Japanese move into Kwangsi in November, and their capture of Nanning, was followed by a protest against the supply of munitions, and a proposal to station Japanese officials in Indo-China, coupled with a disclaimer of designs against it.

The French sent a firm response, but their position changed with the armistice in Europe. Their prime objective was to preserve the continuity of French government in Indo-China, and to that end they formalised and extended the implicit understandings of the prewar phase. Catroux offered the Japanese concessions even before they sought them: he closed the frontier and accepted inspection. That the French ambassador in Tokyo, Arsène Henry, thought would 'enable the Japanese authorities to control their extremists at least temporarily and prevent any direct action against Indo-China'.[23]

But the inspection team, headed by General Nishihara Issaku, and characteristically composed of representatives of the army, the navy and the foreign office,[24] made additional demands early in July, involving the admission of Japanese troops on a scale that would undermine French authority. Nishihara and the intelligence division focused on China, and the demands were 'ostensibly' designed to cut off supplies to the KMT. But the operations division and the local commanders saw Indo-China as a base for the southward advance.[25]

The new Konoe government, installed on 17 July, stepped up the pressure. Its foreign minister, Matsuoka, gave Arsène Henry an *aide-mémoire* asking that Japanese troops might cross Tonkin and occupy French aerodromes. Paul Baudouin, the Vichy foreign minister, decided to negotiate, and a telegram to Tokyo expressed readiness 'to accord exceptional facilities temporarily to Japan in return for a formal assurance that she has no territorial designs in Indo-China'.[26] 'The position is unhappily very simple; if we refuse

[22] q. ibid., p. 100.

[23] q. N. Tarling, 'The British and the First Japanese Move into Indo-China', *JSEAS*, 21, 1 (March 1990), p. 42.

[24] Minami Yoshizawa in Takashi Shiraishi and Motoo Furuta, eds, *Indochina in the 1940s and 1950s*, Ithaca, NY: Cornell Univ. Press, 1992, p. 19.

[25] Hata Ikuhiko in J.W. Morley, ed., *The Fateful Choice*, New York: Columbia Univ. Press, 1980, p. 155. Murakami Sachiko, 'Japan's Thrust into French Indochina 1940-1945', Ph.D. thesis, New York Univ., 1981, p. 105.

[26] q. Tarling, *Pacific War*, p. 152.

Japan, she will attack Indo-China which is incapable of being defended. Indo-China will be a hundred per cent lost. If we negotiate with Japan; if we avoid the worst, that is to say the total loss of the colony; we preserve the chances that the future may perhaps bring us.' The Japanese troops might remain in the country and annex it bit by bit, 'but they might also respect French sovereignty, and withdraw once the fight against Chiang Kai-Shek is at an end'.[27]

He looked for a renewal of the 1907 undertaking; what Arsène Henry got was an exchange of letters, in which the French government recognised 'the supreme interests of Japan in the economic and political spheres in the Far East', while the Japanese government indicated that it had 'every intention' of respecting the rights and interests of France and the integrity of Indo-China.[28] Special military facilities would be available solely for the purpose of resolving the conflict with Chiang Kai-shek. Those it was envisaged would cover three air bases, the stationing of 5,000-6,000 troops, and the right to transport troops for the China operation, but a separate military convention was to be negotiated in Hanoi.

In Hanoi Nishihara, urged by the chief of the operations division, Tominaga Kyogi, pressed negotiations on Catroux's successor, Decoux, even before he had received authority from Vichy. He rejected the approach as an ultimatum, and the Japanese agreed to negotiate. The outcome was the Nishihara-Martin agreement of 4 September, which barred Japanese movements into Indo-China until a definitive pact was signed. Then it envisaged the use of three air bases and also limited the number of troops in Tonkin to a maximum of 25,000. The restless Tominaga thought the French 'not sincere'.[29]

Negotiations were indeed broken off when the Japanese violated French territory on 6-7 September: planes flew over Langson and two companies of infantry crossed the frontier in war formation. On 14 September the Japanese cabinet agreed to introduce troops into Indo-China on the 22nd, whether or not agreement had been reached. Tominaga reopened negotiations in Hanoi by demanding the stationing of 25,000 troops, the use of five aerodromes and the inclusion of Hanoi and Haiphong in the stationing area. This went

[27] P. Baudouin, *The Private Diaries*, trans. C. Petrie, London: Eyre & Spottiswood, 1948, pp. 199, 203.

[28] q. Tarling, *Pacific War*, p. 163.

[29] q. Morley, *Fateful Choice*, p. 178.

beyond his instructions and, despite the operations staff and other extremists, the Japanese made some concessions. The agreement, finally signed on 22 September, covered the stationing of 6,000 troops, the transit of 25,000 and the use of four air bases.

Major incidents were still to occur, both on the border at Langson and at Haiphong. They could have been avoided despite the fact that the agreement was signed only shortly before the Japanese deadline. The reason for them lay in the attitude of Tominaga, the operations division and the armies in south China. 'There is a strong tendency for our local troops to take the initiative', a navy observer said, 'leaving the Tokyo authorities to approve the *fait accompli.*'[30] Decoux feared an effective occupation, and he had therefore tried to ensure that the army sent to attack the Chinese was in Tonkin only transitorily. That was the basis of the agreement of 22 September. Nevertheless the Japanese infiltrated and clashes occurred. Some of the military indeed wanted to occupy Indo-China. Their withdrawal followed an imperial mandate, secured by Prince Kanin.

Baudouin justified his approach by the lack of American support, and Decoux claimed that he spun out the negotiations in Hanoi in the hope of it. For most of the crisis the US had confined itself to verbal protest, and that did nothing to discourage an ambitious policy on the part of the Japanese. On 12 September Roosevelt placed under licence equipment that might manufacture aviation fuel from petroleum or tetraethyl lead. On the 26th the press announced that all grades of iron and steel scrap would be placed under licence and licences issued only for countries in the western hemisphere. Those additional economic steps – taken partly in reaction to the Japanese moves in Indo-China – did not stop them. Nor did they – as he also hoped – halt the Tripartite Pact.

The Burma Road

The border between China and British Burma was less penetrable than that between China and French Indo-China, and while French railway-building had extended into Yunnan, the British stopped at Lashio. The all-weather road completed by late 1938 provided a means of supplying the KMT resistance, which attracted the attention of the Japanese. In the Tientsin crisis of June 1939 it was

[30] q. Sumio Hatano and Sadao Asada in Robert Boyce and E.M. Robertson, eds, *Paths to War*, Basingstoke: Macmillan, 1989, p. 390.

reported that they had demanded that Britain close the road to shipments of arms and munitions. The following year, at the same time as they sought to prevent the transit of war supplies across the Indo-China frontier, they put in what the Vice-Minister Ohashi Chuichi described as a 'friendly communication', the object of which was to obtain Britain's cooperation in stopping the transit of arms, ammunition, fuel and trucks along the Burma Road.[31]

Sir Robert Craigie, the British ambassador, advocated giving way. 'Quite apart from Chinese feelings, if we do, the Americans – or a large section of opinion – will say "the English are beat anyway",' wrote Sir Alexander Cadogan at the Foreign Office. 'And we don't want that.' Winston Churchill declared, however, 'that we could not afford the Japanese navy being added to the German and Italian and possibly even coming round West'. Some thought the Japanese were 'bluffing', Neville Chamberlain wrote, 'but if they were mistaken – and we have to deal not with the Foreign Office but the truculent and ignorant army officers who think we are going to be beaten by the Germans – we have not got the forces to fight Japs, German and Italians at once.'

The British agreed to close the Road for three months on the understanding that during that time attempts would be made to bring about a 'just and equitable peace' in the Far East. 'We've been bluffed,' wrote Cadogan. 'But it was Winston who resolutely refused to call it.' Hull expressed 'much regret and disappointment'.[32]

Negotiations for a Sino-Japanese peace never began. The British cabinet considered reopening the Road. At first it seemed that the Indo-China situation had overtaken the matter: occupation by the Japanese would bring the Road under threat of air attack. The British were, however, surviving the German bombardment. They wished, too, to encourage the US in the firmer stand they were taking, though anxious that it should not consist merely of declarations and embargoes without some indication that force would if necessary be applied. In Clarke's view the September embargoes and the Tripartite Pact were arguments for repudiating the agreement: it would 'encourage the Americans on the right path' and give 'moral encouragement' to the Chinese.[33] The Road was reopened, but not too dramatically.

---

[31] q. Tarling, *Pacific War*, p. 112.

[32] q. ibid., pp. 114–17.

[33] q. ibid., p. 188.

The Kobayashi mission

The end of the phoney war, and the prospect that the Germans would invade the Netherlands, had renewed fears that Japan, uncertain about its supply of American oil, would seize Netherlands India. Arita Hachiro, the foreign minister, wanted to restrain the militarists. He expressed concern 'over any development accompanying aggravation of war in Europe that may affect status quo in Netherlands East Indies'. The Indies government, the acting US consul-general reported, would 'strive to exist ... as an independent nation', even if Germany conquered the Netherlands, though the 1922 identical notes might not apply. However, a Nazi coup was possible, and that might give the Japanese an excuse to offer 'protection'.[34] On 17 April Hull made a firm statement in support of the *status quo*. The French, interested also in the *status quo* in Southeast Asia, welcomed the declarations, and the British told the Japanese they shared Arita's view.

When the Netherlands was overrun, the governor-general insisted that the government's authority in the Indies could be maintained: 'Assistance to this end from abroad from whatever side it may be offered will be refused as being unwelcome.' Craigie and his Dutch colleague, Pabst, thought that 'the main danger probably lies in Navy's taking matters into its own hands'. Arita said that his main concern was to prevent Germany's making a 'paper annexation'.[35] Statements supporting the status quo came from the Americans and British. The Germans were rather slower to indicate their disinterest in the NEI: they did it only on 22 May.

'[W]e must do what we can to cut ground from under feet of those pressing for positive Japanese action,' Craigie thought.[36] The Dutch gave reassurances about the continued supply of oil and raw materials. But, as the British now became aware, the Japanese had already made 'far-reaching' economic demands on Netherlands India. Shortly after the termination of their commercial treaty with the United States, they had presented The Hague with a memorandum of general principles on promoting trade with the Indies. Now, as the Dutch colonial minister saw, there would have to be negotiations at Batavia.

---

[34] q. ibid., pp. 83, 84-5.
[35] q. ibid., pp. 88, 89.
[36] q. ibid., p. 90.

The Japanese planned a new economic mission to Batavia, though, according to the British consul-general, they delayed it 'awaiting the outcome of the present [German] attack on England'.[37] Pabst opposed the appointment of Koiso Kuniaki, who had allegedly declared that 'freeing the Oriental races [was] necessary and destined to be realized',[38] and advocated a 'guarantee-like occupation' of the Indies.[39] Late in August Kobayashi Ichiro, minister of commerce and industry, was appointed envoy, but his agenda was not very different. A member of the mission was reported as saying that he expected 'to have long confidential talks with the Governor General, ending in a secret oral or gentleman's agreement. When asked on what subject agreement was to be, he said that aim of mission was to arrange that Japan will guarantee territorial integrity of the Netherlands East Indies and in return have a free hand commercially there.'[40]

The cabinet indeed declared on 29 August that Japan faced 'an emergency situation', that it must seek resources in the southern region 'in order to cope with the malignant scheme of the United States', and that it must as well 'firmly establish our political leadership over this Dutch territory'.[41] The Dutch resisted Kobayashi's attempt to shift the discussion to the political sphere, as they put it, and they reacted to the Tripartite Pact by stressing that Netherlands India did not fall 'within the living space of any Power, that Dutch will not admit leadership of any foreign Power, and will resist all attempts by others to alter status quo in the Netherlands East Indies'.[42]

The Tripartite Pact

The Tripartite Pact was Konoe's masterstroke. He thought his predecessor, Yonai, had been too cautious, too anxious to await the outcome of the war in Europe, too apprehensive lest a move in Southeast Asia would provoke the United States.

[37] q. ibid., p. 146.

[38] q. Nagaoka Shintaro in Morley, *Fateful Choice*, p. 140.

[39] q. Goto, *'Returning to Asia'*, p. 90.

[40] q. Tarling, *Pacific War*, p. 147.

[41] q. J.B. Crowley in Bernard S. Silberman and H.D. Harootunian, eds, *Japan in Crisis*, Washington, DC: Public Affairs Press, 1974, p. 288.

[42] q. Tarling, *Pacific War*, pp. 214–15.

Whenever a new cabinet is formed these days, the emperor warns the new premier on these points: respecting the provisions of the constitution, avoiding any upheavals in the business world, and co-operating with the Anglo-American powers. ... But politics in Japan today cannot be run in accordance with these imperial wishes.[43]

As earlier, Konoe saw the international crisis through a politician's eyes: he was constructing a new political movement, with the support of Kido and leaders of the Minseito and Seiyukai parties, that aimed to 'strengthen the national defense state', 'renovate foreign policy' and establish a new political system. The resources the New Order required, he argued, could be secured without a war by making a pact with the Axis. 'The Tripartite Pact was the center of Konoe's world policy,' as his adviser Kazami Akira put it.[44]

Early in July officers from the army general staff had drafted 'Main Principles for Coping with the Changing World Situation'. That indicated its new concern with the south. Colonel Usui Shigeki of the operations staff explained the shift at a conference with officers from the navy general staff:

It seems to be an inevitable outcome of the European war that Germany and Italy will establish a bloc extending over Europe and Africa, separating Great Britain from the United States economically as well as strategically. As a counter-measure to this offence, Great Britain will try to secure a line of communication with the United States in the South Pacific, using India and Australia as their bases. In the meantime the enormous expansion plan of the US navy will have been completed in several years from now. The upshot will be the establishment of a strong Anglo-American bloc, economic as well as strategic, in the South Seas.

Japan's trade would be jeopardised, and '[w]e have no choice but resolutely to forestall the United States and Great Britain by establishing ourselves in the South Seas.' Japan could not, however, afford to go south under present conditions: it needed peaceful relations with the Soviet Union, 'disposal' of the China incident, alliance with Germany and Italy.[45] Japan must form 'an economically self-sufficient zone, including the Southern Area, establish a powerful political structure, and institute a planned economy'.

[43] Konoe to a friend, q. B.-A. Shillony, *Politics and Culture in Wartime Japan*, Oxford: Clarendon Press, 1981, p. 37.

[44] q. Crowley in Morley, *Japan's Foreign Policy*, p. 82.

[45] q. Murakami, 'Japan's Thrust', pp. 61-2.

The navy staff agreed, of course, with the new priority, though it wanted southern expansion achieved by peaceful means 'if at all possible'.[46]

The new Konoe government was installed on 17 July, with Tojo Hideki as army minister, Yoshida Zengo as navy minister and Matsuoka as foreign minister. The Outline of Fundamental National Policy was adopted by the cabinet on 26 July and by the liaison conference on the 27th. Strengthening ties with the Axis would neutralise the Soviet Union, promote the 'southern policy' and prevent the United States from entering the war in Europe or interfering in Southeast Asia. Chiang Kai-shek was to be subjugated; Indo-China controlled; the Burma Road closed; the resources of Netherlands India secured, preferably by negotiation. Relations with the United States would deteriorate, but outright hostilities could, it was hoped, be avoided. If the general situation turned favourable and the war with China were settled, military force would be used. Then it might become impossible to avoid a clash with the United States.

The government secured the closure of the Burma Road and the compliance of the Vichy French, though the Dutch proved more obstinate and the United States added to the embargoes. The Japanese remained optimistic: a panel of academics, businessmen and former officials echoed a Tokugawa-period nationalist, Aizawa Seishisai, declaring that '[t]his is a great opportunity that comes once in a thousand years.'[47]

Searching for their place in the world, the Japanese tended to oscillate between the insufficient and the excessive, between the prudent and the ambitious, leaving the position to be determined by others, either by offering them opportunity or curbing their excess. In 1937-8 Konoe had articulated an insouciant optimism. Undeterred by its disastrous outcome, he now shared the panel's views: 'A humble attitude will only prompt the United States to become domineering.'[48] He again attempted a coup in foreign policy, something that would transform the situation at a blow and without a blow.

Yet the pact was made with a Germany that had not succeeded with its policies. Hitler was more ready to turn to the Japanese

[46] q. Crowley in Morley, *Japan's Foreign Policy*, p. 87.

[47] q. ibid., p. 88.

[48] q. ibid.

because his air offensive had failed to bring about Britain's surrender, and the United States had indicated growing confidence in its survival by concluding the destroyers-bases agreement. Moreover the pact, negotiated between 9 and 22 September, did not really resolve the differences that had made it difficult for the two powers to draw closer together in 1938-9.

Germany, Italy and Japan undertook 'to assist one another with all political, economic and military means when one of the three Contracting Parties is attacked by a power at present not involved in the European war or in the Sino-Japanese conflict'.[49] From this the Soviet Union was specifically excluded, so that the Japanese army's reservations were met. The navy sought to avoid an absolute commitment against the United States in an exchange of letters: Matsuoka endeavoured to insist that the question whether an attack had taken place must be the subject of consultation. The pact was a statement that in itself was expected to affect the international situation rather than a commitment to action. It was a piece of bluff. Its main achievement was to deny any claims in Southeast Asia on the part of its ally.

Indeed it was to some extent counter-productive. It alerted American opinion and tended to align the United States more closely with Britain. For a time its impact was muted by the approach of the American elections, but afterwards Roosevelt was to speak of the United States as the 'arsenal of democracy' and lend-lease was introduced. Nor, of course, did it lead the United States to adjust its view of Japan, in turn a factor in the making of Japan's policy. It believed that, if Japan's problems in China, coupled with Western disapproval, did not bring it to a halt, economic embargoes would. That, indeed, had not so far proved to be the case. It was also true, however, that Japan appeared still to act only when others offered the opportunity, and the Tripartite Pact did not undermine that appraisal. Nor – though at times the British and the Dutch expressed concern about the possible fall-out from embargoes – was it thought that the Japanese would turn to force if it was clear that they would be faced with joint opposition from Britain and the United States.

In a sense the experience of the undeclared war was a misleading guide for the policies to be followed in Southeast Asia. The United States would not effectively interpose in China, and the Japanese

[49] q. Tarling, *Pacific War*, p. 131.

could expand their aims, though not necessarily achieve them. In Southeast Asia the United States would interpose, not because of its intrinsic importance, but because of its significance in the European war. Yet the United States failed to see that because Southeast Asia had also become crucial to the Japanese, its assumption that they could be brought to a halt might not work, and that when diplomacy could not achieve their aims, they would resort to force.

Meanwhile the failure to oppose them encouraged them to set out their basic ambitions in a most expansive form, first in East Asia and now in Southeast Asia as well. In the latter half of 1940 the major objective of imperial policy was defined as the creation of the Greater East Asia Co-Prosperity Sphere (GEAPS). The European crisis had also introduced a time factor, because it prompted the expansion of the American naval programme. The Japanese could not wait for Southeast Asia to come to them in the course of a long historical process, as Ashton-Gwatkin had once suggested.

Mediation between French Indo-China and Thailand

After the signing of the pact, Japan achieved some success in Thailand, but not as a result of it. In 1933 Siam had abstained during the League of Nations vote on Manchukuo, and the following year the British ambassador had noted 'a distinct tendency on the part of the younger Siamese to look to Japan'. His successor, Sir Josiah Crosby, suggested rather that Japan was now 'one of the pivotal points around which her foreign policy must turn'.[50] Prime Minister Phahon did not want Siam's contacts with the world limited: 'I think the theory of "Asia for the Asiatics" is unnatural and unsound. It would mean the end of progress.' Pridi Phanomyong asked:

Suppose we do have 'Asia for the Asiatics', what then? Do we have dissension among the Asiatics? Do we have one nation trying to assume dominance?... what has Siam to gain from such a policy? As it is now, open to all countries, we have the benefit of the culture, social and economic advantages, through intercourse with Western nations! And what is more, we have freedom![51]

Yatabe Yasukichi, the Japanese ambassador, himself insisted:

[50] q. ibid., p. 50.
[51] q. E. Th. Flood, 'Japan's Relations with Thailand: 1928-1941', Ph.D. thesis, Univ. of Washington, 1967, p. 68.

Siam wishes to be rid of the white man's oppression, but she has no desire to replace it with Japanese influence in Siam ... if there is anyone who believes that Siam can easily be gathered under the umbrella of the pan-Asian movement ..., that person is badly mistaken.[52]

While the civilian promoters of the 1932 coup mainly focused on getting rid of the remnants of the unequal treaties, however, the military wing increasingly emphasised the irredentist cause articulated by Luang Vichit Vadhakarn, and they were encouraged by news of the Austrian *Anschluss*. In mid-1938 the French had reports that Japan was seeking a deal with Siam, by which it would secure facilities from which to threaten the Burma Road, and that it was urging Siam to join the Anti-Comintern Pact. After he became prime minister in December, Pibun denied the rumours that Siam would associate itself with the pact. The newspapers the Japanese subsidised indeed urged him to join it. Even one of the more neutral ones commented that, if war broke out in Europe, Japan would offer the Southeast Asian peoples support in their struggle for independence, and Siam would have to side with Japan and not the Europeans.[53] Prime Minister Pibun was nervous. But there was no clear indication that the French and the British would come to the aid of the Thais if Japan backed its demands by force, even though the Singapore conference of 1939 recognised that its geographical position made Siam 'a vital factor in the security of Indo-China, Malaya and Burma'.[54]

The conclusion of the Nazi-Soviet Non-Aggression Pact put an end, of course, to any question of extending the Anti-Comintern Pact. On the outbreak of war in Europe, Siam, soon to be called Thailand, declared its neutrality, and the belligerents pledged to respect it. Pibun now took up the idea of a non-aggression treaty that the French had earlier suggested and suggested one with Britain as well. That the British favoured, as preventing the Japanese use of Thailand as a base for offensive operations without encountering Thai resistance. The Thais wanted, however, to couple their treaty with the French with a long-sought modification of the Mekong border. Afraid that this would only encourage irredentism, the French were reluctant, and the agreement was signed only a week before France fell.

[52] To Hirota, 15 December 1935, ibid., pp. 131-2.

[53] J. Stowe, *Siam becomes Thailand*, London: Hurst, 1991, p. 121.

[54] q. Tarling, *Pacific War*, p. 53.

Prince Wan had also invited the Japanese to make a similar treaty. They did not reply, for they were looking not for a Western-style non-aggression pact, but for 'a special political understanding'.[55] In April Direck, the deputy foreign minister, sought an answer. The Japanese determined to secure, not the special political understanding, but an agreement that would forestall any gains the British might make from their pact. The basic points would include respect for territorial integrity and affirmation of friendship and peace, exchange of information on problems of common interest, and obligation not to assist enemy states in time of war. The Japanese minister wanted the agreement signed before the pacts. The Thais offered to sign it on the same day. They accepted in return that it should be signed in Tokyo.

The collapse of France upset the calculations of the Thais, as of others. What was to be the fate of Indo-China? Pibun sounded out the Japanese. Officers of the war ministry and of the army general staff, meeting on 7 August, responded positively to the opportunity Thai irredentism seemed to provide. The agreement with the Japanese of 30 August, however, Vichy saw as a restraint on the Thais as well as the Japanese, and it hoped that the Japanese would uphold the integrity of Indo-China against them.

The semi-occupation of Tonkin and the conclusion of the pact prompted Pibun, however, to make a verbal undertaking to the Japanese: he sent his deputy Vanich to tell the naval attaché Torigoe Shinichi that he had resolved to rely on Japan, and he affirmed the pledge on 1 October, though declining to put it in writing.[56] 'A verbal pledge is quite all right,' said Matsuoka.[57] Pibun would permit Japanese troops to cross Thailand to attack Singapore in return for support for the irredentist cause. He would also agree to supply Japan with all the raw materials it needed. The staff officers in Tokyo were pleased, and pressed Matsuoka to act on these pledges.

Matsuoka now had to reconcile Japan's policies towards Indo-China and Thailand. The answer was a dishonest mediation. The Four Ministers conference of 5 November decided that 'favourable consideration' would be given to Thai claims, 'especially concern-

[55] Stowe, *Siam becomes Thailand*, p. 157.

[56] Charivat Santaputra, 'Thai Foreign Policy 1932-1946', Ph.D. thesis, Univ. of Southampton, 1982, pp. 229-30; also E. Th. Flood, 'The 1940 Franco-Thai Border Dispute', *JSEAH*, 10, 2 (September 1969), p. 324.

[57] q. Flood, 'Japan's Relations with Thailand', p. 337.

ing the recovery of lost territories in the area of Luang Prabang and Pakse', and attention would be given to mediation in Franco-Thai relations. Thailand would have to 'cooperate actively in the New Order in East Asia' and to recognise Manchukuo. Conferences would be held on cooperation in various fields, and far-reaching economic collaboration established. 'A gradual reform in the internal composition of the Thai government will be effected so that a Japan-Thai Alliance may be harmoniously realised.'[58]

On 20 November, after conferring with army and navy leaders, Matsuoka told the legation in Bangkok that Japan would offer its good offices. In the mediation Japan would take Thailand's side and favour the return of Luang Prabang and Pakse. In return Pibun would agree to the conditions of 5 November. Japan would also promise to consider the return of other lost territories in the future, especially those in British hands, and to furnish Thailand with economic and military aid.

Pibun speedily accepted the Japanese proposals, and negotiations culminated in a meeting between him and the chargé Asada Renzo on 28 November. Tension was increasing, and there were border incidents. But the French took their time to reply to Matsuoka's offer, made on 2 December, and then declined it. Matsuoka had indicated that the return of Luang Prabang and Pakse would be involved. France could not accept his offer from the point of view of its territorial integrity. Junior army officers condemned Matsuoka's policy and pressed for an immediate takeover of all Indo-China and Thailand. Tojo argued that this would provoke war with Britain and the United States, for which Japan was not yet prepared, and the officers had to content themselves with supplying war equipment to Bangkok.

The liaison conference of 26 December called for swift establishment of political, military and economic ties with Thailand and stressed the need to coerce Indo-China into accepting mediation, 'a typically ambiguous compromise between the extreme ideas of the army general staff and the more conservative approach of the war ministry, the navy, and the foreign office'.[59]

Decoux's contacts with Singapore, and the loss of a Thai destroyer in a naval engagement, were discussed at a liaison conference on 19 January. The military pressed for complete control of

[58] q. ibid., pp. 337-8.
[59] Ibid., p. 379.

Indo-China and a military pact with Thailand so that Japan could oust Britain from Southeast Asia; they also argued for a show of force to pre-empt British mediation. Matsuoka, however, got his way: a renewed offer to mediate.

His speech to the Diet on 21 January indicated that 'Japan as the leader in East Asia cannot afford to remain indifferent to such a dispute',[60] and he declared that British interference could not be tolerated. The French gave in. 'And it would appear that the Thai leaders in order to acquire their mess of pottage from the prostrate French in Indochina have gone along and deliberately put their heads into the Japanese noose.'[61] Pibun responded to the formal offer of mediation conveyed by the new minister, Futami Yasusato, without even consulting Direck.

The first step was a ceasefire. The French rejected a Japanese proposal to send a peacekeeping force to interpose between the two sides. The Thais deeply disliked the venue of the negotiation, a Japanese ship, the *Natori*, moored in the harbour at Saigon next to the ship that had sunk their destroyer. Difficult negotiations followed, and the ceasefire agreement, to last till 11 February, was signed only on 31 January. A Japanese destroyer, the *Fumitsuki*, was stationed at Paknam. The German, American and British ambassadors in Tokyo thought that a new Japanese move was imminent. In fact the Japanese were still divided.

The army general staff, especially the operations division, saw the mediation simply as a means of extracting agreements from the two parties and wanted to apply pressure on the French. Matsuoka thought that precipitate action would provoke the United States and Britain, and taunted his opponents, asking them if they were ready to attack Singapore. He also opposed favouring the Thais unduly, lest that undermined relations with the French. A liaison conference on 30 January rejected a military plan to use force against Indo-China if Japan's objectives, close ties with Indo-China and Thailand, were not met by 31 March. The policy finally approved called for a military agreement with Thailand and additional facilities in Indo-China without setting a deadline for the use of force.

A conference on 5 February approved Matsuoka's mediation plan. That put up three options for a territorial settlement. Japan would be guarantor of the treaty, secure facilities for carrying out

---

[60] q. Charivat, 'Thai Foreign Policy', p. 235.
[61] Grant/Hull, 27 January 1941, 48. FRUS, V, 44.

its obligation, and participate in the border commission. France and Thailand would make no agreements with third countries and would recognise Japan's leading position in the sphere.

Prince Wan sought the return of Laos and Cambodia. Though Torigoe argued that Japan should favour Pibun, that was far more than Matsuoka contemplated, and, pushing through an extension of the ceasefire to 25 February, the Japanese sought to scale down Thai demands. On 17 February they suggested that France should cede the Luang Prabang and Pakse enclaves, all of Battambang, two-thirds of Siemreap and a third of Kompong Thom. The Thais would make a payment, so as to give the impression of reciprocity that the French sought.

Neither side accepted this proposal. Matsuoka persuaded the liaison conference to extend the ceasefire deadline, and to offer another proposal. He secured the emperor's support on 24 February, and presented it to the two parties the same day. This dropped the payment, but extended the demilitarisation zone that had been proposed. Vichy agreed reluctantly. Matsuoka's notion that it should after all retain Battambang Tojo rejected.

The plan was signed on 11 March, but the treaty itself took some weeks to conclude. The French still sought a payment, and in the end the Japanese insisted on it, and also on total demilitarisation. Letters exchanged by Matsuoka and the chief delegates stipulated that Japan would guarantee the settlement. They also bound Thailand and Indo-China not to make agreements with third parties that might be hostile to Japan.

Indo-China had received a blow, but not a fatal one, Arsène Henry thought; the blow to Thailand was 'absolutely fatal', reducing it to 'the position of Manchukuo'.[62] Thailand had, however, assumed no formal obligations to Japan other than the pledge not to make agreements with others. In the subsequent weeks, moreover, the British still sought to conciliate Thailand, and, partly as a result of their persuasion, the State Department, on 17 June 1941, agreed to offer it a loan and commercial credits, and also help it acquire limited quantities of petroleum products.

The Yoshizawa mission

Whatever their success in Indo-China and Thailand, the Japanese had not done well in the Indies. Kobayashi had departed after a

[62] Grew/Hull, 17 March 1941, 423, FRUS, V, 112.

renewed but vain attempt to start political discussions. The Mitsui representative, Mukai, had accepted the oil companies' offer, about half of the expanded amount the Japanese had sought. The Dutch, their minister in London explained, 'did not want to put the screw in on the Japanese to too great an extent'.[63]

In January the Japanese renewed their efforts. Kobayashi's successor, Yoshizawa Kenkichi, a former foreign minister, produced an agenda for the discussions that, while not specifically invoking the New Order, began, as Van Mook put it, 'with the usual tendentious and incorrect generalities alleging the close economic interdependence of Japan and the Netherlands East Indies and the urgent necessity for the former to help the latter to develop her resources for the welfare of the world'.[64] The desiderata included many old proposals – easier immigration; removal of restrictions on prospecting; freer medical practice; 'favourable' and 'friendly' treatment of Japanese enterprises; fishing in territorial waters; direct air service to Japan by Japanese planes; removal of restraints on coasting trade – and one new one, a Japanese-managed submarine cable and the use of Japanese in telegrams. There were also unspecific proposals over import quotas and exports.

After rebuffing Matsuoka, who had in his Diet speeches included the Indies in the Sphere, the Dutch replied to Yoshizawa in stonewalling style. Netherlands policy was based on welfare, progress and emancipation of the population, which required wide-ranging and non-discriminatory trade, though restrictions were inevitable in wartime. The Japanese enjoyed a larger share of the import trade than of the export trade, but that was possible only because Netherlands India traded with other countries. By mid-February discussions were under way. They were, Van Mook said, 'pervaded by a bland, friendly feeling', but 'should Japan get bases in Indo-China and Thailand', he intended to propose that Yoshizawa should return to Japan, and the discussions be closed. In March the Japanese still seemed 'indifferent to the success of their own proposals', as Van Mook put it.[65] They were divided as to whether to stick to their proposals or go for a compromise on materials. Their mission also provided a cover for espionage.[66]

---

[63] q. Tarling, *Pacific War*, p. 215.

[64] q. ibid., pp. 223-4.

[65] q. ibid., pp. 224-5, 233.

[66] Goto, '*Returning to Asia*', pp. 55, 96.

Britain had been anxious to prevent supplies from reaching Germany through the Japanese. When they joined the Tripartite Pact and announced their intention of building the Sphere, Britain took what it hoped were non-provocative steps to weaken their economy and prevent their accumulating stocks that might make them invulnerable to blockade in future. With their success on the mainland, the Japanese were able to supply their tin and rubber needs. If the Dutch now responded to their economic demands, they would be able to supply Germany and build up their own reserves.

The question of quotas thus became central. The Dutch reply in June indicated that commitments could not extend beyond six months; allowed for the existing quotas of tin and a reduced quota of rubber for the rest of 1941, but suggested that they might need to be cut; allowed one concession for oil exploration; and asked for increased Japanese imports of sugar, ebony and coffee. Though there was some feeling among the British that the quotas were 'generous',[67] Yoshizawa told the governor-general that they were unsatisfactory, and left. Craigie was concerned lest military operations should follow. The army chief-of-staff, Sugiyama Gen, opposed them, but wanted troops sent to Indo-China. Matsuoka pointed to Japan's promise to respect the integrity of Indo-China and thought sending troops might hasten a clash with Indo-China. 'Another reason the occupation needs to be reconsidered is that Russo-German relations are strained at present.'[68]

The Japanese, as Craigie said, were preoccupied with developments elsewhere. Would Germany reach agreement with Russia or go to war? What policy should Japan pursue?

Southern Indo-China

The diplomacy of the Tripartite Pact had not brought the advantages that Konoe had anticipated. Japan explored other options. Talks with the United States began unofficially in March through the activities of the so-called John Doe Associates. A draft understanding was produced on 9 April, largely the work of Col. Iwakura Hideo, attached to Ambassador Nomura's staff by the army ministry. Hull indicated that he wished to put in a statement of fundamental principles, but Nomura did not report that. The liaison

---

[67] q. Tarling, *Pacific War*, p. 235.
[68] q. N. Ike, *Japan's Decision for War*, Stanford Univ. Press, 1967, p. 54.

conference was unwilling to make the 9 April proposal formal, unless it was clear that the United States would allow Japan a free hand in Southeast Asia, in return for its neutrality in the event of American entry into the European war. Iwakura thought Matsuoka was an obstacle to understanding, and advocated a meeting between Konoe and Roosevelt.

For his part Matsuoka was attempting to improve relations with the Soviet Union. That could not be achieved through Berlin, as he had hoped. It was instead achieved in what Matsuoka termed 'diplomatic *Blitzkrieg*'[69] as a result of the worsening relations between Russia and Germany. Japan and the Soviet Union concluded a five-year neutrality pact on 13 April.

Either way the Japanese were seeking to use the relationships among other powers to secure their objectives in Southeast Asia without actually resorting to war. The drastic change in the relations of Germany and the Soviet Union prompted a reconsideration of both direction and method. On 5 June Oshima Hiroshi, the ambassador in Berlin, had warned that it was probable that Hitler would invade Russia. Three tentative choices were discussed: a move into Southeast Asia; compromise with the United States and the preparation of operations against the Soviet Union; strengthening the Kwantung army and securing control of Indo-China. The army general staff favoured the third option, with priority for the Kwantung army. A meeting of the heads of the operations sections of the two general staffs and a representatives of the army ministry on 10 June gave priority to the southern problem, however, and Sugiyama argued accordingly at the liaison conference.

The matter was reconsidered when the German invasion of the Soviet Union began on 22 June. Matsuoka favoured going along with Germany, despite the neutrality pact he had so recently signed in Moscow. 'Great men change their minds. Previously, I advocated going south, but now I favour north.'[70] At the liaison conferences he argued Japan's obligation to its Axis partner. A meeting of staff officers at Tojo's residence reconfirmed the priority of the southern advance, however, and Konoe supported that option. An imperial conference on 2 July sanctioned an 'Outline of National Policies in View of the Changing Situation'.

---

[69] q. Sato Kyozo, *Japan and Britain at the Crossroads*, Tokyo: Senshu Univ. Press, 1986, p. 107.

[70] q. ibid., p. 117.

'Regardless of whatever changes may occur in the world situation, Japan will adhere to the established policy of creating a Greater East Asia Coprosperity Sphere and thereby contribute to the establishment of world peace.' The southern area was vital to Japan's 'self-preservation and self-defense',[71] and it would not be 'deterred by the possibility' of war with Britain and the United States.[72]

Matsuoka continued to resist until he was displaced by a cabinet reshuffle on 18 July. Steps to secure southern Indo-China ensued. Only on 9 August, however, did Imperial HQ formally decide 'to abandon hope for a favorable opportunity to exploit the situation in the north against the Soviet Union, and to concentrate all effort on a southward advance, regardless of any new developments in the German-Soviet War'.[73] The priority was now emphatically on the south. There was still the hope that the objectives there might be achieved by diplomatic means, particularly if the Germans secured a decisive victory.

Ambassador Nomura called on Admiral Turner, director of war plans in the US Office of Naval Operations, on 20 July. The occupation of southern Indo-China was expected in the next few days, and he conveyed the impression that, if the United States were accommodating, 'any action it might take in the Atlantic would not be a matter of any great concern to Japan'. In that he was recurring to the notions of April. The chances of a deal *ex post facto* were small. But the notion had never been realistic, since the Americans connected Southeast Asia with the European war. This Turner now emphasised. The occupation of Indo-China would affect the strategic position of the United States, to which the greatest danger, as he told Nomura, lay in the continued military success of Germany. 'If Great Britain were to collapse, German military power might very well be directed against South America, and such moves would cause great difficulties for the United States.' Anything that affected 'the future security of the UK, in any part of the world', was of interest to the United States 'from the defensive standpoint'. The occupation of Indo-China was

particularly important for the defense of the United States since it might threaten the British position in Singapore and the Dutch position in the

---

[71] q. Crowley in Morley, *Japan's Foreign Policy*, p. 94.

[72] q. Ike, *Japan's Decision*, p. 78.

[73] q. Crowley in Morley, *Japan's Foreign Policy*, p. 95.

Netherlands East Indies. Were they to pass out of their present control, a very severe blow would be struck at the integrity of the defense of the British Isles, and these Isles might well then be overcome by the Germans. It can thus be seen what a very close interest, from a military viewpoint, the United States has in sustaining the status quo in the southern portion of the Far East.[74]

Europe was thus not offering Japan an opportunity but foreclosing it.

In any case the Japanese had already presented their demands to Vichy, and on 21 July Admiral Darlan indicated that, owing to 'extremely strong insistence' on the part of the Japanese, he had been 'forced, with regret, to grant permission for Japan to occupy Indo-China'. He had, however, asked Japan 'to make a public declaration of its intention to respect French sovereign rights over the country, and to promise to withdraw its troops when "emergency" has passed'.[75] Resistance, it had been made plain, would result in the internment of French forces, the proclamation of Annam's independence and the assumption of sovereign power by the Japanese. The Vichy authorities clung to their earlier view: any authority was better than none. '[T]he most important question for France is to remain with some authority on the spot regardless of how restricted such authority may be or how humiliating its curtailment.'[76]

Nishihara's successor, General Sumita Raishiro, presented the demands in Hanoi on 22 July and the agreement was signed on 23 July. It provided for the use of eight air bases in south Vietnam and Cambodia and three naval bases, including Cam Ranh and Saigon. Forty thousand troops would be sent and have freedom of movement. The agreement superseded that of 23 September 1940. Japan guaranteed French sovereignty and the integrity of Indo-China.

An announcement on 26 July alluded to friendly conversations, respect for territorial integrity and sovereignty, and the GEAPS. The same day Sumita arrived in Saigon to superintend the operation. French aircraft and certain French troops, including the Foreign Legion, were sent north. The 'curiosity' of the native population was aroused, as the British consul-general put it: they

[74] Turner/Stark, 21 July 1941. FRUS Japan, II, 518-19.
[75] q. Tarling, *Pacific War*, p. 331.
[76] Leahy/Hull, 22 July 1941, 921. FRUS, V, 221-2.

have collected at street corners as if to watch a procession'.[77]

The same day, 26 July, was also the day on which Roosevelt issued an executive order freezing Japanese assets in the United States, subsequently enforced more rigidly than he had expected. Somewhat nervously, the British and the Dutch followed the American lead, though they had no guarantee of American support should Japan react by attacking their possessions. On 30 July the Americans announced that defending the Philippines was now official policy.[78] The main feature of the reinforcement programme was the supply of B-17 bombers with a range of 1,500 miles, the Flying Fortresses. Based in the Philippines, they might deter the Japanese from attacking the islands or indeed other parts of Southeast Asia. The build-up would be complete by February or March 1942.[79]

Negotiations with the United States

For their part, the Japanese had already concluded 'that the United States and Great Britain were inseparable', and that if there were to be hostilities in the south, they would have to attack the Philippines.[80] They had begun to talk of 'encirclement'.[81] What that meant, of course, was that their expanded hopes were being frustrated. They did not, however, abandon them. For those hopes had also been fears. If they did not secure the resources of Southeast Asia, they would become dependent on the United States. That was not acceptable. Japan had failed to pursue a realistic policy, and others had not stopped it. Now they wanted to. The war had encouraged the Japanese to think that a further expansion might be the answer. It was also the source of the limits upon them. If diplomacy could not succeed, the options were war or dependence. The chances of success in the former would not improve with delay unless Germany won.

On 24 July Roosevelt had suggested that, if Japan refrained from occupying Indo-China, or withdrew its forces, he would

[77] q. Tarling, *Pacific War*, p. 331.

[78] D. Reynolds, *The Creation of the Anglo-American Alliance 1937-41*, London: Europa, 1981, p. 285.

[79] H. Conroy and H. Wray, *Pearl Harbor Reexamined*, Honolulu: Univ. of Hawaii Press, 1990, pp. 171-2.

[80] A.J. Marder, *Old Friends, New Enemies*, Oxford: Clarendon Press, 1981, p. 329.

[81] Crowley in Morley, *Japan's Foreign Policy*, pp. 91-3.

endeavour to secure a commitment from other countries that it should be treated as a neutralised country. Nothing came of this, but in early August the Japanese used it in an attempt to reopen Nomura's discussions. On 6 August he offered Hull a proposal under which Japan would not station further troops in the southwest Pacific, would withdraw those in Indo-China 'on the settlement of the China Incident', and guarantee the neutrality of the Philippines. The United States would suspend military measures and advise the British and the Dutch to do so, too. It would restore normal trade and commerce and cooperate with Japan in procuring the resources it needed, especially in Netherlands India. It would use its good offices to initiate negotiations between Japan and the 'Chiang Kai-shek regime', and recognise a special status for Japan in Indo-China even after its troops had left. The US reply alluded to its views on a broad understanding.

Nomura took up the earlier idea for a meeting between the President and Prince Konoe, but Hull pointed to the need to reshape Japan's policies. Then Churchill and Roosevelt met in Newfoundland, producing the Atlantic Charter, and also a statement opposing further Japanese steps to secure military domination of neighbouring countries. Watered down, this was given to Nomura on 17 August, Roosevelt indicating that conversations might be resumed if Japan were to 'readjust its position' along the lines of the principles to which the United States was committed. On 28 August Nomura brought a message from Konoe, seeking a meeting, and a statement, saying that the principles and 'the practical application thereof, in the friendliest manner possible' were 'the prime requisites of a true peace'.[82] Konoe had taken up the idea of a top-level meeting, in the hope that it could repair the damage evidenced by the unexpectedly strong American reaction to the move into southern Indo-China. He planned to meet the President and get round any obstruction at home by cabling direct to the emperor.[83] Hull was against any meeting before an agreement on 'the principal questions' had been reached.[84]

On 9 August the army general staff had authorised preparations for war in the south starting about the end of November. The navy preferred a mid-October deadline, and that was informally agreed

[82] q. Tarling, *Pacific War*, p. 289.

[83] Oka Yoshitake, *Konoe Fumimaro*, Tokyo Univ. Press, 1983, pp. 136, 139-40.

[84] q. Tarling, *Pacific War*, p. 289.

by staff and ministry officers on 29 August. A liaison conference on 3 September approved 'Essentials for Carrying Out the Policies of the Empire'. The government was prepared to face a war with the United States, Britain and the Netherlands. It would use 'every possible diplomatic means available' to secure its minimal demands, but '[i]n the event that there is no prospect of our demands being met by the first ten days in October, we will immediately decide to commence hostilities with the United States and Britain, and take final measures'.[85]

An imperial conference was convened on 6 September to sanction the decision. Britain, the United States and the Netherlands were 'taking every possible measure to oppose our Empire', Konoe declared: Japan must complete its preparations, 'and at the same time take all diplomatic means to prevent the outbreak of a disastrous war. Only in case such diplomatic means fail within a certain period of time should we resort to the last means of self-defense.'[86]

The demands related both to China and to Southeast Asia. The United States and Britain must refrain from interfering with the settlement of the China Incident, giving no aid to Chiang Kai-shek, closing the Burma Road, accepting a pact between China, Japan and Manchukuo. They must not jeopardise the defence of the empire, must refrain from further military preparations in East Asia and must not build any bases in Thailand, the Indies or the Soviet Union. They must 'cooperate' with Japan's acquisition of necessary commodities, lifting embargoes and encouraging the cooperation of Thailand, Indo-China and the empire. For its part Japan would undertake no offensive operations into adjacent areas except as needed to end the China Incident, would withdraw from Indo-China when a 'fair and just' peace had been made with China and would respect the neutrality of the Philippines.

A version of this was presented to the United States coupled with an indication that Japan would not abide by the Tripartite Pact if it entered the European war. The US reply, made on 2 October, considered that the Japanese statement would circumscribe the application of the general principles, and questioned whether a summit meeting would in such circumstances be 'likely to contribute to the advancement of the high purposes which we

---

[85] q. Crowley in Morley, *Japan's Foreign Policy*, p. 96.
[86] q. ibid., pp. 95–6; also Ike, *Japan's Decision*, p. 138.

have mutually in mind'.[87] Konoe's diplomacy failed. Rather than seek to reverse the decision of 6 September, he chose to resign.

The former premiers found it difficult to offer agreed advice on a successor, finally expressing their 'feeling of negative support' for Tojo.[88] His government re-examined Japan's policy. A liaison conference on 1 November gave the diplomats until 30 November to complete a settlement. War with America and Britain would follow if they failed.[89] Nomura spoke on 10 November of a *modus vivendi*, and on 18 November Hull raised the possibility of 'a relaxation of freezing' so as 'to enable the peaceful leaders in Japan to get control of situation on [in?] Japan and to assert their influence'.[90] On 20 November Nomura offered to remove Japanese troops from southern Indo-China, while the Americans would co-operate in securing commodities from the Indies, drop the freeze, supply oil and refrain from measures prejudicial to endeavours for restoring peace in China.[91] The United States prepared a counter-draft *modus vivendi*, but abandoned it. Instead it reiterated the general principles. Nomura's new assistant, Kurusu Saburo, thought his government would 'throw up its hands'.[92] The reply indeed came only after the attack on Pearl Harbor.

US policy had been based on the assumption that it could halt further Japanese advances if it chose to do so. That notion rested ultimately on an image of Japan's weakness that had a substantial basis in fact. When the Japanese sought to by-pass their weakness by maximising their planning and exploiting the opportunities others gave them, the Americans stepped up the economic restraints, engaged in joint planning with their allies, began reinforcing the Philippines, and, by reaffirming their principles, helped to keep Chiang Kai-shek's resistance alive.

When those steps failed to bring the Japanese into a compliant frame of mind, Hull continued the conversations in the hope that, if it became plain that the Germans would not win in Russia, and the reinforcement programme were completed in the Philippines, Japan might yet refrain from turning to armed action. It was, how-

---

[87] FRUS Japan, II, 660-1.
[88] Crowley in Morley, *Japan's Foreign Policy*, p. 101.
[89] Ike, *Japan's Decision*, p. 204.
[90] FRUS Japan, II, 744-50.
[91] Ibid., pp. 755-6.
[92] Ibid., pp. 764-50.

ever, impossible to win time by a *modus vivendi* that would appear
to sacrifice China, one of the constituents of the policy of restraint.

Time was of the essence to Japan, too, but in a different way.
Earlier, it had seemed that in due course Japan must have a share of
the resources of the outer Nanyo, since the European colonial
powers could not survive in the long term, and the Americans had
indeed put a time limit on remaining in the Philippines. Those
long-term prospects were undone by the European war. 'I do not
believe that the present situation would have developed out of
just the China Incident,' Hara, the president of the privy council,
declared on 5 November. 'We have come to where we are because
of the war between Germany and Great Britain.'[93]

The United States became anxious to keep Southeast Asia open
to the British so that they might continue the war in Europe with
its resources, and perhaps succeed in defeating Germany without
overt American intervention. The European war, moreover, prompted the United States to expand its navy. That was undertaken
above all with an eye to hemispheric defence and as a precaution
against Germany's success. But it would also affect the naval relationship with Japan in the coming years, and put the Americans in a
position to determine its policy, above all by control of oil supplies.
Japan was thus focused more urgently on the resources of the Indies,
and the army came to share the view that Southeast Asia was the
priority provided there was no war with the Soviet Union. An
attempt must be made to ensure its resources before too late.

There was an air of fatalism among Japan's decision-makers.
'The government has decided', said the chief of naval staff, Nagano
Osami, commenting on the imperial conference of 6 September,
'that if there is no war, the fate of the nation is sealed. Even if there
is war, the country may be ruined. Nevertheless, a nation which
does not fight in this plight has lost its spirit and is already a
doomed country.'[94] Tojo told the imperial conference on 5
November:

The first stage of the war will not be difficult. We have some uneasiness
about a protracted war. But how can we let the United States continue to
do as she pleases, even though there is some uneasiness? Two years from
now we will have no petroleum for military use. Ships will stop moving.
When I think about the strengthening of American defenses in the south-

[93] q. Ike, *Japan's Decision*, p. 237.
[94] q. Crowley in Morley, *Japan's Foreign Policy*, p. 98.

west Pacific, the expansion of the American fleet, the unfinished China Incident, and so on, I see no end to difficulties. ... I fear that we would become a third-class nation after two or three years if we just sat tight.[95]

If there was a more rational approach, Nagano had hinted at it. The empire could not subjugate the enemy, nor break its will to fight. But if the first stage of the operation were accomplished promptly, Japan could 'secure strategic points in the Southwest Pacific, [and] even if [the] military preparations of the United States develop as scheduled, we shall be able to establish the foundation for a long war by maintaining an invincible position'.[96] What was missing here was a means of ending it. Indeed, Tojo seemed to think that other powers, engaged elsewhere, would come to accept a *fait accompli*. 'As to what our moral basis for going to war should be', he argued on 5 November,

there is some merit in making it clear that Great Britain and the United States represent a strong threat to Japan's self-preservation. Also, if we are fair in governing the occupied areas, attitudes toward us would probably relax. America may be enraged for a while, but later she will come to understand [why we did what we did].[97]

The liaison conference of 15 November adopted a plan for bringing the war to an end. In it Germany, Italy and Japan were to cooperate 'to put down Britain first so as to induce the United States to withdraw from the war'.[98]

The other powers, it was assumed, would come to accept a Japanese occupation. In that sense the invasion was a further step in the increasingly forceful diplomacy Japan had been adopting. Other powers had defined Japan's objectives since the 1890s. In the interwar period they had been ineffectual in limiting them, and internal pressures had helped to expand them. Even now the premier could persuade himself that they would not contest Southeast Asia, where the approaching end of the colonial system had marked out Japan's destiny and the acquisition of oil had a new urgency. It was characteristic of Japan's policy-making that little thought was give to the means of concluding the new conflict.

[95] Ike, *Japani Decision*, p. 238.

[96] q. Crowley in Morley, *Japan's Foreign Policy*, p. 97; also Ike, *Japan's Decision*, p. 140.

[97] q. Ike, *Japan's Decision*, p. 199.

[98] q. Ikeda Kiyoshi in T.G. Fraser and P. Lowe, eds, *Conflict and Amity in East Asia*, Basingstoke: Macmillan, 1992, p. 44.

'[W]e cannot avoid a long-term war this time', said Hara on 1 December, 'but I believe that we must somehow get around this and bring about an early settlement. In order to do this, we will need to start thinking now about how to end the war.'[99] Instead the Japanese leaders seem to have hoped that something would turn up. 'The general idea must have been', Nagano put it at the end of the war, 'that this would be a very long, protracted war, that in time it would end somehow. That was the idea prior to the outbreak of the war.'[100] 'Before and at the beginning of the war', Admiral Tomioka Sadatoshi recalled,

we all believed in the concept of Limited War ... and anticipated the course of the war as follows: firstly, to attain an overwhelming supremacy over the enemy forces in its early stages and create an equilibrium versus the Allies; then, to seek a favourable opportunity to enter into negotiations with our enemies for a compromise peace, keeping enough potential to continue the war. Such optimistic predictions, it is clear, were not really based on rational or reliable calculations. But, considering the favourable development of the war in Europe where Germany had become an irre- sistible force, and also taking account of possible developments in interna- tional politics, most of the top leaders expected that they would have a good chance to bring the war to a negotiated peace fairly easily.[101]

'This means that Japan is sunk too,' Onozuku Kiheiji, a former president of Tokyo Imperial University, whispered to a colleague in the dining hall after Pearl Harbor.[102] No one indeed believed that Japan could win a total victory against the United States. 'In war', as Ho Chi Minh was to put it in April 1942,

the one who is most consistent and durable in strength will win ... the longer the war lasts, the more will it benefit Britain and America and harm Japan. Japan's victories are preliminary, like a straw catching fire – it burns quickly, and is quickly extinguished.[103]

But the euphoria the initial success brought made it difficult to consider negotiation. A compromise was always going to be diffi- cult to find, given that Japan's decision-making structures were

---

[99] q. Ike, *Japan's Decision*, p. 282.

[100] q. Marder, *Old Friends*, p. 261.

[101] q. Ikeda Kiyoshi in I. Nish, ed., *Anglo-Japanese Alienation*, Cambridge Univ. Press, 1982, p. 145.

[102] q. Ienaga, *Japan's Last War*, p. 141.

[103] q. S. Tonnesson, *The Vietnamese Revolution of 1945*, Oslo: IPRI; London: Sage, 1991, p. 34.

attuned to expansion rather that moderation. A compromise also required the agreement of its opponents. They, however, had become more determined to put Japan in its place, not less.

The move into Southeast Asia was the product of growing fear and unthinking optimism. It followed a long period in which Japan had sought to achieve its aims there by pressure rather than invasion. It was not in fact prepared for the task of occupation. In the case of the Indies, it still hoped to avoid armed force, and it did not declare war. It wanted the Indies 'intact', and it was the Dutch who declared war on the 8th.[104] The administration of the new empire was improvised, borrowing from the practices of metropolis and Manchuria.

---

[104] Togo Shigenori, *The Cause of Japan*, New York: Simon & Schuster, 1956, p. 214. Goto, *'Returning to Asia'*, p. 122.

3

WAR AND PEACE

Pearl Harbor

'We're all astounded over Japan. We never thought she would attack us and America at once. She must have gone mad,' wrote Oliver Harvey at the Foreign Office.[1] General Hastings Ismay heard of Pearl Harbor with 'stunned surprise. It had never occurred to anyone in London, nor I believe in Washington, that such a thing was possible.'[2] Such comments testified, perhaps, to the long-standing depreciation of Japan, and the consequent belief that the Japanese could be contained. They testified, indeed, to the boldness, if not foolhardiness, of the venture. 'Name me', Stanley Hornbeck has asked John Emmerson, then in the Tokyo embassy, 'one country in history which ever went to war in desperation!'[3]

The rationale, such as it was, came somewhere in between boldness and desperation. Force was used in a dramatic attempt to shift the international situation in Japan's failure when diplomacy had failed, and then it was hoped that their opponents would leave them alone or that diplomacy would somehow resume. A somewhat similar concept had lain behind Germany's policy in 1914. A power, frustrated by others seeking to maintain the status quo, even seeing that as encirclement, breaks out, maximising the application of its strength in what it has to hope will be a decisive blow, a coup, to which others will have to accommodate.

Japan was, however, at a double disadvantage. It was already at war in China. And its resource base, no matter how far total mobilisation went, was very much less than that of its opponents. The Kaiser looked for a short struggle. The Japanese knew that a long struggle could not readily be sustained. That was a reason for a short one. But it was easier to envisage its initial success than its successful conclusion.

[1] O. Harvey, *The War Diaries*, London: Collins, 1978, p. 71.

[2] H. Ismay, *Memoirs*, London: Heinemann, 1960, p. 241.

[3] q. Conroy and Wray, *Pearl Harbor Reexamined*, p. 175.

There were enormous risks in both cases. But, while the Wilhelmine Reich might hope that their opponents would not act together, and that the weakest of them could be quickly defeated, the Japanese acted against its major opponents simultaneously. On the other hand, those opponents, as the Japanese were aware, were committed elsewhere. If Germany had not won, it had forced Britain, already at war, and the United States, though not yet at war, to devote resources to helping the Soviet Union. The Japanese were also aware that the colonial territories were in no position to defend themselves if those that held them could not do so by land, air or sea. Their moves in Indo-China and Thailand had given them another advantage.

It was a leap in the dark. But there were glimmerings of light that a desperate man might count on. The war in Europe might yet turn out better for Germany. The United States might in any case become more directly involved. Confronted with a *fait accompli* in Southeast Asia, the Allies might come to accept what Japan did, as, despite protests and embargoes, they had put up with what it had so far done.

Ensuring command over the oil of Netherlands India was Japan's prime objective, and that had indeed to be done as soon as possible if the war were not simply to use up existing stocks. Going straight for Borneo and Sumatra would, however, expose the Japanese to counter-attacks on the way. The staffs agreed that the first step was to defeat the British forces in Hong Kong, Singapore, Malaya and Borneo, and the American forces in the Philippines. Occupying flanking positions in the Bismarck archipelago and southern Burma, they would then converge on Netherlands India. Finally they would complete the occupation of Burma and the Andaman and Nicobar islands, establishing a perimeter which they could defend.

Given its commitments elsewhere in East Asia, the army could allocate only 11 out of its 51 divisions to this venture, together with some 700 of its 1,500 aircraft. Each division in principle consisted of 18,000 men, organised in three infantry regiments, each of three battalions, one field artillery regiment, one engineer regiment and one transport regiment. The Southern Area Army, with its HQ in Saigon, was to be responsible for internal security in Indo-China, and to coordinate the operations of the Fourteenth, Fifteenth, Sixteenth and Twenty-Fifth Armies.

The Fourteenth, including the 16th and 48th Divisions, was to capture the Philippines. The Fifteenth, led by Iida Shojiro and comprising the 33rd and 55th Divisions, was to occupy Thailand, seize airfields on the Kra isthmus and invade southern Burma, with air support from the 5th Air Division after the capture of Manila. The Sixteenth Army, including the 2nd Division and, after it had taken Hong Kong, the 33rd, and also the 48th after Manila had been taken, was to occupy Dutch Borneo, Sulawesi, Ambon, Timor and southern Sumatra. The Twenty-Fifth Army, led by Yamashita Tomoyuki, was to invade Malaya and capture Singapore, southern Sumatra and British Borneo, with the Imperial Guards Division, and the 5th, 18th and 56th.

The navy had more force available. In total it had eleven battleships, six fleet carriers, four light fleet carriers, eighteen heavy cruisers, eighteen light cruisers, 113 destroyers, sixty-three submarines and six seaplane carriers. It had more than one thousand aircraft, about half carrier-borne, and most of the rest based in Taiwan, southern Indo-China and the mandated Pacific islands, and it was able to devote about half the total to direct support of the land-based operations. The planning staff did not think their forces could risk a straight fight with the US Pacific fleet, but they could not allow it to threaten their communications. The strategy had been one of 'Gradual Attrition' (*Zen-gen Sakusen*), but Yamamoto Isoroku, commander-in-chief of the combined fleet, advocated a surprise carrier-based air attack on Pearl Harbor, the nearest base the US could modernise under the Washington agreements.

Clearly he was convinced that Japan would most certainly be involved in a serious crisis if the war were prolonged. Thus, in his view, the only way to avoid this unfavourable development was to annihilate the main body of the American navy in a decisive battle in the early stages of the war, and 'thoroughly demoralize the US Navy and discourage the American people in any wish to continue the war'.[4]

The idea was encouraged by the success of the British torpedo bombers against the Italian ships at Taranto in 1940. Though it surely reduced the likelihood that the United States would accept a *fait accompli*, the project was adopted on 5 November. It was allocated to a Striking Force commanded by Nagumo Chuichi, including six carriers, with 432 aircraft, screened by nine destroyers and a light cruiser, supported by two fast battleships and two heavy

[4] Ikeda Kiyoshi in Nish, *Anglo-Japanese Alienation*, pp. 130-1.

cruisers, and accompanied by three submarines. He was to be re-called by a prearranged signal if the negotiations in Washington succeeded after he had begun his 3,000-mile voyage. Other sub-marines, approaching from the south-west, were to sink any warships that tried to escape.

The code message 'Climb Mount Niitaka' – an allusion to the highest mountain in the empire, in Formosa – warned Nagumo on 2 December that there would be no recall. The attack was fixed for 7 December, and on the evening of the 6th he hoisted the flag flown by Togo at Tsushima in 1905 and set his course for Oahu. Next morning 353 aircraft were sent off, wave after wave. Within two hours eighteen American warships and auxiliaries had been sunk or damaged and 349 aircraft destroyed or damaged. Only the *Arizona* was a total loss, however, and all three of the American carriers were intact.

'While a brilliant tactical success, the attack on Pearl Harbor was an almost unmitigated strategic failure.' The American aircraft carriers were hardly affected (two were at sea, one on the west coast), shore installations were 'hardly touched', and the submarine base was not attacked.[5] Nagumo had ruled against further attacks, and Japan's advantage was even more temporary than it was bound to be, and its perimeter even more insecure. In the meantime, however, it had made rapid advances in Southeast Asia itself.

The Thai alliance

The diplomacy of July-September 1940 had secured Japanese forces a base for the conflict with Chiang Kai-shek, though it could also be a step to the south. The diplomacy of July 1941 had secured the Japanese forces bases for moving south should that move be finally decided upon. But if they were to attack Burma, or attack Malaya overland, and not merely by sea, they would need to pass through Thailand. The main part of the 5th Division was to land at Songkhla (Singgora) and advance south along the west coast to the Perak river, and another element would land at Pattani and push south to flank the British force. A portion of the 18th would meanwhile land at Kota Bahru and seize the British airport. The Fifteenth Army would take over the rest of Thailand, and then attack Burma, descending initially on the airfield at Victoria Point.

[5] Paul B. Seguin, 'The Deteriorating Strategic Position of Japan: 1853-1945', Ph.D. thesis, Univ. of Minnesota, Minneapolis, 1972, pp. 293-4.

The Japanese plans stated that 'close military relations with Thailand will be established just prior to the use of force'. Raising the question too soon would undermine secrecy. 'It is necessary from an operational point of view for us to make landings in Thailand,' said Tojo. 'It will not do to let this be known too early. Therefore, we cannot do other than push this matter by force if they do not agree with us at the talks just before we act.'[6] The liaison conference agreed that Japan should promise to respect Thailand's territorial integrity, and hint that part of Malaya might be ceded to it.[7] When the time came, however, Pibun was absent from Bangkok, and no deal could be made. 'This upset Japanese plans for a smooth entry, and allowed for a brief period of resistance that redeemed the Thai pledge to defend the nation's territorial integrity.'[8]

General Terauchi Hisaichi in Saigon had decided to press ahead. At Songhkla the vanguard force under Tsuji Masanobu did not meet the welcoming reception it expected; instead there was a pitched battle at the police headquarters.[9] There were clashes at other coastal landing sites as well. When Iwakura Hideo's guards crossed the frontier from western Cambodia into Thailand's recently reclaimed territory, they met no resistance. News of the attacks on Pearl Harbor and Malaya had arrived, the prime minister had returned to the capital, and the Thai government had then ordered a ceasefire.

Tsubokami Teiji, the ambassador, broached the question of an alliance. Some of the Thai cabinet were in favour, but the consensus was in favour of the minimal commitment. In the final text the Thais agreed to allow the Japanese forces passage, and a joint military group would watch over implementing the arrangements. Japan pledged to respect the 'independence, sovereignty, and honor' of Thailand.[10] On 11 December, however, the cabinet voted for an alliance, pledging mutual political, economic and military assistance when either signatory was engaged in war.

In a secret annex the Japanese promised to cooperate in the re-

[6] q. Ike, *Japan's Decision*, p. 235.

[7] Flood, 'Japan's Relations with Thailand', p. 665.

[8] E.B. Reynolds, *Thailand and Japan's Southern Advance 1940-1945*, New York: St. Martin's Press, 1994, p. 81.

[9] Ibid., pp. 89-90.

[10] Ibid., p. 96.

turn of Thailand's 'lost territories', while the Thais would provide full assistance to them in their war against Britain and the United States.[11] The prospect of regaining more of the old territories was no doubt appealing. It is also true that through the liaison group Pibun was under pressure from the Japanese, who saw the alliance as a necessary preliminary to the invasion of Burma. News had come, too, of the sinking of the British battleships *Repulse* and *Prince of Wales*.

On 25 January the Thai government took the further step of declaring war on Britain and the United States. Japanese military leaders saw it as a guarantee of full cooperation in the Burma campaign, and the liaison conference had decided on 10 January that Thailand should be 'induced' to declare war when the invasion of Burma began.[12] Pibun was willing to do so, and British bombing of Bangkok on 8 and 24 January gave a pretext. 'Speaking plainly among the Thai, it is about time to declare war with the winner,' Pibun told his cabinet.[13]

The Malayan campaign

The British had been unable to provide support, or, until past the last moment, to promise assistance in the event of a Japanese attack. Nor had they been able to carry through Matador. That was a plan to pre-empt the Japanese by moving into southern Thailand to protect the approaches to Malaya. Of that risk the Japanese were aware. In the circumstances, it was, however, an impractical plan. If done without the Thais' approval, it breached their neutrality, offered the Japanese an argument for invasion and risked alienating the United States. Getting their approval was also impossible, as the British could not offer Thailand protection. The plan could not therefore be operated till the war began. In that case it could be effective only if the Japanese advanced overland rather than by sea. They did both. The British forces, led by Lieutenant-General Sir Lewis Heath, would have to stand at Jitra – on the road from Singgora but within the Malayan frontier – while also sending a small force to block the road from Pattani.

That Matador was ruled out quickly became plain, but the British delayed the decision to seize The Ledge, the best means of

---

[11] Ibid., p. 105.
[12] Ibid., p. 111.
[13] q. ibid., p. 110.

blocking the Pattani road, till it was too late. Some Thai opposition slowed the Punjabis' advance to Betong, and the Japanese reached The Ledge first. The attempt to stop the Japanese on the main road failed. 'Few of the Indian troops in this area had seen a tank before.'[14] On 12 December, in face of the attacks by Matsui's 5th Division and tanks, General Murray-Lyon ordered the 11th Indian Division to withdraw from Jitra. The result was disastrous. 'Some units and sub-units withdrew without incident; others, finding themselves unable to use the only road available, had to make their way as best they could across country. Others again never received the withdrawal orders.'[15] By 14 December Heath believed that it was necessary to retreat right back to the Perak river, and buy time for a safe withdrawal of the British garrison from Penang. That was effected on 16 December, but in the meantime the troops had to fight a number of delaying actions, and also prevent the Japanese on the Kroh road cutting of their retreat. Colonel A.M.L. Harrison wrote on 25 December:

The troops were beginning to attribute almost supernatural powers to the Japanese. ... The Japanese tanks had played a great part in this. The material effect of their fire had been small. It was the moral effect of having no adequate counter and above all of knowing that we had no tanks in Malaya at all (just as we had no Navy and no Air Force) which shook the exhausted men.[16]

Heath chose two positions south of Ipoh. The first, Kampar, the Japanese attacked on 1 and 2 January. On the 3rd the British forces withdrew to the second, Tanjong Malim, putting two brigades to the north at Trolak near the Slim river bridge. The Japanese repeatedly attacked from the air, and on 7 January broke through with tanks and infantry. 'The action at Slim River was a major disaster.'[17] 'It is obvious that tanks caused the disaster, that communications broke down, that bridges were not blown up, and that the troops (both officers and men) were too exhausted to fight the Japanese, who had put first-class, fresh troops into the field.'[18] On 11 January the

---

[14] B. Prasad, ed., *Official History of the Indian Armed Forces in the Second World War, 1939-45. Campaigns in South-East Asia, 1941-1942*, Combined Inter-Services Historical Section India and Pakistan, 1960, p. 149.

[15] Ibid., p. 166.

[16] J. Smyth, *Percival and the Tragedy of Singapore*, London: Macdonald, 1971, p. 55.

[17] S.W. Kirby et al., *The War against Japan*, London: HMSO, 1957-69, I, 281.

[18] Prasad, *Official History*, p. 220.

5th Division entered an evacuated Kuala Lumpur and established its HQ there. Approaching from Port Swettenhan, the Japanese failed to cut off 11th Division as it retreated. It took up its position for the defence of northern Johore as part of 'Westforce' under General H.G. Bennett of the 8th Australian Division.

Yamashita recognised that the withdrawing British forces would defend northern Johore along the Muar river, 'the last natural defensive position north of Singapore Island'.[19] The 5th Division was to drive down the trunk road through Batu Anam and Segamat, while the Imperial Guards thrust at Muar, and also moved to land in the rear of the British near Batu Pahat. The advance was slowed down 'at a tremendous cost' to the British forces.[20] But its success – which included a cruel massacre of wounded Australian and Indian soldiers at Parit Sulong[21] – led General Percival on 23 January to order Westforce to fall back on the Kluang-Ayer Hitam line, and on 25 January he decided to pull out of Batu Pahat. On 28 January he ordered Heath to complete the withdrawal to Singapore by 31 January. That day, after the last man had crossed, a 70-foot gap was blown in the causeway.

The battle in northern Johore was decisive for Singapore. The new supreme commander, Sir Archibald Wavell, had of course recognised that, as Yamashita had. If his forces were forced back into southern Johore, he would not have time or opportunity to build up his defences and prepare for a counter-attack. 'A withdrawal to the island would then become inevitable and, since it had been prepared to withstand neither an assault from the north nor a siege and once invested could be neither relieved nor reinforced, this could end only in surrender.'[22] The attempt to defend northern Johore failed. Now it was 'a question of holding on to Singapore Island in order to deny it to the Japanese and contain their divisions in Malaya as long as possible'.[23]

Wavell believed that Percival, strengthened by the diversion of the 18th Division from the Middle East, ought to be able to hold the island for some months. American aircraft and other reinforce-

[19] Kirby, *War against Japan*, I, 301.

[20] Prasad, *Official History*, p. 274.

[21] Kirby, *War against Japan*, I, 316. Louis Allen, *Singapore 1941-1942*, London: Davis-Poynter, 1977, p. 266.

[22] Kirby, *War against Japan*, I, 342.

[23] Ibid., p. 346.

ments were expected, and even a respite of 6-8 weeks would permit a counter-attack from the Indies. Indeed he had some 70,000 combatant troops, British, Indian and Australian, and some 15,000 non-combatant troops. The Twenty-Fifth Army had no advantage in numbers, but much in morale. Above all Yamashita 'could count on receiving about ten times as much air support as his opponent'.[24] Bombing raids increased in intensity in the latter part of January, and on 22 January two waves of twenty-seven naval bombers from Indo-China bombed Singapore from a height of 22,000 feet. The British had to concentrate their 'exiguous' air resources on protecting the reinforcement convoys.[25]

Starting on 8 February, Yamashita attacked with the 5th and 18th Divisions and the Imperial Guards, concentrating on the northwest corner of the island. There was stiff Australian resistance, but the defending troops failed to hold the Jurong Line, and a counter-attack ordered by Wavell was abandoned. The 12th and 15th Indian Infantry Brigades disintegrated in desperate self-defence. 'The fierce battle that raged in front of Bukit Timah heights was a do-or-die, hand-to-hand battle.'[26] Percival had to fall back on his last line of defence. That he had decided would not be the east of the island, but a perimeter round the built-up area of Singapore town, with its airfield, supply dumps, reservoirs and hospitals. Occupation of it was complete by the morning of the 13th. That, however, made the town, its population doubled to a million, a military target, while the reservoirs were in the hands of the Japanese by the 13th, and damage to the mains and pipelines in any case severely limited supply.

On the morning of the 15th Percival told a conference that there were only two alternatives: to counter-attack in an endeavour to regain the reservoirs and the military food supplies at Bukit Timah, or to capitulate. The commanders were unanimous in thinking a counter-attack impracticable. Percival decided to capitulate. At a meeting at the Ford factory at Bukit Timah, Yamashita demanded unconditional surrender. Before signing Percival asked that the Imperial Forces would protect British civilians, and Yamashita agreed. He had completed his campaign thirty days in advance of timetable.

[24] Basil Collier, *The War in the Far East*, London; Heinemann, 1969, p. 190.

[25] Kirby, *War against Japan*, pp. 323-4.

[26] q. Prasad, *Official History*, p. 329.

Churchill described the fall of Singapore as 'the worst disaster and largest capitulation in British history'.[27] He and Wavell had urged that it hold out, but rhetoric was not enough. 'God knows we did our best with what we had been given,' said Air Vice-Marshal Pulford.[28] Whether that was the case or not was, of course, a question that remained controversial. What they were given was certainly deficient. While the troops were more numerous than the Japanese, many were inexperienced and insufficiently trained. They were, moreover, quickly demoralised by an almost uninterrupted series of defeats and retreats. Air forces were fatally lacking, and the Japanese command of the air was evident from the start. The British were out-generalled, Kirby believes: rather, says Montgomery, 'too often the tasks they were given were beyond the capacities of the untrained young soldiers they commanded.'[29] Certainly the Japanese were greatly helped by the weakness of their opponents, if also by the fact that those opponents had continued to depreciate them. Their opponents, too, were fighting a major war in Europe, while they had secured bases in Hainan and southern Indo-China. 'We should ask ourselves', Duff Cooper had declared at the war council in Singapore on 13 December:

is it possible with barely four divisions (mainly Indian), with only three squadrons of fighter aircraft not all properly trained, without command of the sea, to defend a country the size of England? ... If not possible, then we should consider change of plan. ... There is a need to withdraw to Johore and hold the island [of Singapore] to the last.[30]

Perhaps that was realistic; it was also impractical. How could you start like that? The essential issue was lack of resources. The same was true of the loss of the *Prince of Wales* and the *Repulse*. 'Realistically' Sir Tom Phillips should have retreated: but how could he? 'Had he not done what he did', Admiral Sir Dudley Pound wrote in 1943, 'I do not think there is a shadow of doubt but that everyone would by now attribute the fall of Malaya and Singapore to his inactivity.'[31]

---

[27] W.S. Churchill, *The Hinge of Fate*, London: Cassell, 1951, p. 81.

[28] A.E. Percival, *The War in Malaya*, London: Eyre & Spottiswood, 1949, p. 287.

[29] B. Montgomery, *Shenton of Singapore*, London: Leo Cooper, 1984, p. 122.

[30] q. ibid., p. 94.

[31] q. Marder, *Old Friends*, pp. 500-1.

In a sense the Japanese were once more taking advantage of the opportunities other powers afforded them, no longer by diplomacy, or even diplomacy backed by force, but by force itself. They used it to maximum effect, daringly planned as their operations characteristically were and dauntingly carried through. What that did not guarantee was success in the longer term. Would they be able to retain their gains? Could there be negotiation? The very level of their success, and the depth of the humiliation they had inflicted, did not make it more likely. And yet time would tell. For a while they seemed to be cheating time. But while it was not clear whether Germany would win or lose, the United States had been brought into the war, and that must be decisive.

Yoshida Shigeru thought the fall of Singapore an opportune moment to initiate peace negotiations, but he seems to have taken no step as a result. Kido had similar thoughts, and conveyed them to the emperor to no effect.[32] The moment was not in fact opportune. What moment would be opportune it was, however, difficult to perceive. It was in this context, and in some confusion, that the foreign minister, Togo Shigenori, recognised the crucial importance of the relationship with the Soviet Union. He spoke at this time not merely of preserving its neutrality, but of mediating between it and Germany, whose invasion had got bogged down. He saw this as a way to 'victory in our war', but also believed that 'to bring about an early termination of the war, it would be necessary to introduce peace from this quarter'.[33] The ideas were impractical, but not, as Iriye suggests, 'grotesque'.[34]

The attack on British Borneo

To gain the Sarawak and Brunei oil wells, to guard the flank of their advance on Malaya, and to prepare for their attack on Netherlands India, the Japanese had attacked British Borneo. The British plan was to destroy the oil installations, and to defend only Kuching, since its airfield would give the Japanese access to a Dutch airfield across the border at Singkawang, only 350 miles from Singapore. The former was completed by the evening of the 8th. The Japanese

[32] J.W. Dower, *Empire and Aftermath*, Cambridge, MA: Harvard Univ. Press, 1979, p. 229.

[33] Togo, *Cause of Japan*, pp. 239-41.

[34] Iriye Akira, *Power and Culture*, Cambridge, MA: Harvard Univ. Press, 1981, p. 87.

forces – the 35th Infantry Brigade HQ and the 124th Infantry Regiment – left Cam Ranh in southern Vietnam of the 13th and began landing at Miri on the 15th. One battalion went on to occupy Labuan on 1 January and Jesselton on the 8th, and on the 19th the governor of North Borneo surrendered at Sandakan.

The Japanese had bombed the Kuching airfield and parts of the town on 19 December and machine-gunned people in the streets. That damaged civilian morale, and there were some desertions from the state forces. HQ Singapore was told of the disappointment at the lack of an Allied air force, and replied that Kuching would have to accept air raids like an English town. As Colonel C.M. Lane's report said, it failed to appreciate 'the vast difference between a town in England and the capital of the State of Sarawak, especially in relation to a native population and the native forces wavering between support for the government and possibly the enemy'.[35] Dutch submarines inflicted some damage on the convoy bringing the Japanese down from Miri, but on 24 December they landed and secured the town. The 2/15 Punjabis withdrew into Dutch Borneo. Only on 9 March, after the Allies had surrendered in Java, did they surrender, 'a formed and disciplined body to the end'.[36]

The capture of the Philippines

The Japanese planned to attack not only Malaya and Hong Kong but also the Philippines, within a few hours of the attack on Pearl Harbor. Initially they had to destroy MacArthur's air force and gain command of the air. The carriers were, however, all in the Pacific, and the army aircraft did not have the range to reach central Luzon. Navy aircraft were therefore based on land in Taiwan, with a small detachment at Palau. The attack could not take place till a few hours after that on Pearl Harbor, and it was further delayed by fog. Practically all the American aircraft were found still on the ground at Manila airport, however, and by the end of the day, half the heavy bombers and one-third of the fighters had been destroyed. Fog closed in on the 9th, but further attacks were made on the 10th. The naval yard at Cavite was destroyed, and all the remaining heavy bombers were withdraw south.

[35] q. Prasad, *Official History*, p. 377.
[36] Percival, *War in Malaya*, p. 173.

Command of the air assured, landings began in northern Luzon on the 10th, and on the 11th at Legazpi in the southeast. The 48th Division was landed at Lingayen Bay on 22 December, and the 16th at Lamon Bay on the east coast opposite Manila on 24 December. The capital was thus threatened from the north and the southeast, and, declaring it an open city, MacArthur withdrew the garrison and retreated into the Bataan peninsula. Isolated, the forces on Bataan held out till 9 April. The island fortress on Corregidor was overwhelmed on 6 May.

The Japanese had also attacked the southern Philippines in December, since it was to be a base for their operations against Netherlands India. A force from Palau landed at Davao on 20 December. Though the port was bombed by the Dutch on the 23rd, a part of the force was sent to Jolo, taken on the 25th. Admiral Takahashi assembled the 3rd Fleet at Davao and the first convoy of troop-laden transports set off for Borneo on 7 January.

The conquest of Netherlands India

Netherlands India was to be attacked by three forces. One based on Cam Ranh Bay would invade southern Sumatra, one source of oil, as soon as the fall of Singapore was assured. A central force was to move down the Makasar Straits from Davao to occupy the oilfields at Tarakan and Balikpapan and then capture Bandjermasin. An eastern force was to take Menado in northern Sulawesi, then the Kendari air base and Makasar in the south, and it was also to capture Ambon, so as to protect the left flank of the advance, and Timor, so as to cut the air route between Australia and Java.

The convoy from Davao was sighted on its way, but American bombers from Java failed to bring it to a halt. The Dutch garrison destroyed the Tarakan oilfield before surrendering on the 12th. On 9 January another convoy had left Davao for Menado, landing troops on the 11th, also dropping paratroops. By the evening of the 12th, the Japanese had command of the whole area, and had thus also extended the range of their aircraft three hundred miles south, and prevented the Allies from reinforcing the Philippines except with long-range bombers.

On 20 January a force left Tarakan for Balikpapan. It was preceded by a demand that the oil installations be surrendered intact on pain of reprisals, but the Dutch destroyed them, and columns of smoke greeted the Japanese on the 23rd. An Allied naval attack did little damage, and by late on the 24th Balikpapan was occupied. The reprisals followed one month later, when eighty Dutch men and women were executed.[37] On 24 January the Menado forces had occupied the Kendari air base. Fighters from Balikpapan and bombers from Kendari attacked airfields in eastern Java and the naval base at Surabaya on 3 and 5 February.

A new convoy left Davao on the 27th to attack Ambon. Dutch and Australian forces there resisted till 3 February. Wavell sought additional forces for Timor, which was less an outlying post than a staging post for reinforcements. There the Australians had joined the Dutch in December and, over Portuguese protests, also occupied East Timor. Now the Australian government was anxious about Japanese attacks on Rabaul and the weakness of the garrison at Darwin, and was not persuaded to reinforce Timor till 7 February. Meanwhile, however, the British forces had retreated to Singapore island. Most of the remaining aircraft, exposed to Japanese attack, had been withdrawn to southern Sumatra, from which operations to reduce the scale of the attacks on Singapore might be carried out. Now the object was to hold southern Sumatra pending the arrival of Australian reinforcements, due at the end of February.

The Japanese did not wait for the surrender of Singapore, however, before launching their attack on southern Sumatra. On 9 and 11 February the 229th Regiment left Cam Ranh Bay with naval support. Admiral Ozawa's ships cut off many of the small ships carrying official or unofficial parties fleeing from Singapore and massacre resulted. The convoy was attacked on 13 and 14 February by all available bombers, but they did little damage. More damage was done when the Japanese vessels entered the Musi river on the 15th, but troops got ashore, and joined up with paratroops sent in on the previous day. Naval forces under the Dutch Admiral Karel Doorman failed to deflect a second convoy. Palembang was occupied on the 16th, and by the 17th all the Allied forces had, prematurely, left for Java.

The fate of Java was, however, sealed. That the Japanese intended to invade it without delay was apparent. They moved on Bali on 18 February with the aim of securing an advanced air base, and Doorman's Dutch and American ships failed to prevent them. The convoy of Australian and American troops for Timor was attacked by aircraft from Kendari on 15 February, and Wavell ordered it to

[37] J. Th. Lindblad, *Between Dayak and Dutch*, Dordrecht: Foris, 1988, p. 115.

turn back. Darwin itself was devastatingly bombed on 19 February. The attack on Timor, using some of Nagumo's carriers, followed on the 20th. On the 23rd the Allied force at Kupang surrendered. The Dutch and Australians who had been based at Dili carried on guerrilla warfare with the aid of the Timorese till the end of 1942, when they were finally withdrawn.

The loss of southern Sumatra and of Timor, and the destruction of aircraft at Darwin and in Java itself, meant that resistance could not long continue. A last attempt to bring in air reinforcements failed. USS *Langley*, carrying a number of fighters, was attacked *en route* to Cilacap on 27 February. The cargo vessel *Seawitch* arrived on the 28th, but there was no time to assemble the crated planes.

On 19 February 4th Division, concentrated at Jolo at the end of January, had left via Balikpapan for eastern Java. A western invasion force, including the 2nd Division, had left Cam Ranh Bay the previous day. Nagumo's ships, returning to Kendari after the attack on Darwin, were joined by his colleague Kondo's, and sailed on 25 February for the Indian Ocean in order to cut off the Allied escape route south of Java.

The invasion of Java began with engagement off Surabaya on 27 February, the battle of the Java Sea. The Japanese were victorious, and Doorman went down with his flagship *De Ruyter*, which 'burst into flames to burn like a matchbox'.[38] Only four of the Allied ships survived the main battle and subsequent actions. Not a single Japanese ship was lost. Four American destroyers reached Fremantle on 4 March. On 1 March the Allies ordered the other ships gathered at Cilacap to disperse. Some escaped to Ceylon and Australia, but others were sunk by Kondo and Nagumo.

Hardly delayed, the two invasion forces landed on 28 February. The eastern convoy, pursuing which had cost Doorman his fleet, began landing on 1 March. By 8 March the Japanese had occupied Surabaya and Malang, and had also crossed the island to take Cilacap. The western force split in two, one attacking east of Batavia, one to the west. The former was within reach of Bandung by 7 March; the latter, meeting Dutch opposition but taking the road junction at Serang, was halted short of Buitenzorg by a mobile striking force under Brigadier A.S. Blackburn. That covered the

---

[38] q. A.J. Marder *et al., Old Friends, New Enemies*, Oxford: Clarendon Press, 1990, II, 69.

withdrawal from Batavia and Buitenzorg, upon which General ter Porten decided on 4 March.

On 5 March, however, he declared that Bandung could not hold out for long, that the Dutch would not, in view of 'the uncertain attitude of the local population towards the Europeans',[39] attempt guerrilla warfare, but that resistance was to continue, even if he issued an order to cease fighting. On the 8th he issued a proclamation that resistance was about to cease. That afternoon he met the Japanese commander-in-chief and agreed to the capitulation of all the forces in the Indies. There was no alternative but to comply, despite his instructions of the 5th.

On the same day the Imperial Guards Division, sailing from Singapore, landed at a number of points in northern Sumatra. Air and naval support was provided for the landings at Sabang and Kuta Raja. Little opposition was met, and by 28 March the Japanese had occupied the whole island. That day the Dutch surrendered in Aceh.

The invasion of Burma

The occupation of Burma would protect the northwestern flank of the occupied territories, procure additional supplies of oil and rice and block the Burma Road. The conquest of Malaya and Singapore facilitated the operation. The southern flank was secure, large forces were freed for the operation and the sea route to Rangoon was open.

At the outset of the war, a detachment of the 55th Division had landed at Chumphon on the Thai side of the Kra isthmus, and it seized the Victoria Point airfield on 14 December. On 19 December it took the airfield at Bokpyin to the north. The Oki detachment crossed the border on 4 January, and after heavy fighting secured Tavoy. The object of these operations, as of the air raids on Rangoon on 23 and 25 December, was to assist the Malayan campaign by protecting it from the air. The large-scale invasion of Burma was delayed while the Malayan campaign was driven forward and while a motor road was constructed from Rahaeng to Ban Mae Sot, from which the Japanese planned to invade. They began on 22 January.

The British in Burma were even more under-resourced than in Malaya. Burma had not been regarded as liable to attack by a major power. Its regular forces included two British battalions, the Ist Glosters and the 2nd King's Own Yorkshire Light Infantry, and

[39] Kirby, *War against Japan*, I, 447.

four battalions of the Burma Rifles, until recently composed solely of Chins, Kachins and Karens, rather than Burmans. Burma relied for internal security and for watch and ward on the land frontiers mainly on the six battalions of the Burma Frontier Force. Some expansion took place after 1939, but Burma received a low priority. The air force was limited: when war with Japan began the RAF had sixteen Buffalo aircraft in Burma. Some Indian troops were sent in 1941. The 13th Indian Infantry Brigade Group arrived in March/April and the 16th was still arriving when war started.

Rangoon was of prime importance, since there was no land link with India, and it was the only port with communications into the interior. It was also exposed to attack from the air, from the sea and by land. It had seemed likely that a land attack would be directed against the Shan States, but, as news came of the concentration of Japanese troops at Rahaeng, the 16th Brigade was moved to Moulmein. On the 26th Gen Iida ordered the 55th Division to capture it. They met determined resistance from the 2nd Burma Brigade – Burmans and Indians domiciled in Burma – outnumbered, ill-equipped and inadequately trained as they were.[40] The Japanese secured their objective, but their opponents were able to withdraw with much of their equipment. On 3-4 February, the 33rd Division secured Pa-an, a ford across the Salween, after 'a brisk engagement'.[41]

On 15 February General J.G. Smyth moved his forces, the 17th Indian Division, back across the Bilin river. There his troops delayed the Japanese, but on 20 February he gave the order to withdraw. Now he had to get his forces back over the Sittang bridge before he destroyed it. Only 3,000 got across. The destruction of the bridge left many soldiers to their fate – about half the Gurkhas drowned[42] – and a great deal of equipment fell into the hands of the Japanese. Nor did the destruction in fact delay them, as the British hoped. The 15th Army operations order of 17 February instructed the 33rd and 55th Divisions to advance to the Sittang, and then prepare for future action, and staff officers stressed that

---

[40] Yoon, 'Japan's Occupation of Burma', pp. 127-8.

[41] Kirby, *War against Japan*, II, 38.

[42] Alan K. Lathrop, 'The Employment of Chinese Nationalist Troops in the First Burma Campaign', *JSEAS*, 12, 2 (September 1981), p. 410.

they were to await instructions. The main reason for that was, however, logistical: even the road the Japanese had built was inadequate, and bullock-carts had to be used. Iida said:

I was then extremely worried ... because of the increasing shortage of supplies. In order to pass through the rugged jungle of the Thai-Burma border, the quantity of equipment and supplies was reduced to a minimum. ... Under these circumstances, it was quite impossible to attempt to march further forward beyond the Sittang.[43]

General T.J. Hutton now became apprehensive about holding Rangoon. Wavell thought him pessimistic, and General Harold Alexander was put in charge. The fact was that Burma needed early reinforcements. Following the fall of Singapore, Wavell had told the chiefs of staff that the loss of Java, though a severe blow, would not be fatal, but that Australia and Burma were vital for the war against Japan. The Australian 7th Division, on its way to Java from the Middle East, should go to Burma instead. This, however, the Australian government declined to sanction. 'We feel a primary obligation to save Australia not only for itself, but to preserve it as a base for the development of the war against Japan,' Prime Minister Curtin declared.[44] Wavell told Alexander to hold Rangoon:

If however that is not possible, the British force must not be allowed to be cut off, but must be withdrawn from the Rangoon area for the defence of upper Burma. This must be held as long as possible in order to safeguard the oilfields at Yenangyaung, keep contact with the Chinese and protect the construction of the road from Assam to Burma.[45]

On 2/3 March Iida's forces crossed the Sittang, their object the capture of Rangoon. Alexander made an attempt to hold Pegu against the 55th, which proved vain. Meanwhile, the 33rd had crossed the Pegu river, and Iida had concluded he might take Rangoon by *coup de main*. Late on the 6th, however, Alexander decided that it could not be held, and that the right course was to evacuate the city, from which many civilians had already been evacuated or fled. A denial scheme was put into operation on the 7th, but a great deal was left behind. 'The port when evacuated was still capable of maintaining more divisions than the Japanese were

---

[43] q. Yoon, 'Japan's Occupation of Burma', p. 137.

[44] q. Kirby, *War against Japan*, II, 58.

[45] q. ibid., p. 86.

ever likely to use in Burma.'[46] The withdrawal, however, took the Japanese by surprise, and they failed to cut it off.

This error of judgment allowed the British to dispute Burma for another two and a half months. Once Rangoon was lost to them, however, the Chinese forces could no longer be supplied, except by air from Assam, and the British could not continue the fight in Burma for very long. They were virtually cut off from outside assistance, since there was no through road from India, and only a trickle of reinforcements and supplies could be brought in by air. The Rangoon airfields and refineries had been lost. For supplies the British would have to depend largely on what they had earlier backloaded from Rangoon, and for oil on improvisation at the oilfields themselves. The Japanese were also free to reinforce Burma by sea rather than by land, and their capacity to do so was enhanced by their taking the Andamans, already evacuated on 12 March. On 23 March they occupied Port Blair.

Iida received new orders on 7 March. The next tasks were to crush the Chinese forces in the Mandalay region and to seize strategic areas, such as Bassein, Yenangyaung and the Akyab air base. On 10 March the Fifteenth Army began its thrust north. The 33rd Division pushed up the Irrawaddy valley through Prome, Yenangyaung, Monywa and Kalewa, while the 55th went up the Sittang through Toungoo, Meiktila, Mandalay, Bhamo and Myitkyina. Reinforcements were provided by General Mutaguchi Renya's 18th Division from Malaya, which landed at Rangoon on 26 March, and the 56th, under General Matsuyama Sukezo, which followed it on 8 April. The former proceeded to the Shan States, and the latter to the Salween valley, with the object of encircling the Chinese forces.

Alexander knew that the length of time he could retain control of central and upper Burma was dependent on the size of the force which the Japanese decided to deploy in the theatre: all he could hope to do was to impose the maximum delay and make them expend resources which they could otherwise use elsewhere.[47]

The Chinese 200th Division put up a stubborn defence at Toungoo, but finally withdrew on 30 March. Iida moved his headquarters there on 2 April. He now planned to cut the Burma Road, and thus the Chinese line of communication, in the vicinity of Lashio,

[46] Ibid., p. 95.
[47] Ibid., p. 147.

and encircle the Allied forces in the Mandalay area. The 56th Division was given the first task. The 18th and 55th were to advance along the main road and railway, and the 33rd to advance along the Irrawaddy to Myingyan, outflanking the Allied right.

Prome was occupied on 3rd April. Alexander and Chiang Kai-shek agreed that the time had come to stand and fight. By the 15th, however, the destruction of the Yenangyaung oilfields had become necessary, and the 33rd Division occupied the town on the 17th, inflicting heavy casualties on the 1st Burma Division. The 56th occupied Loikaw on the 20th and Loilem on the 26th. The fall of Lashio was only a matter of time, and Alexander decided to withdraw across the Irrawaddy, telling General Slim not to uncover the line of retreat of the Chinese formations until their rearguard had reached a point on the Mandalay-Myitkyina railway some thirty miles north of Mandalay. Iida thus failed to trap the Allied troops in the loop of the Irrawaddy. The last of them crossed the Ava bridge after darkness on the 30th and at midnight two of its huge spans were destroyed.

Iida now sought to cut off the retreat of the Allied forces. After taking Lashio the 56th was to swing northwest to Bhamo and Myitkina, while the 33rd headed up the Chindwin. Bhamo was taken on the 3rd and Myitkina on the 8th, but two of the three Chinese divisions that were cut off managed to make their way to Imphal in India through the Hukawng valley, their looting and brutality wreaking havoc among the Kachins en route,[48] and the other marched to China from Fort Hertz. Alexander's British, Indian and Burmese forces completed 'the longest retreat ever carried out by a British army'.[49] Harassed by the Japanese, they crossed the Chindwin at Shwegyin, and made their way to India through the Tamu pass shortly before the monsoon made the tracks impassable. They finally reached Imphal on 18 May.

Many refugees accompanied the British forces on their way to Shwegyin. There were thousands of others, and the forces were not always helpful. The exodus of Indian civilians had begun with the first air raids on Rangoon on 23 December, though many were cajoled into returning so as to keep the port and services going. Some 70,000 left by ship in January, and others joined the general stampede in February. Between 100,000 and 200,000 escaped by

[48] Lathrop, 'Employment of National Troops', p. 426.

[49] Kirby, *War against Japan*, II, 210.

the Chittagong route, though many died on the way. Joined by those from up-country towns, others moved north to Mandalay. There the camps were bombed on Good Friday. An attempt to speed the evacuation to Manipur was in fact hampered by Alexander's decision to withdraw the army: it had priority. The trek by land was undertaken by some 400,000-450,000 refugees: perhaps 10,000-50,000 died.[50]

Both the army and the civilians feared a further Japanese advance. Slim believed that it was stopped by the monsoon: 'The monsoon which so nearly destroyed us and whose rain beat so merciless on our bodies did us one good turn – it stopped dead the Japanese pursuit.'[51] Frank Owen thought that 'this curtain of rain saved India'.[52] In fact 'the lines of communication had been stretched too far to undertake an invasion into India.'[53] Nor was one undertaken after the monsoon. The Japanese had reached their perimeter.

Midway

They had also established a perimeter elsewhere. While the British Eastern Fleet was based on Ceylon, any Japanese convoy in the Bay of Bengal was exposed to danger. Taking out the Ceylon bases might also embarrass the British in India at the time of the mission on its future led by Sir Stafford Cripps. Nagumo's First Air Fleet was chosen again, and again a Sunday was chosen, in the hope of finding the fleet at harbour. No Pearl Harbor or Darwin followed. But he sank an aircraft carrier, two heavy cruisers, two destroyers and a corvette, while his own fleet suffered no losses. Admiral Somerville sent his slower ships to Kenya, but kept the faster ones in Asian waters. But after an attack on Trincomalee on the 9th Nagumo withdrew. 'Looks as if the Japs have gone east again but they're damn fools if they have,' Somerville wrote to his wife.[54]

At the same time a naval force under Admiral Ozawa sank nineteen unconvoyed merchant ships off the coast of Madras. On the 6th bombs were dropped on Cocanada and Vizagapatam and a panic spread to Madras itself. No invasion followed, however.

[50] Hugh Tinker, 'A Forgotten Long March...', *JSEAS*, 6, 1 (March 1975), pp. 1-15.

[51] W. Slim, *Defeat into Victory*, London: Cassell, 1956, p. 87.

[52] q. Yoon, 'Japan's Occupation of Burma', p. 146.

[53] Ibid., p. 147.

[54] q. Marder *et al.*, *Old Friends*, II, 140.

The incursion was a raid designed to cover the convoys to Rangoon. If the Japanese had pressed westward, the British chiefs of staff recognised, they could have placed India in danger, and threatened the British in the Middle East from one direction while the Germans threatened them from the other. But they did not do so. 'A Japanese fleet never again ventured into the Indian Ocean.'[55]

Yamamoto had favoured a more ambitious strategy, and the navy, emboldened by easy success, wanted to invade Australia. Imperial HQ compromised on attempts to 'isolate' it by seizing Samoa, Fiji and New Caledonia, as well as Papua New Guinea,[56] 'closing the ring round their newly-won empire in the Pacific'.[57] That went less successfully. Rabaul had been captured on 23 January and made into an advance base. An attack on New Guinea followed in February, and, while preparing for an attack on Port Moresby, also included in the defence perimeter, the Japanese put landing parties on Buka and Bougainville. In the battle of the Coral Sea that followed, the US Navy lost the *Lexington*, but the invasion of Port Moresby was held off.

A dramatic air raid on Tokyo had taken place on 18 April. The Japanese chiefs of staff as a result decided to bring about a decisive naval action with the remnants of the US fleet in the central Pacific. Yamamoto's plan was to create a diversion in the Aleutians, and seize Midway. Forewarned, Chester W. Nimitz, commander of the Pacific fleet, avoided his trap. Nagumo, by contrast, lost four of his carriers, and Yamamoto ordered a retirement. 'This was the most decisive defeat tasted by Japanese naval forces since the days of Toyotomi Hideyoshi.'[58]

That was, in the view of Kirby and others, though not of all, 'the turning point' in the war. Without his carriers Yamamoto could not risk a fleet action outside the range of his land-based aircraft. Seeking to expand an 'already overstretched perimeter', rather than concentrate on defensive operations, the Japanese had lost their naval supremacy. Without it they could not retain what they had. And certainly they would not be able to regain it.[59]

[55] Kirby, *War against Japan*, II, 131.

[56] Marder *et al.*, *Old Friends*, II, 84.

[57] Kirby, *War against Japan*, II, 221.

[58] q. Hata Ikuhiko in S. Dockrill, ed., *From Pearl Harbor to Hiroshima*, Basingstoke: Macmillan, 1994, p. 67.

[59] Kirby, *War against Japan*, II, 233; Hata, *From Pearl Harbor*, p. 69.

Acquiring the resources of Southeast Asia, and the strategic points necessary to defend their position, had been the requirements, as Nagano had seen them, of a long war. The Japanese had secured Southeast Asia in an extraordinary series of triumphs. If they had pushed on in the west, that would, as the British recognised, have threatened the whole position of their opponents, particularly if Germany had attacked in the Middle East at the same time. The Japanese had resolved, however, simply to create havoc on their Indian perimeter. The Germans, for their part, focused on their Russian campaign. By the time that, after the fall of Tobruk on 20 June, they opened their offensive on Suez, the Japanese had been defeated at Midway.

Thoughts of peace

Wars may be easier to start than to stop: the euphoria of victory encourages continuance, and setbacks are not a good basis for negotiation. Perhaps this was particularly true of the open-ended wars in which the Japanese engaged. The Japanese war in China had started without being declared: it had not proved possible to conclude it. What in any case would represent victory? With whom, if anyone, would you negotiate peace? Could you declare that you had won what you had never admitted starting?

The war in Southeast Asia had more explicit objectives and more explicit limits. The colonial territories were to be acquired, and placed behind a defensive perimeter. That could be achieved in the short term and lay the foundations for a longer struggle. What was more difficult to envisage, let alone achieve, was the ultimate acceptance of Japan's predominance in Southeast Asia by the other powers. In the past they had in a sense defined Japan's policy by the extent of their collusion, complaisance or opposition. In 1941 they had then set limits which the Japanese resolved to overcome by force. In that they enjoyed stunning success. But it could only be temporary, unless the other powers accepted the outcome, either by refraining from further contest or as a result of negotiation. If, however, the Japanese had no strategic concept, and could not, with the Axis partners, aim at victory, neither did they have a means of securing a compromise.

The navy was always apprehensive of the great powers. They defined its policy more effectively than they defined the army's. In the prewar phase it was the advocate of caution, while the army, though running up against the Soviet Union, could enjoy success after success in pursuit of the almost limitless ambitions it generated in China. The caution extended into the wartime phase. The navy's plans were bold, but that was a sign of weakness, not strength, a recognition that Japan's advantage was temporary and its forces had to be used to maximum effect, yet, if possible, not expended. The attack on Pearl Harbor was a triumph, but Nagumo did not risk a second one, and he was content with one sortie against Ceylon.

Before the war began Yamamoto himself was apprehensive about slipping into an unlimited war against the United States. A letter he wrote to Sasakawa Ryoichi early in 1941 was published during the war as a means of raising morale. A crucial passage was omitted:

If there should be a war between Japan and America, then our aim, of course, ought not to be Guam or the Philippines, nor Hawaii or Hong Kong, but a capitulation at the White House, in Washington itself. I wonder whether the politicians of the day really have the willingness to make sacrifices, and the confidence, that this would entail?[60]

He appears to have looked for negotiation. In September 1941 he told Sasakawa that Japan would have everything its own way for a while, 'stretching out in every direction like an octopus spreading its tentacles. But it'll last for a year and a half at the most. We've just got to get a peace agreement by then. The right timing would be when Singapore falls.'[61] By that time, however, the Japanese were studying the next stage of the operations. They finally resolved on the Pacific option, and Yamamoto himself advocated it. It was, as Kirby puts it, a means of destroying the remnants of the US Pacific fleet before it could be rebuilt.[62] The idea in Yamamoto's mind, Agawa suggests, was 'to score a victory that would give a second chance for an early peace settlement'.[63] Either way, it failed. Yamamoto and Nagumo had made continued war more likely, not less.

The defeat at Midway did, however, prompt Yoshida to approach Konoe, suggesting that he should 'settle down in a neutral country', such as Switzerland, apparently to observe the situation.

---

[60] q. Agawa Hiroyuki, *The Reluctant Admiral*, Tokyo and New York: Kodansha, 1979, p. 291.

[61] q. ibid., p. 292.

[62] Kirby, *War against Japan*, II, 226.

[63] Agawa, *Reluctant Admiral*, p. 321.

Diplomatic personnel with him could 'secretly make overtures to the politicians of various countries and arrange for them to approach you'. If the war went well for Germany, the United States and Britain 'should seek a way out of the impasse through you', and vice versa. Then Japan might be 'in a leading position insofar as peace is concerned.'[64] Kido was non-committal, though Konoe was willing to try. The matter died there.

In face of setbacks as in the euphoria of victory, the civilians had little chance of initiating a negotiation. The Japanese were faced with 'a war of attrition with the greatest industrial power among all the belligerents – a type of war she could not win'.[65] Japan made 70,000 planes between 1941 and 1945; the United States 300,000.

Fighting in the Pacific

The Midway disaster made the seaward attack on Port Moresby impractical. Instead the Japanese decided on an overland advance from the north coast. They also planned to supplement their seaplane base on the southern Solomons by constructing an airfield on Guadalcanal. The Allies, while giving priority to the defeat of Germany, decided that did not preclude their securing bases for an eventual offensive against Japan. A step-by-step approach was to start with the seizure of the Santa Cruz islands and the establishment of a firm foothold on the southern Solomons. The struggle for Guadalcanal ensued. Renewed in October and November, it went badly for the Japanese, and on 31 December Imperial HQ decided to abandon the island. Some 13,000 were able to make their escape. The struggle meanwhile hampered the Japanese effort in New Guinea.

Troops of the new Seventeenth Army had begun to land at Buna on 21 July, and they occupied Kokoda on 29 July. Their strength was quickly raised, but the difficulties of supply proved insuperable. Even so they were brought to a halt only 32 miles from their destination. In appalling conditions, the Australians drove them back, entering Kokoda on 2 November. American and Australian troops secured the coast and Japanese resistance was at an end by 21 January 1943.

The Allies were now able to think in offensive terms, although Roosevelt and Churchill, meeting at Casablanca in January, still

[64] q. Dower, *Empire and Aftermath*, p. 230.
[65] R. Spector in Dockrill, *From Pearl Harbor*, p. 78.

gave priority to Europe. In the southwest Pacific, the advance through New Guinea and the Solomons was to continue until Rabaul was taken and the Bismarck barrier broken. Expecting an offensive, the Japanese sought to pre-empt it in early April by air raids on Guadalcanal, on Oro Bay, near Buna, on Port Moresby and on Milne Bay. Yamamoto believed them successful. He did not live to learn the truth.'[66] American intelligence gave warning of his visit to Bougainville, and he was shot down on 18 April. 'This became my parting with him forever,' Admiral Ugaki realised before his own plane was shot down.[67]

The Allied offensive began late in June. Lae was occupied on 16 September, and on 1 October the Japanese withdrew from Finschhafen. By late January 1944 the Japanese had been driven from the Huon peninsula, and western New Britain was in Allied hands. MacArthur planned to encircle Rabaul. In March his forces secured the Admiralty Islands. Approaching from a different direction, Halsey had begun to contest Bougainville late in October. A desperate Japanese attack on the American perimeter – 'a course of despair'[68] – led to a week-long battle in March, abandoned after great losses. By May some 140,000 Japanese soldiers and seamen were cut off from the main body of the Japanese forces.

The Americans also built up their fleet in the central Pacific, based on Pearl Harbor. In late November they secured the Gilbert Islands. Nimitz then advanced on the Marshall Islands. These the Japanese had resolved to defend, as outposts of the new perimeter, extending from the Kuriles through the Carolines to Timor and to Burma, the Absolute National Defence Sphere, upon which they had decided in September 1943. Their chances of success were reduced by the endeavours of Yamamoto and his successor, Koga, to prop up the defences of Bougainville and Rabaul. In February the Americans took Kwajalein and Eniwetok. Koga withdrew most of his fleet to the Palau Islands in time to avoid destruction, though he himself was lost on a flight to Davao.

MacArthur moved west, with almost undisputed command of the sea and air, with 50,000 troops, and 30,000 in reserve. Hollandia was taken at the end of April 1944. That had been an outpost for the new Japanese perimeter, and in May Imperial HQ had to adjust

[66] Kirby, *War against Japan*, II, 378.
[67] Ugaki Matome, *Fading Victory*, Univ. of Pittsburgh Press, 1991, p. 354.
[68] Kirby, *War against Japan*, III, 105.

it. The main position was to be pulled back to a line between Sorong and Halmahera, and Biak and Manokwari to be held only as outposts. That decision was itself revised as the Japanese garrison at Biak counter-attacked, but signs of an impending assault on the Marianas prevented Admiral Toyoda from sending strongly escorted reinforcements from Davao. Even so the Allied forces were able to complete the occupation of Biak only on 2 July. MacArthur now needed a foothold in the Halmahera group so as to give his land-based bombers a base for attacking the Philippines. Morotai was secured in September.

Nimitz was meanwhile approaching the Philippines from the west. In June the Americans attacked the Marianas, starting with Saipan. They also dealt a devastating blow at the fleet Toyoda had assembled, almost annihilating the Japanese fleet air arm, and the remnant retreated to Okinawa. '[D]ue to lack of oil and fleet tankers, the Battle of the Marianas was fought only with carriers and planes.' Moving the Northern Carrier Force from Palau to engage the Americans at Saipan, Ozawa had to adopt a direct course 'due to shortage of fuel'. The result was the 'turkey shoot': a US carrier force met the Japanese head on and shot down 402 planes.[69] The Saipan troops, encouraged by the suicide of Admiral Nagumo and General Saito, made a death-or-glory charge, and almost all were killed. The island was captured on 9 July, giving the United States a base for long-range bombers within reach of Tokyo. A bitter struggle for Guam followed. By August it was clear that Japan was facing defeat. The raids brought it home.

On 17 July 1944 the former prime ministers decided that Tojo must go. In the new cabinet, formed on 22 July, General Koiso Kuniaki became prime minister, and Admiral Yonai navy minister and in effect vice-premier. While continuing an offensive in China – Ichi-go – Imperial HQ focused on preparing to defend the Philippines, Formosa and the Ryukyu islands, the homeland and the northeast front. At a meeting attended by the Emperor on 19 August, the new Supreme War Direction Council, which had replaced the liaison conference, also emphasised the importance of improving relations with the Soviet Union, and the desirability of bringing about the end of hostilities between the Soviet Union and Germany.

MacArthur believed that the United States should liberate the

---

[69] Oi Atsushi, q. Marder *et al.*, *Old Friends*, II, 379.

Philippines before going further, and that it was good strategy to do so. Admiral Ernest J. King, and, less certain, Nimitz preferred an earlier attack on Formosa and the China coast. Either way, the Japanese links with the south would be severed: the forces there would be without ammunition, and the fleet in home waters without oil. In September the joint chiefs of staff directed MacArthur to occupy Leyte, by-passing Mindanao, with Nimitz's forces, having taken Palau, joining in the attack.

Having lost most of their carrier-based aircraft, the Japanese assembled as many land-based aircraft as possible, with the object of attacking the American carriers. Under this air umbrella they would use the combined fleet, brought from Singapore and the Inland Sea, to destroy the invading fleet. Terauchi decided that priority was to be given to the defence of Luzon, and Yamashita, the conqueror of Malaya, was brought from Manchuria to take command of the Fourteenth Area Army. Over his protests Imperial HQ decided to fight the decisive battle on Leyte, not on Luzon.

The Japanese threw in *kamikaze* or suicide bombers. 'To think it has come to this .... And yet, they have done nobly,' the Emperor is alleged to have remarked.[70] 'Is this spiritual strength?', a domestic critic wondered. 'Or is it something like compressed air put into a torpedo? Instead of sending tubes of compressed air, they now send men with special valour. Material has been substituted by spirit.'[71]

The sea battle of Leyte Gulf imposed devastating losses. 'Although six of the nine Japanese battleships survived, the loss of supporting forces and especially of the carrier forces was so great that never again were Japanese forces able to offer any serious challenge to the American fleet.'[72] To resist the American advance, the Japanese had to rely on shore-based aircraft. Yamashita still managed to reinforce Leyte itself, and it was only at the end of December that Japanese resistance ceased.

MacArthur's next step was to take Mindoro on 15 December, and then move on Luzon itself. Halsey supported the Luzon landings, and then early in 1945 moved into the South China Sea, where no American ship had ventured since 1942. No capital ships

---

[70] q. ibid., p. 403.

[71] q. B.-A. Shillony, *Politics and Culture in Wartime Japan*, Oxford: Clarendon Press, 1981, p. 133.

[72] Kirby, *War against Japan*, IV, 83.

were found at Cam Ranh Bay, but merchant ships and tankers were sunk. The landings were at Lingayen. Clark Field was captured on 1 February. Yamashita's plan was to delay the invading forces as much as possible, and then withdraw into three strongholds, from which to undertake a protracted defence and harass the Americans. Manila, he decided, should be an open town. Admiral Iwabashi insisted on defending it, however, and the struggle developed into 'a desperate house-to-house combat'.[73] Japanese resistance ceased only on 4 March. Resistance on Corregidor did not cease till the 26th.

Raids on Japan had intensified from late November, and Imperial HQ believed that they would be followed by an invasion. The US might launch this by way of China and the Ryukyus, or by advancing on them from Formosa. The second route was thought the more likely as it was the shorter, and the Americans would be anxious to end the war as soon as possible after the defeat of Germany. While relying on diplomacy to preserve the neutrality of the Soviet Union, Imperial HQ resolved to prepare for a last-ditch resistance, in the hope that, facing a long war, the Allies would after all advocate a compromise peace.

The China Expeditionary Force was to abandon long-range operations against Chungking and concentrate on fending off any American attempts to land and establish air bases within range of Manchuria or Japan itself. The Southern Army, virtually cut off, could still delay the invasion of Japan. Terauchi was to hold areas vital to the security of the Southern Region and maintain control of areas with essential natural resources. As far as possible, his forces were to become self-sufficient, since they could not be supplied or reinforced. He was to give special attention to Indo-China now open to invasion from the Philippines. But he was also to send back men and material to the homeland, particularly air units and oil.

The coup in Indo-China

In Indo-China the Japanese had still not dislodged the Vichy authorities. After September 1943, when they decided on their new perimeter, the Japanese had begun to re-examine their policy towards Indo-China. They were also influenced by the establishment of a Free French mission in Kunming, and by the possibility that Thailand would go the way of Italy. The local military argued for a

[73] Ibid., p. 99.

takeover, and so did foreign office officials, who, however, saw it as a step towards offering independence. HQ and the liaison conference rejected a change.[74] A plan for a takeover was prepared in March 1944, but it was not implemented.[75] The invasion of France in June, the fall of Paris in August and the declining cooperation of the Decoux regime again raised the question. So, too, did the failure of the Burma offensive and the growing isolation of the Southern Region. The US navy's incursion into the South China Sea might be a precursor of invasion.[76] Was it better still to leave the French in occupation, or to replace them, and, if they were replaced, with what?

Concentrating on the Philippines, the army had been opposed to a takeover, though Koiso was in favour of it, hoping to offer Tonkin to Chiang Kai-shek to induce him to abandon the war.[77] The foreign minister, Shigemitsu, an advocate of independence, had hesitated to act while Japan was sounding out the Soviet Union on mediation. On 10 December the Soviet Union and France signed a treaty of alliance and assistance: a harsh policy in Indo-China might make it difficult to preserve Russian neutrality, let alone get its help in securing peace. The defeat at Leyte followed, then the American naval attacks in the South China Sea, while the British forces took Akyab on 2 January. On 17 January the army and navy HQs agreed to overthrow the French by a surprise attack, Operation Meigo.

The ambassador, Matsumoto Shunichi, argued for cancelling or delaying the decision. By February it was clear that a US invasion was unlikely: American forces landed on Iwojima on the 19th. He also argued that a coup would antagonise the Soviet Union. That argument, however, Shigemitsu now rejected. A coup against Vichy would do little to harm Soviet-Japan relations, particularly if presented as the prelude to liberation rather than a

[74] Shiraishi Masaya and Furuta Motoo in Shiraishi Takashi and Furuta Motoo, eds, *Indochina in the 1940s and 1950s*, Ithaca, NY: Cornell Univ. Press, 1992, pp. 66-9.

[75] Kiyoko Kurusu Nitz, 'Japanese Military Policy towards French Indochina during the Second World War', *JSEAS*, 14, 2 (September 1983), p. 335.

[76] R.B. Smith, 'The Japanese Period in Indochina and the Coup of 9 March 1945', *JSEAS*, 9, 2 (September 1978), p. 278. Martin Thomas, 'Free France, the British Government and the Future of Free Indo-China', *JSEAS*, 28, 1 (March 1997), p. 155. Tonnesson, *Vietnamese Revolution*, p. 190.

[77] Shiraishi and Furuta, *Indochina in the 1940s*, p. 73.

takeover.[78] The coup was carried out on 9 March. The French put up some resistance in Hanoi and at Langson, where the Japanese killed French officers who surrendered.[79] 'Most of the native inhabitants were greatly delighted when we resorted to military action,' a Japanese report declared. 'They considered this situation a good opportunity to achieve their independence and their deep feeling toward Japan greatly increased.'[80]

Imphal

The battle in the Coral Sea and the defeat at Midway diminished Wavell's fears that the Japanese would mount a full-scale invasion of Ceylon and the eastern coast of India. He had felt that, until he had air superiority, he could undertake only a limited operation in late 1942 and early 1943, the object of which would be to secure part of upper Burma north of Mandalay and re-establish a front with the Chinese. As Churchill wanted, however, he planned a larger offensive, Anakim, with Rangoon as the objective. That was put off by the Germans' successes in Libya and their thrust towards the Don, together with the 'Quit India' movement. A coastwise attempt at the end of 1942 to take Akyab, thus reducing the air threat to Calcutta and increasing that to the Japanese, was turned back by Koga's 55th Division. But the 77th Indian Infantry, the Chindits, a special long-range penetration force under Colonel Orde Wingate, was allowed to go ahead early in 1943, even though it could not be followed up.

The venture, however, showed that forces could be sustained in the jungle by air supply, though the popular endorsement of Wingate's achievement increased the risk that the more orthodox operations that were also needed would be neglected. The venture also affected the Japanese. On the Burma frontier their stance had hitherto been defensive. Now they concluded 'that the British, having evolved new tactics, might repeat the operation on a larger scale in conjunction with a major offensive'.[81] Their policy ceased to be merely defensive. General Mutaguchi, now commanding the

[78] Tonnesson, *Vietnamese Revolution*, p. 220. Murakami, 'Japan's Thrust', pp. 519-20.

[79] D. Marr, *Vietnam 1945*, Berkeley: Univ. of California Press, 1995, pp. 59-60.

[80] Monograph No. 24, p. 27, in Donald S. Detwiler and Charles B. Burdick, comp. *War in Asia and the Pacific*, New York: Garland, 1980, vol. 6.

[81] Kirby, *War against Japan*, II, 329.

Fifteenth Army, believed that the defence of upper Burma required him to advance his line to the Chindwin and even beyond the frontier. He convinced his superiors that he should aim at seizing Imphal in the 1943-4 dry season.

On 7 August 1943 Southern Army instructed Burma Area Army to completed preparation for U-Go, a counter-offensive against Imphal, designed to forestall a British offensive. The Burma Area Army's order of 12 August instructed the Twelfth Army to 'advance to Imphal before enemy preparations for a counter offensive could be completed. After crushing the enemy at Imphal, our forces will seize the Arakan Mountain Range and establish the defense line there.' Upon the occupation of Imphal, the provisional government of Free India would be established there 'in order to accelerate the political campaign in India'.[82]

Given that the sea route to Rangoon from Singapore was long and exposed to attack by Allied submarines and aircraft, the Japanese had to find an alternative line of communication to Burma. The road from Rahaeng to Moulmein had been hurriedly improved at the time of the invasion, but was not adequate. In June 1942 Imperial HQ therefore ordered the construction of a single-line railway across the Three Pagodas Pass. Work began in November 1942, the labour drawn from Allied prisoners of war and conscripted Burmese, Malays, Tamils, Chinese and Javanese. When in early 1943 it became clear that Burma would have to be reinforced, construction was speeded up, and the men on the 'Death Railway' more mercilessly treated as a result. Perhaps 60,000 died.[83] Even so the railway was not opened till 25 October 1943.

Anakim was still not feasible in 1943. In those circumstances the Americans preferred to concentrate on regaining upper Burma, so reopening the Burma Road and supporting the struggle in China. While maintaining the air route to China, the British wanted to contain the Japanese in Burma and prepare amphibious forces that would be used for a breakthrough in the south, starting with an attack in Sumatra. Their preferences were influenced by political as well as strategic concerns. Though keeping Southeast Asia free of the Japanese had been the Americans' objective before the Pacific war began, returning it to the colonial powers was not a priority.

[82] Monograph no. 134, pp. 38-9, in Detwiler, *War in Asia*, vol. 6.
[83] J.W. Dower, *War without Mercy*, New York: Pantheon, 1986, p. 47

At the Quebec Conference in August (Quadrant) the strategy Roosevelt outlined for defeating Japan did not involve reconquering their conquests. 'He likened the area held by the Japanese to a slice of pie with Japan at the apex and the island barrier formed by the Netherlands East Indies as the crust.'[84] The strategy of the Allies should be to advance along the edges of the slice to enable them to bomb the Japanese mainland and shipping on the routes to the various points on the crust. They should advance across the Pacific towards Formosa and the China coast and from Burma into China proper, rather than nibbling at the crust. The Americans' view prevailed, helped by Wingate's persuasiveness.

The fall of Mussolini in July 1943 meant that the British could at last plan the reinforcement of their Eastern Fleet. An amphibious operation in the Bay of Bengal became more feasible. The meeting with Stalin at Teheran, however, convinced the Western Allies that they must invade the continent of Europe in 1944, and the assault shipping was needed there. The priority of the European struggle was thus reaffirmed, while Stalin undertook to enter the war with Japan when Germany had been defeated. These moves also suggested that the campaign in the Pacific was taking priority over the campaign in China/Southeast Asia as a means of defeating Japan, and that operations in the latter were to be conducted in support of those in the former. The new Supreme Allied Commander Southeast Asia, Mountbatten, had to concentrate on preparing an overland advance in Arakan and limited operations in the Chindwin area, coupled with Wingate-style activities.

Churchill still cherished hopes of an operation, more or less bypassing Burma, that would strike at the south, his favoured objective being northern Sumatra (Culverin). For that, however, the force was not at once available, and the Americans did not accept it as a priority. The British chiefs of staff, moreover, had themselves come to prefer a Pacific strategy, using British ships, based in Australia, in the attack on Japan. If the British might still thus make a telling contribution to the struggle against Japan, they would not, however, be seen to be liberating the peoples it had conquered. That Churchill could not accept:

A decision to act as a subsidiary force under the Americans in the Pacific raises difficult political questions about the future of our Malayan posses-

[84] Kirby, *War against Japan*, II, 422.

sions. If the Japanese should withdraw from them or make peace as a result of the main American thrust, the United States Government would, after its victory, feel greatly strengthened in its view that all possessions in the East Indian Archipelago should be placed under some international body upon which the United States would exercise a decisive control.[85]

In any case the contribution that the British might make in the Pacific could not be substantial.

While this argument was waged over several months, a campaign had begun in Burma that in fact decided what contribution the British would make to the defeat of the Japanese, did something to redeem their military reputation and allowed them to start the liberation of Southeast Asia. Their essential instrument, the Indian army, was being made into a force that could face the Japanese. And the Japanese 'played into Slim's hands by launching their 1944 offensives'. The way was thus opened, as Callahan puts it, 'not only for the counter-stroke that made possible the long-sought American goal of reopening the Burma Road, but for a culmination of Britain's war in the east that made all the strategic argumentation in London after "Quadrant" irrelevant.'[86]

As the British were debating what they might do, Imperial HQ authorised Mutaguchi's offensive on 7 January 1944: 'In order to defend Burma the Commander-in-Chief, Southern Army, may occupy and secure the vital areas of north-eastern India in the vicinity of Imphal by defeating the enemy in that area at the opportune time.'[87] On 15 January the Southern Army instructed the Burma Area Army to carry out the Imphal campaign. The object was to complete it by mid-April, giving the Japanese enough time to consolidate their positions before the monsoon and the Allies insufficient time for a counter-attack. Prompt success was important, above all because of the weak supply position. Yet some of the troops, coming overland from Thailand via Kengtung, would not be there in time.

The 55th's diversionary offensive in Arakan, Ha-go, was beaten back. Slim, now in command of the Fourteenth Army, was able to use his air power to drop supplies to the forward troops when the Japanese attacked. Their stealthy infiltration was no longer successful. Instead their troops might, as Slim put it, be caught between

[85] q. R. Callahan, *Burma 1942-1945*, London: Davis-Poynter, 1978, p. 119.

[86] Ibid., p. 106.

[87] q. Kirby, *War against Japan*, III, 76.

the anvil of the forward troops and the hammer of the reserves.[88] The success of these tactics made the battle of Ngakyedauk pass, though it took place on 'a not very important part of the Burma front', 'the turning point in the war in South-East Asia'.[89] 'This was to be our first major test against the Japanese in our comeback. ... Completely to destroy a Japanese offensive would, I thought, have the greatest moral effect on our troops.'[90]

Air support was crucial to Slim in dealing with U-Go itself, which began in the second week of March. By early April the Japanese were besieging the British and Indian troops in Kohima and Imphal. Mountbatten drew on the airlift, despite some American opposition, as well as from the Middle East, and the DC 3s were decisive. 'Air supply, made possible by borrowed resources, turned Imphal-Kohima into a Stalingrad in reverse for the Japanese Fifteenth Army.'[91] The Japanese had supplies for only twenty days. Failing to secure Imphal by the end of March, they did not, however, break off. Only on 8 July did Mutaguchi and Kawabe at Burma Area Army accept defeat. The 15th Army had been destroyed. On this outcome, it seems, the heroic endeavours of the Chindits had, however, limited effect. Nor were they well used by General Joseph W. Stilwell after Wingate's death on 24 March. The advance on Myitkyina was costly.

The Japanese had not only failed to pre-empt an Allied offensive in Burma: they had precipitated it. There were, however, other reasons for the British to continue with the conquest of Burma. The Americans were now less interested in it, since, with the success of their Pacific campaigns, China was playing less of a role in their plans to defeat Japan, either in terms of a military contribution or as a base for bombing the Japanese homeland. In a strategic if not a political sense, it was no longer necessary to conquer Burma so as to sustain China. The focus of the war was now on the Pacific side of Roosevelt's slice. The Americans were attacking the homeland from the Pacific and securing the Philippines.

While the British chiefs of staff argued for taking part in the Pacific struggle, Churchill was anxious for a different kind of British participation. He told them:

[88] Collier, *War in the Far East*, p. 410.
[89] Kirby, *War against Japan*, III, 150.
[90] q. Callahan, *Burma 1942-1945*, p. 133.
[91] Ibid., p. 137.

[O]ur policy should be to give naval assistance on the largest scale to the main American operations, but to keep our own thrust for Rangoon as a preliminary operation, or one of the preliminary operations, to a major attack upon Singapore. Here is the supreme British objective in the whole of the Indian and Far Eastern theatres. It is the only prize that will restore British prestige in this region.[92]

A seaward attack on Sumatra had been in Wavell's mind and in Churchill's. Until the war in Europe was over, however, Mountbatten had no means of undertaking it, and it soon became apparent that the war in Europe would not end in 1944, as had been hoped. The success of Slim's 14th Army in Burma, precipitated by the Japanese, opened up another prospect. 'The war in Burma', as Callahan puts it, 'was turning into a peculiar sort of sideshow – an almost private war between Slim's army and the Japanese, in which the political object of the campaign was less important than simply winning it. Mountbatten was also affected, since it began to look as if victory in Burma might be the only victory in SEAC's grasp.'[93] In February Mountbatten's objective became the capture of Rangoon from the north before the monsoon. A schedule of future amphibious operations would bring him to Singapore by March 1946.

In Burma, indeed, the Fourteenth Army had been doing well. After the failure of the campaign in the north, Imperial HQ had considered withdrawing from Burma altogether. That, however, was ruled out, as it would risk the chain of defences extending from Burma to Sumatra that protected the western flank of the Southern Army's area. In September, Terauchi was told that the security of southern Burma had priority, and that interrupting India-China communications was a secondary task. Kumura, Kawabe's successor as commander of the Burma Area Army, realised the importance to his army of the rice-producing Irrawaddy delta and the Yenangyaung oilfields. Slim's objective came to be to prevent his falling back with his surviving armies. That was done by a master-stroke, capturing Meiktila, while also thrusting at Mandalay. With them in his hands, Slim rushed to beat the monsoon to Rangoon. On 1 May, some thirty-eight months after it had met disaster at the Sittang bridge, 17th Indian Infantry Division reached Pegu. On 3 May seaborne elements of the 3th Indian

---

[92] Churchill, *Hinge of Fate*, p. 146.
[93] Callahan, *Burma 1942-1945*, p. 141.

Infantry Brigade entered Rangoon. The Japanese had evacuated it on 29 April.

Mountbatten now planned to launch Zipper, the attack on Malaya. It was never to take place, for Japan was forced to surrender in August. The capture of the Marianas had brought the homeland more effectively within the range of bombers, since those based in southern China could reach only Kyushu. Initially the target was the aircraft factories. In February and March the Americans shifted to dropping incendiaries on the industrial areas. A raid on a densely populated part of Tokyo on 9/10 March was particularly devastating and killed 80,000 people. Others were sent against Nagoya, Osaka and Kobe, and it was clear that Japan's cities were open to complete destruction.

A desperate battle for Okinawa followed. The largest battleship ever built, *Yamato*, little used because of her fuel consumption, but now sent out on a virtual suicide mission code-named Kikusui, was sunk on 7 April. The struggle was seen a portent of what would happen when the homeland was invaded, and an even greater armada was exposed to *kamikaze* attacks. Those were included in the plans Imperial HQ drew up to resist the expected invasion of the homeland (*Ketsu-Go*). That MacArthur and Nimitz were instructed to begin on 1 November 1945.

Surrender

Those Japanese leaders who thought in terms of negotiation had faced insuperable difficulties, at home and abroad and in combination. The war had begun when diplomacy failed, and the way in which diplomacy might resume was left uncertain. Tojo indeed seems to have hoped that a peace could be made if the perimeter were secured and held. It was rapidly secured but not held for long. The early victory made it difficult to seek a settlement, given Japan's success and the consequent hubris of the military. The subsequent deterioration of its position also made it difficult. Not only would the military find it difficult to accept. Japan would also appear to be negotiating from a position of weakness.

In any case Tojo's judgment of the Allies was faulty. He seems to have thought that, involved in Europe and facing a *fait accompli*, the United States would not fight to undo what Japan had done. He had, of course, some reason to think along those lines, for the US had not committed itself to resist Japan until the European war began, and had been planning to leave the Philippines. In the war, moreover, the Allies made the defeat of Germany their priority. They did not, however, intend to accept the *fait accompli*. At Casablanca in January 1943 they committed themselves to unconditional surrender, and the joint Anglo-American declaration at Cairo in December 1943, repeating that, also indicated that Japan would be required to give up all the gains it had made since 1895. Those who thought in terms of negotiation had an impossible gulf to bridge. If the military leadership had never accepted negotiation, it would certainly not accept humiliation.

An advocate of a new policy towards China as Tojo's foreign minister from April 1943, Shigemitsu also, like Togo, looked to the Soviet Union, with which the neutrality pact made by Matsuoka in April 1941 had been loyally sustained. On the fall of Mussolini in July 1943 Kido had broached the idea of ending the war through the good offices of the Soviet Union,[94] and in September the foreign minister instructed Ambassador Sato to speak to Molotov about sending a Japanese envoy to Europe. If Japan's idea was to end Russo-German hostilities, he replied, Russia could not accept. Shigemitsu repeated the idea in April 1944, again in vain.[95]

In September the navy minister, Yonai, directed his thinking towards a general peace, encouraging Rear Admiral Takagi Sokichi, 'a sort of one-man "brains trust" within the IJN',[96] to take up a study he had begun the previous year that had led him in that direction, too.[97] For his part Shigemitsu had the foreign office prepare a draft on diplomatic measures to be taken *vis-à-vis* the Soviet Union. The purpose was to maintain the pact, to promote peace between Germany and the Soviet Union, and to utilise Soviet assistance in improving Japan's situation if Germany collapsed. If Germany made a separate peace, or if a general peace were secured through the good offices of the Soviet Union, Japan would accept a number of Soviet demands. So, too, if it was necessary to guard against a Soviet attack. Such demands could include a sphere of interest in Manchuria, peaceful activities in

---

[94] R.C.J. Butow, *Japan's Decision to Surrender*, Stanford Univ. Press, 1954, p. 88.

[95] G.A. Lensen, *The Strange Neutrality; Soviet-Japanese Relations during the Second Word War, 1941-1945*, Tallahassee: Diplomatic Press, 1972, pp. 113-15, 117.

[96] Marder *et al.*, *Old Friends*, II, 395.

[97] Butow, *Japan's Decision*, p. 38n.

China and title to southern Sakhalin and the northern Kuriles.[98] Hirota, a former ambassador and prime minister, was in his mind as special envoy. Molotov again rejected the idea.[99]

On 7 November Stalin denounced Japan as an aggressor, but Shigemitsu did not give up. Standstill diplomacy was impossible, he told Sato. 'To tell the truth, we have already passed the decisive stage of fighting. War thereafter is unreasonable ... we must pursue unreasonable diplomacy.'[100] Sato got nowhere with Molotov, however, even with an attempt to discuss the question of French Indo-China,[101] and he was evasive over the Yalta meeting in February. The Japanese did not give up the hope of a negotiation, however. Nor was the hope entirely destroyed when, shortly after the invasion of Okinawa began (1 April), the Soviet Union announced that it would not renew the neutrality pact when it expired in April 1946.

The same day Koiso resigned. A new cabinet was headed by Admiral Suzuki Kantaro. 'This is the end,' Tojo declared. 'This is our Badoglio cabinet.'[102] Significantly, the new foreign minister and minister for Greater East Asia was Togo Shigenori, once an ambassador in Moscow. He, like his predecessor, was ready to make large sacrifices, should the German collapse make it possible for the Soviet Union to bring about a general peace or should relations with the Soviet Union deteriorate so as to threaten an attack on Japan.[103] He told Ambassador Malik on 20 April that Japan-Soviet relations were 'the only bright spot' on the world scene, and hoped they could be a nucleus round which peace could be restored.[104] Involving Russia might be a means of avoiding the demand for unconditional surrender that a direct approach to the Allies would involve. The object was a negotiated peace. The Japanese still had some hope that the Soviet Union, originally pushed into alliance with the West by Nazi Germany, could be won over. They were not aware, though Togo suspected,[105]

[98]   Ibid., p. 89.
[99]   Lensen, *Strange Neutrality*, pp. 119-20.
[100] q. ibid., p. 122.
[101] Ibid., p. 126.
[102] q. Shillony, *Politics in Wartime Japan*, p. 81.
[103] Butow, *Japan's Decision*, pp. 89-90.
[104] Lensen, *Strange Neutrality*, p. 132.
[105] Butow, *Japan's Decision*, p. 77.

that the Western Allies had already outbid them at Yalta.

Germany surrendered on 8 May. On 14 May Togo suggested to his colleagues that Japan should make new offers to the Soviet Union, designed to win assistance or neutrality, surrendering Port Arthur, even the Kuriles, though not Korea. Secret talks between Hirota and Malik in Hakone were, however, ineffectual, though Japan offered a 20-30-year non-aggression pact, and was ready to withdraw from Manchuria as well as the territories it had occupied in the Greater East Asia war.

Before the Allies met at Potsdam, Togo cabled the Emperor's desire for peace, and his wish to send Konoe to Moscow. The Soviet Union declared the proposal 'unclear' and said it could not give 'any definite reply'.[106] Sato sought definition rather than 'phrases beautiful but somewhat remote from the facts and empty in content'.[107] The aim was peace, Togo replied, short of unconditional surrender: 'at the same time, it would also be impossible as well as disadvantageous, in view of the domestic situation as well as of external relations, to set forth concrete terms of peace immediately now.'[108]

The fact was, it seems, that there was no agreement in the Japanese cabinet. The output of new vehicles by March was only 18 per cent of that in 1941; imports of oil had ceased and only 4 million barrels were in stock; aircraft fuel would run out by September.[109] But the military did not admit they were beaten, and hoped that Russia might even aid Japan. The peace faction, on the other hand, wanted it to mediate.[110] The approaches to the Soviet Union had been ambiguous and formulaic. The proposal to send Konoe was intended, like a similar proposal in 1941, to cut through the differences and invoke imperial authority. Sato told Lozovsky that Konoe had proposals both for ending the war and for closer Soviet-Japanese relations.[111] Even at this stage, the Japanese were leaving it to others to define their policy. On 8 August Molotov finally replied that war would begin the following day.

---

[106] Lensen, *Strange Neutrality*, p. 147.

[107] q. J. Samuel Walker, *Prompt and Utter Destruction*, Chapel Hill: Univ. of North Carolina Press, 1997, p. 49.

[108] q. Lensen, *Strange Neutrality*, p. 148.

[109] Kirby, *War against Japan*, V, 98.

[110] Walker, *Prompt and Utter Destruction*, pp. 47-8.

[111] Lensen, *Strange Neutrality*, p. 147.

The Potsdam declaration of 26 July had repeated the demand for unconditional surrender, though, as Butow points out, adding the phrase 'of all Japanese armed forces'.[112] The Japanese government did not accept it, though it did not dismiss it, as a phrase Suzuki used, *mokukatsu*, seemed to imply.[113] It sought to ascertain Soviet intentions, but in vain.

On 6 August, the atomic bomb was dropped on Hiroshima. That had been developed initially by the British, and from 1942 as a joint Anglo-American enterprise. The test version of the plutonium bomb was exploded in New Mexico on 16 July, shortly before the Potsdam conference opened. The Potsdam declaration was intended to be an invitation to surrender before extreme measures were taken, though it included no assurance over the imperial house such as Stimson had suggested.[114] On the way home from Potsdam, Truman sanctioned the dropping of two nuclear bombs, already delivered to the Marianas. The second bomb was dropped on Nagasaki.

On 14 August the Japanese decided to surrender. The Emperor avoided using the word: his broadcast referred to the enemy's use of 'a new and most cruel bomb'.[115] He recalled the Meiji emperor's attitude to the Triple Intervention: 'As he endured the unendurable, so shall I, and so must you.'[116] The instrument of surrender was signed on board USS *Missouri* in Tokyo Bay at 9 a.m. on 2 September, one day short of the sixth anniversary of the opening of the war in Europe.

MacArthur and the Philippines

The Pacific war thus ended even before the approach to Japan along the eastern side of Roosevelt's pie was complete, while the approach along the western side had already lost much of its significance. Both approaches had, with the exception of northern Burma and part of the Philippines, attributed little importance to Southeast Asia, the original bone of contention. MacArthur had, however, been anxious, partly for political reasons, to regain, rather than bypass, the Philippines. The British, partly for political rea-

---

[112] Butow, *Japan's Decision*, pp. 133. The text is on p. 243.

[113] Ibid., pp. 145ff; Walker, *Prompt and Utter Destruction*, pp. 72-3.

[114] Collier, *War in the Far East*, p. 473.

[115] q. Walker, *Prompt and Utter Destruction*, p. 88.

[116] q. Butow, *Japan's Decision*, p. 208.

sons, also wished to play a role in the defeat of Japan. What that could or should be was less clear. A naval role in the Pacific would clearly be only a subordinate one. A role in retaking Southeast Asia would restore Britain's prestige, but not contribute to concluding the war, given the shape it had come to take. The answer was in a sense provided by the Japanese, whose offensive in Burma opened up an opportunity that the British forces were now prepared to exploit, and the Americans, not without some uncertainty, made the necessary air support available.

By the time of the surrender, therefore, neither Singapore nor Malaya had been regained by the Allies, and the main work of SEAC, started only after the surrender was signed on 2 September, came to be not reconquest or liberation but occupation. At Potsdam it was also given responsibility for Borneo and eastern Indonesia. These were parts of Southeast Asia that had been reconquered, following the advances the Allied forces had made in the southwest Pacific.

The reconquest of the Philippines involved US forces. The Sixth Army and later the Eighth contended with the three groups into which Yamashita had divided his forces on Luzon, but, despite severe privations, they held out in the mountainous areas till the end of hostilities in August. In the south the Eighth Army invaded Palawan on 28 February, and met little resistance. On 10 March Zamboanga and Basilan were occupied, the Tawi-Tawi islands on 2 April and Jolo on the 9th. In the Visayas Filipino guerrillas welcomed American landings near Iloilo on 18 March, and the Japanese, leaving much of the town in flames, fled to the hills. Cebu City was occupied on 27 March. Most of Mindanao yet remained in Japanese hands. MacArthur had intended to attack it first, before he was directed to bypass it and attack Leyte, and the Japanese had prepared for an attack from the south. The US forces entered Davao on 3 May. As elsewhere the Japanese continued fighting in the interior.

The large Japanese forces which had been bypassed in New Guinea, New Britain and Bougainville were left to the Australians. There, somewhat controversially, General Blamey took the offensive. The Australians were also to play a role in Borneo. In February MacArthur declared that he intended to use I Australian Corps to retake the oilfields, and that it should then go on to Java. Tarakan was occupied on 5 May, but organised resistance did not cease till

24 June, and some of the garrison held out to the end of the war. There was determined resistance to the Australians at Balikpapan in July, though by the end of the month the Japanese had withdrawn into the interior. On the northwest coast, landings on Labuan and at Brooketon on 10 June had met no opposition, and by the 15th Brunei Town had been occupied. Beaufort followed on 28 June, while to the south Seria had been taken on 21 June, and the whole area had been secured by 1 July.

The peoples and the war

All Southeast Asia had been involved in the war. In that sense it was a unique event in Southeast Asia's history. Even so, the experience varied across the region. Some parts of it, for example, had been fought over twice, some only once, some not or hardly at all. While the destruction of the colonial regimes that covered all the region but Thailand was a common feature, that in Indo-China was not finally displaced till some three years after the others. Japan's empire in the region was throughout an embattled one, but its reaction to that differed from area to area. Not only were the areas different in character: Japan's policy-making was contingent and variegated.

The involvement of the Southeast Asian peoples themselves in the struggle over the region also varied. The colonial powers rarely risked calling upon them, though they did not dispose of the strength to defend their possessions from the outside. The war was, as it were, to be fought over their heads. 'Confidence, resolution, enterprise and devotion to the cause will inspire every one of us in the fighting services', declared the British order of the day of 8 December, 'while from the civilian population, Malay, Chinese, or Indian, we expect that patience, endurance and serenity which is the great virtue of the East and which will go far to assist the fighting men to gain a final and complete victory.'[117]

'The majority of the natives of Sarawak did not view Japanese aggression with any great concern,' wrote J.L. Noakes, the state's secretary of defence. 'They had never experienced modern warfare and had no desire to be embroiled in a conflict which they neither understood nor wanted. ... A war with Japan would not be their concern.'[118]

[117] q. Tarling, *Pacific War*, pp. 367–8.
[118] Report Upon Defence Measures... JJ/KK C/A/d2, Sarawak Museum, Kuching.

The Indian National Army

Though varying among themselves, the Japanese shared something of the reluctance to arm the natives, though what they did, under the pressure of emergency, was revolutionary enough. Even their treatment of the Indians was equivocal. Indians, of course, constituted a large part of the British forces, some 700,000 men. 'The prewar Indian Army', as L.S. Amery, then Britain's Secretary of State for India, had put it, 'was ... a mercenary army in so far as the men were volunteers, seeking a means of livelihood, not conscripts: but it was a professional army of men who chose the profession of arms as good in itself and were imbued, as part of their professional instinct, with a devotion to their regiment and to the Sirkar.'[119] What it was not was a national army. The Japanese, pressed by the Indian revolutionaries, tried to turn national feeling to account, but only half-heartedly.

Fujiwara Iwaichi's original task in October 1941 was to head an intelligence operation, *kosaku*, in Bangkok. He moved into Malaya with the invading forces, encouraging the surrender of Indian troops, among them Mohan Singh and his men. They formed the core of a volunteer army, the Indian National Army, joined by thousands of prisoners of war in February 1942 after an inspiring speech by Fujiwara in Farrer Park.[120] Imperial HQ saw it, however, mainly as a propaganda outfit, useful for controlling prisoners of war and maintaining law and order among the Indian population.[121] It was also at odds with the Indian Independence League, led by R.B. Bose, one of the exiles in Tokyo. Numbers dwindled, and in December Mohan Singh was stripped of his command by Bose and arrested by the Japanese.[122] In 1943 a Provisional Government of India was established under Subhas Chandra Bose. The army was reconstituted as Azad Hind Fauj and recruited local civilians, including many Malayan Tamils, as well as ex-prisoners of war.[123]

[119] q. Callahan, *Burma 1942-1945*, p. 94.

[120] Fujiwara Iwaichi, *F. Kikan*, trans. Akashi Yoji, Hong Kong, Singapore and Kuala Lumpur: Heinemann, 1983, p. 17.

[121] T.R. Sareen, *Japan and the Indian National Army*, Delhi: Agam Prakashan, 1986, p. 78.

[122] Fujiwara, *F. Kikan*, pp. 244-5; Sareen, *Japan and INA*, p. 101.

[123] U. Mahajani, *The Role of Indian Minorities in Burma and Malaya*, Bombay: Vora 1960, p. 78.

The Ist Division INA was placed under the Fifteenth Army for U-Go, though of course there was no chance of the March on Delhi for which some may desperately have hoped.[124] In this case, as in Southeast Asia itself, the achievement of the Japanese was indirect rather than direct. Postwar the British became anxious about using the Indian army to deal with the nationalist movements in Southeast Asia, making the restoration of the Europeans' position, already doubtful, even more impractical.

The main effect of the Japanese venture was to dislodge the colonial regimes. The long-term prospects of those regimes were no doubt in any case limited, and their position was transitional. Once interrupted, however, colonial rule could not be resumed. The judgment the French made was, in that sense, the right one. The regimes, always fragile, could not be restored, either in Burma, which was reconquered, or in Malaya or Indonesia, which were not. Not only had the 'prestige' of the Europeans suffered an irreparable blow. They now had no effective means of winning that collaboration without which the deployment of such force as they had would operate in a political vacuum.

The break in colonial continuity was sufficient to allow the nationalists their chance. To them, again, the Japanese offered little that was positive. Their structures and their ideology were a pragmatic mixture of East and West, home and colonial. They made it up as they went along.

Though the Japanese had indeed spoken of Greater East Asia, their idealism was limited from the start and qualified by wartime necessity. If there was nevertheless some reason for Southeast Asian peoples to be grateful to the Japanese, even though their contribution to the end of colonialism was not whole-hearted, such was eroded, not only by their economic greed and administrative incompetence – which might be partly blamed on wartime conditions – but also, perhaps even more, by their violence and their cruelty. Those features also undermined the readiness of their opponents to see justice in their cause or to admire the almost incomprehensible determination and endurance of their soldiers.

---

[124] Cf. T.R. Sareen, ed., *Select Documents on the Indian National Army*, Delhi: Agam Prakashan, 1988, p. 364.

4

CONQUEST AND LIBERATION

Racism and rhetoric

While its prewar leaders had been certain that Japan would come
to play a larger role in Southeast Asia and that the colonial structures there could not endure for ever, they had developed no more
specific vision of its future or of their role in it, still less any more
definite plans. Information had been collected, societies formed,
pamphlets published. Commercial interests had been established,
either private or, increasingly, with government backing. In 1936,
the government had authorised 'footsteps' in the south. But, while
the resources of Southeast Asia became more important, there was
no plan to take it over. Those most interested in them, the naval
leaders, were indeed those most apprehensive of the opposition of
the maritime powers. Their army colleagues were more concerned
about the Soviet Union.

It was the European war that changed such attitudes. Even
then, it was initially hoped that it would provide opportunities in
Southeast Asia that might avoid the need for force. When force
was resolved upon, indeed, there was a residual notion that it was
but a step beyond the previous diplomacy, and that the other
powers would accept a *fait accompli* as in Manchuria. The conquest
of Southeast Asia was not therefore the result of a long-term plan,
but of a sudden frustration.

It was clearly partly as a result of this timing that, when the
venture was begun, military objectives predominated, and that
planning for the empire was limited and largely improvised. The
previous history of Japan's policy-making suggests, of course, that
time was not the only factor in its incoherence. There were struct-
ural as well as personal reasons for its failure to develop strategic
concepts and its tendency to resort to the cumulation of objectives
and to formulae. Outside factors had also contributed to Japan's
special kind of policy-making, shaping its actions, contributing to

125

its opportunism, allowing it to avoid realistic appraisals, even, as it were, relieving it from the burden of decision.

These processes were combined with a visionary rhetoric that spoke first of equality with the West and then increasingly, as Japan 'returned' to Asia, of some kind of leadership in Asia. That did not help in defining a policy. It was itself contested in the process of making policy at home and also indeed in carrying it out. It also affected outside perceptions of Japan, those held by the Chinese, the Western powers and the peoples of Southeast Asia. Even if the rhetoric rallied opinion at home it might not appeal abroad. What might seem idealistic aims to the Japanese might not – even if implemented – seem so to others. Would it win support and avoid war? Would it help to bring victory in war? Would it make the empire acquired easier to sustain?

The answers had seemed doubtful even in East Asia. Japan shared a Confucian background with China and Korea, but it had no special bond with its neighbours, and handling them was complicated not only by the interests of the West but by Japan's emulation of the West. '[A]s England might say of Ireland or Russia of Poland, proximity made neither for successful imperialism nor co-prosperity.'[1] The New Order rhetoric of 1938 was, as Kumitada Miwa says, presented in traditional terms so as 'to have a readier appeal to the sentiments of the Japanese public. It was also hoped that it would have a similar effect on the Chinese.'[2] It was a forlorn hope.

The acquisition of Manchuria prompted attempts to accommodate national self-determination and pan-Asian rhetoric. The Great Asia Society (Dai Ajia Kyokai) was founded in 1933 on the day Manchukuo was proclaimed. Its emphasis was neotraditionalist: it spoke, for example, of the harmony of the five races. The Showa Study Association (Showa Kenkyukai), a think-tank for Konoe[3] informally inaugurated in November 1933, sought a more 'scientific' approach. But if proximity did not help in defining Japan's relationships, nor did distance. Extending the rhetoric to cover the non-Sinitic world was still more challenging.

---

[1] Lone, *Japan's First Modern War*, p. 124.

[2] White, Imegaki and Havens, *Ambivalence of Nationalism*, p. 149.

[3] James B. Crowley in James W. Morley, ed., *Dilemmas of Growth in Prewar Japan*, Princeton Univ. Press, 1971, pp. 324-5.

Characteristically it was seriously attempted only in 1940. Konoe's New Order had not been concerned with Southeast Asia.

[I]ts definitional extension to include Southeast Asia was the result of a sudden turn in international events and of Japan's opportunism in seizing upon this turn, rather than the consequence of a long-considered or widely held interest in the co-prosperity of the Southeast Asian peoples.[4]

Its rhetoric could not emphasise a common Sinitic heritage. It tended therefore to emphasise 'liberation'. Four days after the war began the government announced that the Anglo-American war would be called a Great East Asia War 'because it is a war for the construction of a new order in East Asia'. It entailed the 'liberation of East Asian peoples from the aggression of America and Britain', which was to lead to 'the establishment of a genuine world peace and the creation of a new world culture'.[5]

That was as hard to reconcile with Japan's own interests and attitudes, however, as pan-Asianism had been earlier, if not harder. The task force on ideology at the navy ministry in June 1941 had voiced its dismay over the contradictions within the concepts *hakko ichiu* (eight corners of the world under one roof, universal peace) and imperial 'benevolence' as the guiding principles of the Greater East Asia Co-Prosperity Sphere. The terms seemed limited to a Japanese audience. 'Don't we have any "slogan" comparable with the universality of America's "democracy"?', asked a naval officer. One adviser suggested redefining *hakko ichiu* as 'universal brotherhood', but soon all agreed that 'although we say "universal brotherhood", it probably means that we are equal to the Caucasians but, to the peoples of Asia, we act as their leader.' An academic adviser declared in October: 'The Greater Asia Co-Prosperity Sphere is not a reality, nor is it capable of becoming so. We are deceiving the world.'[6]

The Total War Institute, an officially sanctioned think-tank, struggled with the task early in 1942.

The Japanese empire is a manifestation of morality and its special characteristic is the propagation of the Imperial Way. It strives but for the achievement of *Hakko Ichiu*, the spirit of its founding. ... It is necessary to foster the increased power of the empire, to cause East Asia to return to its original form of independence and co-operation by shaking off the yoke

---

[4] M. Peattie in Duus *et al.*, *Japanese Wartime Empire*, p. 211.

[5] q. Iriye, *Power and Culture*, p. 64.

[6] q. Crowley in Siberman and Harootunian, *Japan in Crisis*, pp. 293, 294.

of Europe and America, and to let its countries and peoples develop their respective abilities in peaceful cooperation and secure livelihood.

The desire for independence of peoples in the Co-Prosperity Sphere was to be respected, 'but proper and suitable forms of government shall be decided for them in consideration of military and economic requirements and of the historical, political and cultural elements peculiar to each area'. Independence was to be based on the construction of the New Order, differing from

an independence based on the idea of liberalism and self-determination. ... The peoples of the sphere shall obtain their proper positions, the unity of the people's minds shall be effected and the unification of the sphere shall be realised with the empire as its center.[7]

Meanwhile the troops had been told in a pamphlet *Read This Alone – and the War Can Be Won* that 'after centuries of subjugation to Europe and exploitation by the Chinese' the natives of Southeast Asia 'have reached the point of almost complete emasculation. We may wish to make men of them again quickly, but we should not expect too much.' To the natives, it continued, the British, the Americans, the French and the Dutch were 'armed robbers, whilst we Japanese are brothers. At least, we are indubitably relatives.'[8]

Care should be taken, the cabinet information board had declared in December 1940, to avoid an 'image' of aggression or 'exploitation of the underdeveloped nations'. If Japan were seen as avaricious, the races would not 'identify their aspirations for national independence with Japan's help'.[9] If the racialism of the Japanese stood in the way of the Co-Prosperity Sphere, so, however, did the anxiety to secure the resources of Southeast Asia. Before the war its rhetoric took different shapes and assumed different meanings. That continued to be the case during the war and as it approached a conclusion.

The Greater East Asia Co-Prosperity Sphere

Arita had already begun to evoke the rhetoric in April 1940, when urging the maintenance of the *status quo* in the Indies. He referred to the 'intimate relationship of mutuality' binding Japan and Southeast Asia, and especially the Indies. Extending the war to

[7] q. Tsunoda, *Sources of Japanese Tradition*, II, 294ff.

[8] q. R.H.W. Reece, *Masa Jepun*, Kuching: Sarawak Literary Society, 1998, p. 116.

[9] q. Crowley in Silberman and Harootunian, *Japan in Crisis*, p. 290.

Southeast Asia would interfere with maintaining and furthering 'economic interdependence' and 'co-existence and co-prosperity'.[10] On 29 June he went further:

The countries of East Asia stand in close relationship to the regions of the South Seas in terms of geography, history, race, and economy. They are destined to enjoy prosperous coexistence by mutual help and accommodation and, by so doing, to promote the peace and prosperity of the world. It is a matter of course, therefore, to unite these regions into a single sphere on the basis of common existence so that the stability of that sphere be ensured.[11]

The Konoe government, and its foreign minister, Matsuoka, put forward the vision of the Greater East Asia Co-Prosperity Sphere. But it was still a piece of rhetoric that could be and was subject to many interpretations.

Whatever it might mean, however, it was, at least at this point, no promise of liberation. The Japanese had made a deal with Vichy, and Kobayashi sought one with Netherlands India. It is not easy to share the view put forward by *Greater Asianism*, the magazine of the Dai-Ajia Kyokai, at the time of the occupation of northern Indo-China: 'We are only gratified and admire the wholesome way of Heaven, imagining the joy of the inhabitants there welcoming the Imperial troops with heartfelt joy and gratitude, now that those people in Vietnam have come to look up to the Imperial wind and bask in the Emperor's benevolence....' The occupation was 'the first in a series of great leaps forward toward war to liberate all of Asia'. The move into southern Indo-China was greeted as egregiously: 'Who can imagine the feelings of the people in southern Vietnam without deep emotion?'[12]

Already it was clear that the vision of Greater East Asia was something that was contested among Japanese policy-makers. It influenced their arguments among themselves and the presentation of the outcome to the Japanese public. It was also employed outside Japan, but as a matter of expediency. It did not determine their objectives. That was again made clear when the war began.

Army and navy came together in their operational planning, making use of the military intelligence Japan had acquired, and it was speedily and brilliantly, if daringly, conceived and later ex-

[10] q. Nagaoka Shinjuro in Morley, *Fateful Choice*, p. 128.

[11] q. Tarling, *Pacific War*, pp. 72-3.

[12] q. Goto, '*Returning to Asia*', pp. 150, 151.

ecuted. The planning for the administration of the south put its priority on Japan's economic needs. On that, too, army and navy were agreed. Characteristically the area was to be divided between them, with the army to have primary responsibility, and the navy secondary, in the Philippines, Malaya, Sumatra, Java, British Borneo and Burma, and the reverse to be the case in respect of Dutch Borneo, Sulawesi, Maluku, the lesser Sundas and New Guinea. Both, however, put their priority on the administrative status quo and on the extraction of the materials that Japan required.

In a sense Japan was going only one step beyond the policy already followed in Indo-China and attempted in respect of Netherlands India. That affords further evidence that the endeavour was not only developed in the short term but that, other than the acquisition of resources, its objectives had not been finalised, and the possibility of a deal was not ruled out. Invoking the rhetoric of the Sphere, when it was done, was a matter of expediency.

No deal was made. The result was, of course, that the Japanese stayed on. The policies they adopted were improvised and variegated. The men on the spot responded to the diverse conditions they found. But they responded in ways that were further diversified by the nature, spirit and structure of the two armed services, which continued to be responsible for the southern area, and by the need to sustain the empire against continued attack. Their methods borrowed from the earlier empires of Japan, from Korea and Taiwan, and also from Manchuria. They borrowed, too, from the homeland. They employed the rhetoric of Greater East Asia whenever and in whatever way it seemed appropriate. They responded, with more or less reluctance, to the instructions they received from Tokyo. There the Imperial HQ was responsible for the overall direction of the war. There, too, were those who vainly sought for some kind of negotiated conclusion. Both the continuance of the war and the possibilities of peace also inflected the policies in the south, and in particular the attempts to interpret and give meaning to the concept of the GEAPS.

The guidelines

The cabinet planning board's statement of 6 August 1940, 'Outline of Economic Measures for the Southern Regions', 'set the tone', as Mark Peattie puts it.[13] In the creation of a Southeast Asian bloc Japan's

---

[13] Peattie in Duus *et al., Japanese Wartime Empire,* p. 236.

military requirement for raw materials was to have priority. This priority was followed in the first serious study of the problems of a possible occupation, which was undertaken by the operations division of the army general staff. Its research office produced a draft study, 'Principles for the Administration and Security of Occupied Southern Regions', in March 1941. The planners set forth the three main principles that the government was to adopt later in the year: the restoration of public order, the acquisition of strategic materials and the economic self-sufficiency of the occupation forces.

'It is not clear how much thought the General Staff Research Office, or indeed any element of the Japanese government, gave to these matters between March and November of 1941.'[14] Not till 15 November did the liaison conference adopt the principles. On 20 November it agreed that the occupied areas were to be administered by military personnel, 'making use of existing organs of government as much as possible'.[15] The task of filling out the guidelines was made over to the sixth committee that the planning board set up on 26 November.

The guidelines repeated the objectives enunciated in March, and then set out the principles to be followed. 'In the implementation of military administration, existing governmental organizations shall be utilized as much as possible, with due respect for past organizational structure and native practices.' The occupation forces were, so far as military operations permitted, to 'take measures to promote the acquisition and development of resources vital to national defense so far as military operations permit.' Those were to be integrated into the resources mobilisation programme of the central government in Tokyo. 'Economic hardships imposed upon native livelihood as a result of the acquisition of resources vital to the national defense and for the self-sufficiency of occupation troops must be endured; and pacification measures against the natives shall stop at a point consistent with these objectives.'

American, British and Dutch nationals were to be 'induced to cooperate with the military administrations', 'appropriate measures, such as deportation' being adopted in respect of 'recalcitrants'. The interests of Axis nationals were to be respected, but the expansion of their interests restricted. Chinese residents were to be 'induced' to defect from the Chiang Kai-shek regime. 'Native inhabitants

[14] q. ibid., p. 236.
[15] q. Iriye, *Power and Culture*, p. 67.

shall be so guided as to induce a sense of trust in the Imperial forces, and premature encouragement of native independence movements shall be avoided.' No military governments were to be established in Indo-China or Thailand. 'Further measures necessitated by drastic changes in either country shall be separately determined.'[16] An army document of 25 November, repeating most of this, spoke also of gradually indoctrinating the local people with 'the policy of liberation in East Asia, so that they will be available for use in our operational schemes. Security of property rights and destruction of the hated white races' power should be played up in our propaganda.'[17]

Tojo's speech to the House of Peers on 20 January 1942 went somewhat further. Explaining the aim of the triumphing invaders, he echoed the rhetoric of the War Institute. Japan wanted to enable each country and people in the Sphere 'to have its proper place and demonstrate its real character, thereby securing an order of co-existence and co-prosperity based on ethical principles with Japan serving as its nucleus'. Japan would deal with areas 'absolutely essential' for defence, such as Hong Kong and the Malay peninsula.

As regards the Philippines, if the peoples of those islands will hereafter understand the real intentions of Japan and offer to cooperate with us as one of the partners for the establishment of the Greater East Asia Co-Prosperity Sphere, Japan will gladly enable them to enjoy the honour of independence. As for Burma what Japan contemplates is not different from that relating to the Philippines.[18]

The following month Singapore fell, and in March the Indies. The navy's outline on the conduct of military administration in occupied areas of 14 March 1942 extended one of Tojo's remarks:

The occupation of areas where the Navy shall act as principal administrative authority shall be directed toward their permanent retention under Japanese control. To this end, administrative and other policies shall be so devised as to facilitate the organic integration of the entire region into the Japanese empire.[19]

[16] q. H.J. Benda *et al.*, *Japanese Military Administration in Indonesia*, New Haven, CT: Yale Univ. Press, 1965, pp. 1–3.

[17] q. Ooi Keat Gin, *Japanese Empire in the Tropics*, Athens: Univ. of Ohio Press, 1998, p. 30.

[18] q. Joyce C. Lebra, *Japan's Greater East Asia Co-Prosperity Sphere in World War II*, Kuala Lumpur: Oxford Univ. Press, 1975, pp. 79–80.

[19] q. Benda *et al.*, *Japanese in Indonesia*, pp. 27, 29.

Independence was not at hand elsewhere. The superintendent-general of military administration in Singapore indicated in August that the national policy was 'to defer final decisions on the eventual status of the occupied areas'. Local military authorities should not 'prematurely reveal the Empire's intentions or make commitments to the local inhabitants'. The Philippines and Burma would have independence 'after they have evidenced their cooperation with the empire', but 'military affairs, foreign affairs, economics, and other affairs shall be placed under the firm control of the empire.'[20]

The Ministry of Greater East Asia

Britain's destiny was sealed, the popular magazine *Kaizo* had proclaimed in February. The Anglo-Saxons 'prate of civilization, and rave of justice and brotherly love as though they had a monopoly of them, the while they exploit and despoil the backward peoples of Asia and Africa merely for their own pleasure and ease.' The Japanese had challenged their oppression.

We must ponder carefully how in India, Burma, the Straits Settlements, Borneo and Malaya we are to reconstruct in the wake of people who have merely been extortionists. Our policies for the people we shall free, will require sagacity and great boldness.[21]

So far, however, they had been limited and *ad hoc*.

In the following months a less haphazard approach was adopted. Yet even that resulted less from the idealism some associated with the Sphere than from the practical difficulties that 'adhockery' had produced, and the approach was itself the subject of intra-bureaucratic wrangling. The discussions, moreover, again illustrated the provisional nature of Japan's empire and the recognition that its continuance still depended on the attitude of other powers.

An advisory Council for the Construction of Greater East Asia had been set up in February 1942. Some officials now saw the need for a central planning agency for the occupied areas. The haphazard nature of the policies of the occupying forces was an argument for it, put forward by civilians on the planning board and in the colonial ministry. With that they invoked the need to prepare for the new Asian order. Even so, they noted that the major goal of the goal of the new organisation would be 'to carry out the establish-

[20] q. ibid., p. 187
[21] q. Usui Katsumi in Nish, *Alienation*, p. 96.

ment of a great Asian order properly and expeditiously so as to enable all regions of Asia to concentrate their resources on the strengthening of [Japanese] fighting capabilities'. Japan, as Tojo put it to the privy council, must compel all parts of Asia, autonomous or occupied, 'to unite with Japan and contribute their respective resources to Japan'.[22]

There was opposition. Some of it originated in bureaucratic rivalry, but by no means all. Former financial leaders, like Fukai Eigo, thought it a mistake to separate Asian countries from others. They thought, too, that the agency would symbolise compulsion and alienate those whom it was intended to win over. After Midway the proposal was also criticised by the foreign minister, Togo Shigenori.

Like the privy councilors, he thought an East Asian ministry would represent a point of no return in Japan's determination to separate the region from the rest of the world. It would be particularism in the extreme, making it more difficult than ever to come to terms with the Western powers.[23]

Though now flushed with victory and inflamed by hatred, the Japanese should be making plans to end the war. That task would be more difficult if policy towards Asia was left to a new ministry. It would, he told the prime minister, make it 'impossible to conduct a unified and consistent diplomacy' and 'affront' the pride of East Asiatic countries.[24] He argued in vain and resigned. The new ministry was established on 1 November 1942.

The concept of Greater East Asia had not, however, thus received a final definition. It remained part of the debate among the Japanese, and its role changed as their fortunes changed. Overall the trend was to emphasise its 'liberationist' aspect. The military leadership could see that as a means of recruiting support as the war turned against them, though they remained cautious. Others could see it as a means of universalising Japan's war aims, and so perhaps facilitating a settlement, while yet persuading the Japanese themselves that they had not fought in vain. In that Togo's successor, Shigemitsu, who had argued a new policy in China, was following Togo's line. Later Togo returned to office.

[22] q. Iriye, *Power and Culture*, p. 69.

[23] Ibid., pp. 69-70.

[24] Togo, *Cause of Japan*, pp. 250-1.

On 14 January 1943 the liaison conference decided to determine the future status of occupied areas according to two principles.

When considered suitable as Imperial territory, areas of strategic importance which must be secured by the Empire for the defense of Greater East Asia, as well as sparsely populated areas and regions lacking the capacity for independence, shall be incorporated into the Empire.

The administrative systems adopted were to take account of traditions and cultural and other factors.

Independence shall be bestowed upon such areas as qualify for it in the light of their past political development, if this is deemed advantageous to the prosecution of the Greater East Asia war and the establishment of Greater East Asia.[25]

Shigemitsu argued for the independence of Burma and the Philippines. The military were more doubtful. The liaison conference of 10 March agreed that Burma's independence should be coupled with complete military collaboration and a treaty of alliance. The Philippines were to have independence 'when they have made substantial efforts to render hearty collaboration', it had been agreed in January.[26] The liaison conference of 26 June agreed on a deal like Burma's.

Tojo addressed an extraordinary session of the Diet that month. He insisted that the Imperial forces were repelling the enemy's counter-offensives. The war situation was 'increasingly grave', but Japan would 'win through after fighting a battle of will against will'. New policies were necessary, given that situation, and 'in response to the sincerity and cooperation of the various nations and peoples'. Among them he listed Manchukuo and the Chinese Republic under President Wang. He envisaged 'increased strengthening' of Japan's cooperation with Thailand, and noted the preparations for Burma's independence. He affirmed that the Philippine people, 'who hitherto vainly pursued an illusory independence under the insincere administration of the United States', would gain the real thing later in the year. He spoke of 'an increasingly intimate coalition with French Indo-China', but proffered 'political participation' in the Indies, particularly in Java.[27]

---

[25] q. Benda, *Crescent and Rising Sun*, p. 48.

[26] q. Iriye, *Power and Culture*, p. 115.

[27] q. Benda *et al., Japanese in Indonesia*, pp. 49–52.

The prime minister thus put a new emphasis on the liberationist aspect of the Sphere. But it remained opportunistic and variegated. The treatment afforded the nationalist movements in Burma and the Philippines differed from that afforded the Indonesians, while French rule was retained in Indo-China.

Even so, the war was increasingly presented in terms of liberation. The Allies were fighting to regain their colonies. Japan's aims were quite different, as Shigemitsu told the Diet in October 1943:

To East Asia and its peoples, this is a war of racial awakening – a war for the renascence of East Asia. No wonder that all the peoples of East Asia have risen *en masse* to join this supreme and stupendous enterprise. ... The present war is to us a war of national emancipation, which to our enemy is nothing but a war of aggression. ... The war of greater East Asia is a war for justice to combat aggression. It is a war of liberation.[28]

For the foreign minister, the rhetoric was a means of persuading the Japanese that they had won, as well as a means of stirring fellow Asians to greater efforts. It was, according to the summary he later made of his Diet speeches, something else as well:

We must be prepared to make peace so soon as our aims have been attained. The emphasis on our war aims and the limits we assign to them will provide the groundwork for the restoration of peace.[29]

A Greater Asia Conference met in Tokyo in November, attended by leaders from Free India, Burma, the Philippines, though not by Pibun, who failed to come, or by the Indonesians, who were not asked, and to whom only Laurel referred.[30] The liaison conference had seen it as an opportunity for Asian countries to declare their 'firm resolve to continue the war and to establish the great East Asia co-prosperity sphere'. Shigemitsu had determined to clarify the meaning of the war 'as much for the benefit of the Japanese as for wartime propaganda purposes'.[31] Tojo's welcoming speech used the rhetoric he had used in 1942. In Greater East Asia, each nation was to have 'its proper place', 'enjoy the blessings of common prosperity' and 'practise mutual help'. Such was the

[28] q. Duus *et al.*, *Japanese Wartime Empire*, p. xxvi.

[29] Shigemitsu Mamoru, *Japan and her Destiny*, trans. O. White, London: Hutchinson, 1958, pp. 289-90.

[30] Goto Ken'ichi in Donald Denoon *et al.*, eds, *Multicultural Japan*, Cambridge Univ. Press, 1996, p. 166.

[31] Iriye, *Power and Culture*, p. 118.

'spiritual essence of the culture of Greater East Asia'.[32]

The declaration of principles adopted on 7 November was rather different. The countries of great East Asia were to 'cooperate together in order to secure the stability of East Asia and establish an order based on the principle of coexistence and coprosperity'. They were to 'respect their mutual autonomy and independence, extend aid and friendship to each other, and establish an intimate relationship throughout East Asia', and to 'respect their respective traditions, promote each people's creativity, and enhance the culture of the whole East Asia'. The countries were to cooperate closely 'according to the principle of mutuality, plan their economic development, and promote the prosperity of East Asia'. They would also 'maintain friendly relations with all nations, abolish systems of racial discrimination, undertake extensive cultural exchanges, voluntarily open up their resources, and thus contribute to the progress of the entire world'.[33]

The declaration had been drafted in the foreign ministry. Kase Shun'ichi had the Atlantic Charter by his side when he drafted it, and it was, as many Japanese newspapers observed, a kind of answer to it. Indeed, while retaining key concepts like coexistence and co-prosperity, it was more universalistic in tone than pan-Asianist. 'It is Japan's tragedy', the diarist Kiyosawa Kiyoshi noted, 'to have had to draft a declaration which is similar to the Atlantic Charter, granting all peoples their independence and freedom.'[34]

Yet while the statement was adopted at a conference designed to support the war, its invocation of universal principles could also be a means of working towards peace. If they were accepted in Tokyo, they would give the Japanese a sense of achievement and avoid humiliation. At the same time they might also be accepted in Washington and, less readily, in London, and also perhaps in Moscow. 'In retrospect it can be seen that Shigemitsu and others were preparing themselves and the nation for accepting defeat by calling it a victory for certain universalistic principles.'[35] The three-power declaration issued at the end of the Teheran conference, as Kiyosawa thought, indeed read like that of 7 November.[36]

[32] q. Lebra, *Sphere*, pp. 88ff.

[33] q. Iriye, *Power and Culture*, p. 119; also Lebra, *Sphere*, p. 93.

[34] q. Iriye, *Power and Culture*, p. 119.

[35] Ibid., p. 121.

[36] Ibid., p. 164.

On both sides, as Iriye recognises, there was a strong element of propaganda: if the Allies failed to clarify the future of their colonies in Asia, Chinese, Indians and Indonesians could detect the hypocrisy in the rhetoric of the Japanese. 'Consciously or unconsciously', he adds, however, the Japanese 'were beginning to persuade themselves that the physical outcome of the fighting was less important than the future of Asia and the Pacific – and, indeed, the future of their own country.' It was, Iriye suggests, 'but a step from such a view to the belief that the war should be terminated now that Japan had demonstrated the nobility of its war aims.'[37] Late in 1943 Shigemitsu was indeed in touch with his predecessor, Togo Shigenori, and with Kido Koin and others, on the means of securing peace. The propaganda was, as it were, partly intended for the military leadership.

Independence

Kido thought Germany might surrender during 1944. The affairs of the Pacific, he wrote in his diary, might in future be determined by the major powers, Japan, the Soviet Union, China, the United States and Britain. They would set up a commission, charged with administering the occupied areas, which, with the Pacific islands, would become non-fortified zones. Independent countries, with the exception of Manchuria, would become neutrals, like Switzerland. Economic policies would be based on freedom, reciprocity and equal opportunity. For a settlement to be conceivable, the Allies had to abandon their demand for surrender, and the Japanese military their sense of humiliation. Kido was persuading himself that a yet more drastic revision of the Greater East Asia policy might be the means. Could he persuade others? When could the idea be put forward – and how? The best approach might be to request the good offices of the Soviet Union.[38]

'Vague and often contradictory as their ideas were, men like Shigemitsu and Kido were clear that they were hoping to salvage the war from a complete disaster by devising a formula for a symbolic "victory".'[39] It would, of course, be far more than symbolic. For any such plan, while bringing an end to the exclusivity of the Sphere, would also bring an end to the treaty system in China and

[37] Ibid., p. 165.

[38] Butow, *Japan's Decision*, p. 24.

[39] Iriye, *Power and Culture*, p. 170.

to the colonial system in Southeast Asia. That, in a sense, was what they wanted their Tokyo colleagues to see as a victory, so as to make a settlement possible. They might also hope that the Americans might accept such a formula, particularly if the other superpower put it forward.

In Cairo, indeed, George Kerr, a naval officer with the military intelligence section of the joint chiefs, thought that the Japanese might offer negotiations before Japan itself was attacked, rationalising that it was but a 'stage in the evolution of Japan's manifest destiny'. They might reason, he said, that by losing the war they were laying the groundwork for a continuous struggle in which they could 'count upon the awakened race consciousness of the Orient. ... If the Japanese can make their forced withdrawal seem to be a further invasion of Asia by imperial white powers, they can leave behind them the foundation for another effort some time in the future.'[40]

The Japanese might also assume that the United States and Britain would want a reasonably strong Japan to counter-balance Russia and China. The Allies, however, adopted a policy of unconditional surrender, and Germany did not fall in 1944. Even so the ideas had some influence on the policies the Japanese adopted for Southeast Asia as their military position deteriorated.

The memorandum on the independence of Java produced by the ministry of foreign affairs early in 1944 suggests the accuracy of Kerr's analysis. In 1943, it said, the emphasis was on 'the obvious necessity of meeting the various military and economic requirements of the Empire in the successful prosecution of the Greater East Asia War – a course considered indispensable in completing the material foundation of the Empire which will become a stabilizing power in East Asia as a powerful defensive state after the war'. While an 'adverse turn in events' was conjectured, 'it is open to question whether the current rapid developments were then considered a realistic problem.' It was in those circumstances that the status of Java should be considered.

Granting independence would, the memorandum argued, 'naturally contribute to winning the hearts of the natives', and 'demonstrate the consistency of the Empire's moralistic Greater East Asian policies and contribute in no small way to the unity of Greater East Asia'. The 'tide' of the war was, however, 'running

[40] q. ibid., p. 166

disadvantageously', and it might reach the Indies. Granting independence in such circumstances might retrict 'the Empire's pressing military and economic measures and obstruct military operations in no small degree'. Taking such a step when the military situation was becoming unfavourable might also 'lead to misinterpretation of the Empire's true intentions as a mere stratagem, thus giving the impression that the Empire is weakening.' Altering one part of the policy would affect others. 'This matter requires the fullest consideration from the standpoint of domestic policies.'

The memorandum went on to consider the advantages and disadvantages from the point of view of the postwar period. 'Temporarily leaving aside the possibility of an overwhelming victory for either side, should a stalemate be reached, and should a delicate situation arise making it necessary to terminate the war because of internal and external factors, it will obviously be of the utmost importance to leave everything on an open basis as much as possible to assure diplomatic flexibility.' Since, moreover, the area was not British or American, 'there is the very great possibility that it may become a subject for negotiation', and 'a hasty "commitment" of our diplomacy concerning Indonesia at this time may be harmful'.

Nevertheless [the memorandum continued] the Greater East Asia war is fundamentally a struggle against the Anglo-American world order – in essence, a war between two world outlooks. Even if America and Great Britain, with their utilitarian outlook, do not comprehend the significance of the present war, regardless of whether or not the war is viewed as a clash in terms of the old concepts of national interests, and no matter whether circumstances are even now enabling complete restoration of the old order, the ideological foundation developed through the war of liberation in Greater East Asia by the Empire is, regardless of the course of the war, an eventuality which even the enemy must follow and accept; there should be a deep-seated conviction in this development.

The Empire would find it difficult to achieve its war aims if government and diplomacy remained 'chained to the concepts of the old order, and there were no 'deep conviction' in the principles that would 'govern the next stage of history'. Even if the independence of Indonesia were not finally 'upheld by diplomatic negotiations after the termination of the war' and were 'temporarily left in abeyance as a future problem', not even the enemy would be able to 'deny the fundamental truth that independence inevitably follows the formative development of a people; if so, and if independence is granted by us, then half the victory can be acknowledged as ours'.

Independence, moreover, could be modified to meet the Empire's requirements

should circumstances resolve in our favor; but should the war end completely disadvantageously, with the Empire also unable to honor its other international commitments, the granting of independence, if viewed on a long-term basis, would leave an invincible foundation which could be used in the future resurrection of Japan.

Clarifying Japan's position at this stage would 'make the Empire's war objectives more coherent and provide a constructive legacy for the future; moreover, it should not necessarily prove obstructive after the termination of the war'.[41]

Displacing Tojo in July 1944, the former premiers still nominated a military man as successor, Koiso, then governor-general of Korea, but added in Yonai, an opponent of the war whom Konoe had tried to get into the Tojo cabinet in 1943, as a kind of vice-premier. In September this government announced its plans for Indonesia. Officials had drawn up draft statements for Koiso to use when announcing them in the Diet. Those alluded to the goals of Greater East Asia, invoking 'stability', 'independence of national states', 'fraternal cooperation', 'co-existence and co-prosperity', and quoted the examples of Burma and the Philippines. The natives, said Koiso, had, since their participation was extended in 1943,

thoroughly comprehended the Empire's true intentions and consistently continued their tremendous efforts toward the successful climax of the Greater East Asia war; moreover, their cooperation with local military government has been truly something to behold. In response to these circumstances and in order to ensure the permanent welfare of the East Indies, the Empire here states that their independence will be sanctioned in the future.[42]

At the end of the year the future of Indo-China came into question. While the military saw it in strategic terms and now looked towards a takeover, Shigemitsu clearly saw this, too, in terms of an international diplomacy, and in particular in terms of Japan's relationship with the Soviet Union. His final decision was that a

[41] q. Benda *et al.*, *Japanese in Indonesia*, pp. 240-3.
[42] q. ibid., pp. 257-9.

coup, if followed by declarations of independence, would not be damaging.

His successor, Togo, convened a second Greater East Asia conference in Tokyo on 23 April 1945, attended only by ambassadors, rather than heads of state, because of the physical conditions. One aim was to demonstrate Asian solidarity at the time of the United Nations conference in San Francisco. It 'set forth' the independence of the Indo-China states, and looked towards that of the Indies. Its declaration stressed, not Japan's leadership, but cooperation, political equality, economic reciprocity, non-aggression.[43] Iriye's adjective is 'Wilsonian'. It was a response to the nations of Greater East Asia. It was also, perhaps, a signal to enemy nations, a means of conveying peace terms. 'More important', peace would not be a disgrace: 'it would simply mean an agreement with the enemy about an acceptable framework for Japanese foreign affairs'.[44]

War and empire

If interpreting the concept of the Sphere was part of the interplay over grand strategy in Tokyo, the concept was also interpreted within Southeast Asia itself. There officers of the military administrations, or their civilian advisers, might argue their policies among themselves, or with the higher authorities, in terms of its ideology, as well as of the practical needs and necessities as they saw them. They might also argue about, interpret or reinterpret the instructions they received from Tokyo, which were still often formulaic and reflective of imperfect compromise. If the instructions were unwelcome, or were deemed impractical, their implementation might be subject to delay. In every empire local authorities had found time and distance a useful weapon, either for *faits accomplis*, or for evading instructions.

Other Japanese were also involved as the attempts to 'develop' the new empire got under way. The initial principles focused on the military control of vital resources and infrastructure. Contractors were to be sought for the restoration of mines and, except for tin and iron, the development of new mines. For the time being, there were to be no new Japanese enterprises in agriculture, forestry or fishing.

[43] L.D. Meo, *Japan's Radio War on Australia 1941-45*, Melbourne Univ. Press, 1968, p. 189.

[44] Iriye, *Power and Culture*, p. 241.

As a basic principle, no manufacturing industries shall be promoted in the areas concerned with the exception of certain industries (such as ship-building, and maintenance industries required for the upkeep of equipment needed in the development of resources). This rule, however, shall not apply to industries whose products would significantly decrease transport tonnage, thereby alleviating the strain on transportation, and for which production facilities already exist.[45]

Different interpretations of 'co-prosperity' emerged as the occupation continued and the war situation deteriorated.

This empire was indeed peculiar in the extent to which it was shaped by wartime conditions. It remained largely under military administration, and military needs retained priority. It also shared, however, the problems of other empires. To what extent should the needs of the metropolis prevail? How were they to be reconciled to the ideals propounded by imperialist rhetoric? Like other empires, too, the Japanese empire was shaped not only by the rulers, but by the ruled. The elites were used by the Japanese, but also sought to use them, in the hope of sustaining their role, often, too, in the hope of using one imperialism to displace the others, even of displacing them all. The masses felt the burden of new economic policies, of the collapse of intra-regional shipping, of inept administration, and in some areas of destructive fighting and guerrilla warfare. Yet they, too, might witness, albeit in rather different terms, the prospect of a new and more just society emerging from crisis and chaos.

Though initially anxious to emphasise continuity and order, the Japanese upset it, deliberately reversing colonial policies, and, as their position deteriorated, opening up opportunities for those who would in fact be left with the task of creating a new order whatever glory the Japanese might try to claim.

---

[45] Benda *et al.*, *Japanese in Indonesia*, pp. 20-1.

5

CONTROL AND MOBILISATION

Politics and administration

'How pleasing it is to hear of the great victories at sea, land, and in
the air of the Great East Asia War', Tenkai Juro, who had been in
the Indies in 1906-29, wrote in his diary on 31 December 1941:

... Great victories in the war are fine, but what is more pleasing is that
Japan has embarked on the construction of a New Order, which is Japan's
real aim. But I am much concerned about the postwar administration. To
what extent are we capable? I am very anxious. We must set about the
reconstruction of the Netherlands East Indies, but how much understanding do the military men have?[1]

It was a valid question.

The policies of the Japanese towards Southeast Asia shifted
over time. Before the war they had been conscious that the days of
the colonial system were numbered and that their role in the
region would grow. That did not mean a political takeover, but it
did mean a larger economic role. It also gave the Japanese a great
interest in the nationalist movements, which in some measures
their own success – both in their struggle with the Russians, and,
more generally, in modernisation – tended to encourage. The
European war changed the timing of their expansion, the nature of
their interest in the region and the mode of attaining their objectives. Their occupation of the region, short though it was, again ran
through a number of ill-defined phases, and their policies were
influenced successively by the scale and rapidity of their initial
successes, by the problem of defining the limits of their empire, by
the need for a defensive approach and by the prospect of negotiation.

The occupation policies had been set out in general terms in
1941. They put priority on restoring order, securing strategic materials and providing for the self-sufficiency of the forces, and en-

[1] q. Goto, 'Returning to Asia', p. 184.

visaged using existing organs of government. Those principles were to be everywhere in evidence. Subsequently the Japanese allowed a great measure of political mobilisation, even participation, while at the same time they became less and less able to cope with mounting economic problems and ever more oppressive.

Their policies varied, however, not only over time, but according to the nature of the particular country they were dealing with, and the nature of their interest in it. The application of the general policies was inflected by the relative strategic and economic value of the various territories and by the interpretation of that value by the Japanese in Tokyo, government and corporate, and by those in the country concerned, officers of the army and navy, civilian officials, merchants, contractors and investors. They were also inflected by the nature of the regimes they found in those countries, and of the nationalism they met. Of these they were not always well informed. But the army and navy administrators – and relatively few civilians were involved at least initially – did not necessarily wish to accept the cooperation of the nationalists in any case. The Japanese connections with nationalism – during the prewar period, the invasion and the occupation – were discontinuous.

Despite the variations over time and by place, the Japanese period was marked by some commonality of experience. Among its components in the ex-colonial territories were the overthrow of the European rulers and the new political opportunities that offered, both actual and potential; new approaches to politics, attitudinal and organisational, offering alternatives to both traditional and European models; and the creation of military and paramilitary forces. These changes took place within a wartime context and amid economic dislocation and deprivation and even, in places, famine. It was out of all this that Southeast Asian leaders were left with the task of fashioning independent states after the defeat of the Japanese. Whatever they owed the Japanese, their gratitude was bound to be qualified as a result of their greed, violence and incompetence, and, later, by their sense that postwar Japan continued to take advantage of the information it had gained, and the economic strength it had regained.

In their task they were often influenced, however, by their experience in the occupation. They would establish 'New Orders' and recognise 'Asian values'. Yet much of what they admired was, if not completely alien, only somewhat coincidentally related to their own culture. The Japanese indeed had their own experience in mind, and, perhaps even more, that of Manchuria. The *tonarigumi* or neighbourhood associations, which became a feature of the occupation, had been made compulsory in the homeland in September 1940.[2] Konoe's Imperial Rule Assistance Association, itself based on Manchukuo's Kyowakai, Concordia Association, was in turn the model for Putera in the Indies and the Kalibapi in the Philippines.[3] The emphasis was on control, but also on leadership, consensus, solidarity and harmony.

Burma

Two countries, Burma and the Philippines, were fought over twice. They were also, as it happened, the countries in which the Japanese saw fit to offer the greatest measure of constitutional advance. The last to be conquered, Burma was the first of the Southeast Asian countries to secure independence within the Sphere. Constitutionally, it had been one of the two most advanced countries in the region in 1939. While its electorate was larger than that of the Philippines, it had, however, received no similar promise of independence within a given period of time.

With the completion of their conquest of Burma in 1885, the British had displaced the monarchy, rather than, as in many parts of India itself and in Malaya, retaining it and using it. Much of the resistance they faced in the 'pacification' of the late 1880s and 1890s took monarchical forms, and they reappeared in the rebellion led by Hsaya San in the depression years of 1930-1. There were other political currents. Educated Burmans, stimulated by the success of the Japanese in 1905, founded the Young Men's Buddhist Association in imitation of, but also in rivalry with, the YMCA. Popular Buddhism focused, however, on the monks, the *pongyi*, men like U Ottama, who visited Japan in 1910, and it was they who were able to create a mass political movement. The response to the political institutions that the British introduced in the 1920s, although in part the result of a nationalist demand that Burma should share the constitutional advance of neighbouring

---

[2] Iritani Toshio, *Group Psychology of the Japanese in Wartime*, London: Kegan Paul International, 1991, p. 129.

[3] Louise Young, *Japan's Total Empire*, Berkeley: Univ. of California Press, 1998. p. 49.

India, was deeply ambivalent. Some, like Ba Maw, a lawyer, were prepared to try to work the new institutions, others were not.

In 1935 the British introduced a new constitution, which came into effect in 1937. Under it a cabinet was responsible to a House of Representatives, elected on a suffrage that in effect qualified about one-third of the male population and one-tenth of the female, and there was also a Senate, half elected, half appointed. The governor, appointed by the British government, yet retained extensive powers in the field of defence, foreign relations and monetary policy, and he was also responsible for the Scheduled Areas – hill regions occupied by non-Burman peoples, Chins and Kachins, also Karens, though some of the latter also lived in parliamentary Burma and were represented in the House. No promise was made of Dominion status. That was the status Canada, Australia, New Zealand and South Africa had acquired in the British Commonwealth, in effect independence though with the British monarch as head of state. Ba Maw, leading the Sinyetha, was the first premier. His major rival, and a successor, was Saw.

The building of the Burma Road aroused controversy in Burma. Was it not an imperial interest rather than a Burmese one? Was Burma being exposed to unnecessary risk? The opening of the war in Europe 'caused an acceleration in the pace of Burmese politics'.[4] Ba Maw formed a Freedom Bloc, and that goaded Saw to push for greater self-government. The Pu ministry managed to secure a statement on 24 November that the goal for Burma was indeed Dominion status. Even in the crisis of mid-1940, however, the British declined to promise that it would be reached at the end of the war. As their situation in East Asia deteriorated late in 1941, Saw, as premier, tried again, and, despite the Atlantic Charter, again in vain. 'We were engaged in a struggle for our very lives,' Churchill told him, and this was not the time to raise such constitutional matters.[5] Saw was quite unsatisfied, and distributed a pamphlet, 'Burma's case for full self-government'. Before he got back to Burma, the Japanese had bombed Pearl Harbor. It was then that he allegedly offered them his services through their consul in Lisbon. That was to lead to his detention.

Other Burmans anxious to speed the regaining of independence

---

[4] Robert H. Taylor, 'Politics in Late Colonial Burma', *MAS*, 10, 2 (1976), p. 173.

[5] q. Tarling, *Pacific War*, p. 354.

had pursued a different course. Three seats in the 1936 elections had gone to a new faction, young nationalists from the All Burma Youth League who had come to call themselves 'Thakins', some of them Marxist, all of them radical, distrustful not only of the British but of the old lawyer politicians and their reliance on *pongyi*-led mass support. Their focus was the University of Rangoon, where, with Nu as president of the union and Aung San editor of the student newspaper, they had led a strike in February 1936, but they found mass support more difficult to acquire. The Thakins cooperated with the Freedom Bloc, starting 'rather nebulously' in October 1939.[6] They were an obvious target for Japanese intelligence.

Japan's initial concern was with the closing of the Burma Road, and its secret activities began soon after it was opened in December 1938. A self-appointed secret agent, Kokubu Shozo – a retired naval officer, who had been farming in the Shan States, then moved to Rangoon, where his wife was a dentist – established contact with the group of Thakins led by Ba Sein, who showed him a plan for a revolt. An attempt to send Ba Sein to Tokyo failed, as he was arrested at the border. Officers of the Japanese consulate made contact with Ba Maw in September 1939, and his friend, Thein Maung, visited Japan late in 1939. The group of Thakins led by Kodaw Hmaing, including Aung San, wanted foreign aid for an uprising, and, since it could not be secured from the Chinese communists, looked to the Japanese. Their contacts with Ba Maw led him to facilitate Aung San's escape from arrest in August 1940, when he fled to Amoy.

The Japanese army provided a third channel of intelligence activity. Colonel Suzuki Keiji was instructed in 1939 to collect intelligence on the nationalist movement, and to investigate conditions on the Road. Funding was provided by Okada Kosaburo, owner of the Ensuiko Sugar Manufacturing Company in Taiwan. The *Yomiuri* agreed to employ him as a correspondent, and he adopted the alias Minami Masuyo. He also became secretary of the Japan-Burma Society, founded when Thein Maung visited Japan. So prepared, he reached Rangoon in June 1940.[7] There he made contact with Kodaw Hmaing. He boldly promised help in

---

[6] Ba Maw, *Breakthrough in Burma*, New Haven, CT: Yale Univ. Press, 1968, p. 59.
[7] Joyce C. Lebra, *Japanese-trained Armies in Southeast Asia*, New York: Columbia Univ. Press, 1977, pp. 46-7.

gaining independence, arguing that it would precipitate a revolt, and thus secure the blocking of the Road. Hiroshi Tamura, the attaché in Bangkok, would receive youths smuggled out of Burma, and they would be given training, then sent back to lead an uprising. Aung San and Hla Myaing were located in Amoy and sent on to Tokyo in November.

In an interview with Australian journalists on 17 January 1941 Matsuoka insisted that Japan's expansion to the south would be peaceful and economic. He included Burma in the area of expansion. That, Craigie thought, was a novelty in a public statement by a responsible statesman. Matsuoka replied that Japan did not enjoy 'equality of economic opportunity in Burma', and that was what it sought. He also referred to 'spiritual and intellectual leadership'. Craigie 'observed that the use of the word "expansion" to describe this vague aspiration was bound to arouse hostility and resentment in countries which felt their interests to be threatened.'[8] It was in fact at this time that Imperial HQ decided to set up a secret organisation headed by Suzuki, the aim being to cut the Road as well as to aid the independence movement.[9]

Formally established on 1 February 1941, the Minami-Kikan, headed by Suzuki, included five other army members, three naval members, five civilians, including Kokubu, and three Burmans, Aung San, Hla Myaing and Ko Saung, a student then in Japan. A meeting with an IGHQ representative on 3 February adopted its guiding principles. These followed the scheme developed in Rangoon. Thirty young nationalists were to be taken to Tokyo, trained in Taiwan or Hainan, and sent back to lead a revolt, starting, it was envisaged, in June 1941. Guerrilla forces would attack and occupy southern Burma and Tenasserim, and an independent government would declare Burma's independence. 'The guerrilla forces would then advance towards the north, and cut off the Burma Road.' Minami-Kikan members would be installed at key points along the Burma-Thailand border to establish supply depots and training camps. The transport of arms, ammunition and subotage equipment from Bangkok would be 'carried out under

[8] q. Tarling, *Pacific War*, p. 276.
[9] Won Z. Yoon, 'Military Expediency: A Determining Factor in the Japanese Policy Regarding Burmese Independence', *JSEAS*, 9, 2 (September 1978), p. 246. Lebra, *Armies*, p. 56.

the pretext of engaging in commercial business'.[10] There indeed Suzuki set up Nampo Kigyo Chosa Kai, the Research Association for Southern Region Enterprise.

In February Aung San was smuggled back into Burma. In March 26 Thakins were smuggled out on ships belonging to the Daido Shipping Co., and two others made their way to Bangkok overland. With Hla Myaing and Ko Saung they constituted the 'Thirty Comrades'. They trained in a Hainan camp, the so-called San-ya Peasants Training Centre, under great pressure, for time was short. But the operation was deferred, and the trainees were disappointed when in July it became clear that Indo-China had priority.[11] The fact was that Japan's policy had shifted. It was now a question of invading Southeast Asia, rather than destroying the Burma Road by sponsoring an independence movement. Suzuki and his Thakins had to assume a different role.

In October, somewhat demoralised, the group was transferred to Taiwan. In accordance with the imperial conference decision on 6 September to prepare for a war, Aung San and other comrades were invited to map-manoeuvring exercises, and it was decided that on the opening of the war, a Japanese brigade would occupy Moulmein, while the core members of the Burma Independence Army (BIA) would organise throughout Burma and lead an independence movement. Suzuki had begun infiltrating the Thakins, despite a counter-order from Tokyo, when Terauchi ordered the suspension of all the Kikan's operations on 21 November. The members all moved to Saigon.

On 11 December the Minami-Kikan was sent to Bangkok, where it was to organise the BIA, for which the Thai-Japanese agreement would afford transit rights. On 23 December it was placed under the Fifteenth Army. According to the 'Plan for the Burma Operation', drawn up by Suzuki in December, its major objective was 'to facilitate the operation of the Japanese forces in Burma by disrupting the enemy's war effort, and inducing the Burmese to cooperate with Japan in prosecuting a successful war effort'.

This was a more modest role than had been envisaged earlier. But Suzuki still proposed that a provisional government should be created after the takeover of Tenasserim, that the foundation of

[10] q. Yoon, 'Japan's Occupation', p. 94.
[11] Izumiya Tatsuro, *The Minami Organ*, trans. Tun Aung Chain, Rangoon: Higher Education Dept, 1981, pp. 48, 59.

an independent regime should be established after the seizure of Rangoon, and that the conquest of Upper Burma should follow that. The Minami-Kikan would lead the military administration of the conquered areas, though 'the existing autonomous structures' were to be 'respected as long as they do not hinder military operations or the establishment of an independent regime'.[12]

The Southern Area Army did not, however, approve the plan. Col. Ishii Akiho, its senior staff officer, believed that a military administration would be able to act more freely, if need be taking measures of an unpopular nature impossible for an independent government. Instead of an independent government, autonomous committees were to be established in areas the Japanese occupied, to maintain order and assist the Japanese forces. At the proper time, a new regime would be set up, which 'shall have on the surface the appearance of independence, but in reality ... shall be induced to carry out Japanese policies'. The commander of the Fifteenth Army was to direct the new government, which should be recognised after the war.[13]

Suzuki argued that early independence would win greater support. He pointed in vain to the expectations aroused among the nationalists, and also to Tojo's speech of 20 January. His group was now fitted into an invading force, and its needs had priority.

The BIA was divided into four main groups. The bloodiest battle in which any were involved was at Shwedaung, south of Prome, at the end of March, where the Hirayama group suffered 770 casualties. The Tavoy group followed the 55th Division, setting up a civilian administration in that town, but being prevented from so doing in Moulmein. The Main Force, led by Suzuki, sought in vain to reach Rangoon before the Fifteenth Army, which arrived on 8 March. The fourth group was the Interior Sabotage group, led by Ne Win (Shu Maung). That had got to work in Rangoon in early February.

Gen. Iida Shojiro established a military administration in Rangoon on 15 March 1942, based on the machinery already established in Moulmein, and headed by Colonel Nasu Yoshio, deputy chief of staff of the Fifteenth Army, as *gunseikan* or superin-

---

[12] Yoon, 'Japan's Occupation', pp. 152, 153.

[13] q. Frank Trager, ed., Burma: *Japanese Military Administration: Selected Documents 1941-1945*, trans. Won Zoon Yoon, Philadelphia: Univ. of Pennsylvania Press, 1971, pp. 32-3.

tendent. The objectives were 'to establish public peace and order, to secure unrestricted supplies for military operations, to procure rapidly the resources essential for national defense and to make the necessary preparation for its disposition and management in the future.' Burma was to be 'entirely liberated from the British yoke' and to 'establish close military and economic ties with Imperial Japan. Although there are plans to establish an independent government in Burma in the future, its realization is expected *after* the Greater East Asian War.' For the time being, therefore, 'independence shall not be mentioned,' but 'the Burmese must be carefully guided so as not to lose hope for the future.'[14]

The guidelines for the military administration were consonant with those approved in Tokyo. As long as they did not hinder military administration, 'the existing organizations, native customs, various laws, ordinances, and systems shall be respected, followed and utilized as much as possible.' 'The pressure upon the people's livelihood, due to the procurement of resources for national defense and self-support of the Japanese army in the areas, shall be applied to the utmost of their endurance.' Qualified Burmese officials might be used, and consideration given, too, to using members of the Minami-Kikan. '[P]rejudice against one party or faction ... shall be avoided, but great effort must be made to harmonize and unite many personal elements.'

If it were in agreement with the policy of Japan, men even from hostile countries might, 'for the time being, and as occasion demands, be enlisted to cooperate with Japan in the enforcement of the military administration'. Chinese were to be led to collaborate, and Indians, too, but no new immigrants were to be permitted. Natives not hostile to Japan, including the Indians and Eurasians, were to be 'so guided as to foster gradually the concept of brotherhood with the Japanese'. Independence movements were to be treated 'with sincerity and kindness in accordance with the purport of the statement of the prime minister of Japan'. But 'promises of the time and terms of independence shall not be given.'[15]

On 23 March Iida addressed members of the military administration department. The Burmese, like the natives of the South Seas areas, had been 'turned into inactive peoples with almost no vigorous aspirations' by the 'tyranny and exploitation' of colonial

[14] q. ibid., p. 45.
[15] q. ibid., pp. 46, 47, 50-1.

rule. 'They shall be given, therefore, the best guidance possible in order that we together may establish the Greater East Asia Co-Prosperity Sphere.' The Japanese must show 'a sincere parental affection in guiding and educating them'. The customs of the natives differed from those of the Japanese, and their cultural standard was 'extremely low'. But too much intervention, Iida cautioned, would be as damaging as too little.[16] He thus tried to balance the task of the new imperialists with their fraternal rhetoric.

The *gunseikan*, Jiko Shiji, stressed that the relationship between the military administration and the nationalist movement was 'extremely delicate'. '[W]e must not give the impression that the Japanese Empire is replacing Great Britain in Burma. It is extremely important to give the Burmese the hope that was announced in the statement of the Prime Minister.'[17] In Burma's case, after all, there was a government-in-exile, including Governor Dorman-Smith, the premier and other Burmans.

In April 1942 the military administration authorised Suzuki to set up the Burma Baho Government, or central government, based in Rangoon, and selected Thakin Tun Oke as administrator. This was, however, soon displaced. Failing to reverse the army's policy towards the Thakins, Suzuki was transferred. On 21 May Iida set up a preparatory committee 'for the restoration of the Central Administrative Organ'. Military administration had to be maintained, Iida declared at Maymyo on 2 June. The goal, as Tojo said, was independence. 'It is my hope that the glorious Burmese nation will be established as rapidly as possible,' he declared, though the most urgent task was to win the war. 'Every effort must be made to facilitate the preparation for establishing an independent nation upon a solid foundation.'[18]

The BIA was to take no further part in administration. Indeed in July it was replaced by the Burma Defence Army (BDA), into which selected personnel were admitted. Its programme was directed by the Heibikyoku, or military preparation bureau, under Fukui Yoshisuke, using the Japanese army as a model, and a Burma Military Academy was established at Mingaladon in September.

[16] q. ibid., p. 59.
[17] q. ibid., pp. 61, 62.
[18] q. ibid., p. 112.

On 1 August the Burma Civil Executive Administration had been set up, with Ba Maw as chief administrator. Final authority lay with Iida, and each department had Japanese advisers attached to it. The elected legislature was replaced by a Legislative Deliberative Assembly (*Hosei Shingikai*), but the commander of the Japanese army had the right of approval and veto. The members of the executive included Thein Maung, finance; Thakin Than Tun, agriculture; Tun Oke, forestry; and Hla Pe, commerce. It was a combination of followers of Ba Maw and Thakins, but Aung San, Aung Than (Set Kya) and Let Ya, who were appointed to the BDA, were not included. 'I decided to keep out of our highest posts in the civil services those whose only claim to them was the backing they got from either the Japanese or the Burmese army.'[19] Thakin Mya, without portfolio, had the task of uniting all the parties. In fact he created an amalgamation of Sinyetha and the Thakin's Dobama Asiayon. It adopted as its slogan 'One Party, One Blood, One Voice and One Command', and Ba Maw was its head.[20] The other mass organisations were the East Asian Youth League, started in June 1942 with ex-BIA youths, and its 'tired old brother', the Wundan (National Service Organisation).[21]

The deterioration of Japan's position and the desire to ensure Burmese collaboration prompted the liaison conference on 14 January 1943 to favour the early independence of Burma. The Japanese also hoped that it would have an impact on India, encouraging the anti-British movement that would disrupt the British war effort. Tojo told the Diet on 28 January that 'Japan has the intention to recognize Burma as an independent state within the year.'[22] Now Ishii could not but give in. But the new government was still, of course, to be a government that cooperated with Japan within the Sphere.

The liaison conference of 10 March adopted 'Guiding Principles for the Independence of Burma'. The objective was

to create, under the guidance of the Japanese government, a new Burma as one of the members of the Greater East Asia Co-Prosperity Sphere. Japan must promptly set to the task of guiding the new Burma to prepare herself

[19] Ba Maw, *Breakthrough in Burma*, p. 270.

[20] Trager, *Burma*, p. 132.

[21] D. Guyot, 'The Political Impact of the Japanese Occupation of Burma', Ph.D. thesis, Yale University, 1966, pp. 287, 298.

[22] q. Yoon, 'Japan's Occupation', p. 226.

both physically and spiritually so that she will be able to cooperate closely with Japan for the successful prosecution of the Greater East Asia War.

The military commander was to guide the Burmese in forming a preparatory committee, headed by Ba Maw, to plan the new Burma. It was to be proclaimed on 1 August, and to declare war on the United States and Britain immediately after.

The form of government would have to be dictatorial. In the event that a parliament were created, 'attention must be paid to prevent the Parliament from interfering with the head of State and his execution of the affairs of state'. The national domain was to include all Burma, except Karenni and the Shan States. 'The Burmese Government shall maintain an army and navy for the essential defense of Burma. But Japan shall in reality direct their decisions as to the size and manner of organizing Burmese forces.'[23]

Ba Maw, Thakin Mya, Thein Maung and Aung San arrived in Tokyo on 18 March for ten days' discussion. 'It is the firm belief of Nippon', Tojo told them, '... that the new Burma will be established upon the basis of ethical principles as a member of the Greater East Asian Sphere of Co-Prosperity in order to contribute to the creation of a new world order.'[24] The delegation was also granted an imperial audience on 23 March.[25]

Back in Burma a Burmese Independence Preparatory Committee was set up, including members of the executive administration, Aung San, the chief justice, six politicians including Kodaw Hmaing, Nu and the Karen leader San C. Po. The deputy chief of staff of the Burma Area Army, Isomura Takesuke, attended the meetings, but the talk was in Burmese. The main debate was about the form of government. Ba Maw argued for a dictatorship. To avoid his becoming a dictator, the Baho faction argued that Burma should again become a monarchy. They also opposed Ba Maw's election as head of state. In both cases the Japanese decided against them.

The constitution provided that Burma would be ruled by a head of state with 'full sovereign status and powers'.[26] He appointed the ministers. He also appointed the privy council, an advisory

[23] q. Trager, *Burma*, pp. 145-8.

[24] q. H. Benda and John A. Larkin, *The World of Southeast Asia*, New York: Harper and Row, 1967, p. 228.

[25] Ba Maw, *Breakthrough in Burma*, pp. 312-14.

[26] q. Trager, *Burma*, p. 158.

body. Legislation was the responsibility of the head of state, who would normally consult the cabinet, which itself would normally secure the views of the privy council. The head of state would appoint the chief justice, and he would be supreme commander-in-chief of the armed forces. Within a year, if conditions permitted, but in any case within a year of the end of the war, a constituent body would draw up the definitive constitution. Its members would be appointed by the head of state.

On 1 August Ba Maw read the declaration of independence. In this he denounced the British and expressed Burma's gratitude to the Japanese. Established on the principle of one blood, one voice, one leader, Burma, 'now not only Burmese but East Asiatic as well', entered the 'free and equal partnership' of the Sphere. It pledged itself to the creation of a new Asiatic order, to be established as part of a new world order. It regarded the Great Asiatic War as its war.[27] The same day Ba Maw, as head of state, *Nainggandaw Adipadi*, declared war on the United States and Britain.[28] As in Japan – though Ba Maw was 'against these Japanese ideas'[29] – the defence minister was a serving officer, Aung San. Ne Win became commander-in-chief of what was now called the Burma National Army.

Ba Maw and the newly appointed Japanese ambassador, Sawada Renzo, also signed a treaty of alliance. The Japanese military wanted to refer to co-prosperity and co-existence; Shigemitsu wanted reciprocity. By compromise it referred to co-existence only.[30] Other states, besides Japan, recognised the new Burma: Germany and its satellites, Croatia, Slovakia, Bulgaria, and others in the Sphere, Thailand, Manchukuo and the Nanking regime. Thein Maung became ambassador to Japan, Tun Oke to China, Ba Lwin to Thailand and Ba Sein to Manchukuo.

Yet, while it was the first Southeast Asian state to gain independence, its puppet nature was apparent. Nu records his humiliating position as minister of foreign affairs: 'We received the Japanese Ambassador on his first arrival and he came to call on us once afterwards. That was all we saw of him at the Foreign Office. If I wanted to discuss anything I had to go to his office.' If he wanted

---

[27] Ibid., pp. 164-8; Benda and Larkin, *World of Southeast Asia*, pp. 230-4.

[28] q. Trager, *Burma*, pp. 168-70.

[29] Ba Maw, *Breakthrough in Burma*, p. 321.

[30] Iriye, *Power and Culture*, p. 114.

to discuss anything, he went direct to the Adipadi.[31]

While the Heibikyoku was disbanded, its duties supposedly assumed by the defence ministry, in fact the Japanese military advisory group retained decision-making power. 'This independence we now have is only a name. It is only the Japanese version of home rule', Aung San told Ba Maw a little after the Normandy landings.[32] In September the Japanese government agreed that Burma could take over the Shan States. But, as Tojo had told Ba Maw, two of them, Kengtung and Mongpan, would be made over to Thailand.

In August 1944 Ba Maw set up a new mass organisation, Maha Bama, a 'last-ditch attempt to overcome political divisions'. The Wundan became its core, which tied it to 'a failing government in a losing way'.[33]

Political disappointment and economic crisis prompted army officers to discuss resistance, and Aung San approached the communist Than Tun, also a minister in Ba Maw's government. The rising by younger officers planned for June 1944 was postponed, but their scheme helped to bring about the creation in September of the Anti-Fascist People's Freedom League (AFPFL), with Aung San as leader and Than Tun as secretary. The other factor was, of course, the commencement of the British reconquest, precipitated by the failure of the Japanese pre-emptive strike at Imphal. The Burmese had no wish again to replace one foreign domination by another. Out of the war they sought to win independence. The programme was set out in a manifesto 'Drive Away the Fascist Japanese Marauders'. The rising was now set for October. It was then postponed because the arms secretly sought from the British failed to arrive.[34]

The British were indeed divided. They had already armed hill-tribe guerrillas, especially Kachins. Alienated by Chinese looting, the Shans on the whole accepted the Japanese, who recognised their *sawbwas*.[35] The Karens, however, had not been won over. The BIA's entry into Burma had indeed been marked by comm-

[31] Nu, *Burma under the Japanese*, London: Macmillan, 1954, p. 87.

[32] Ba Maw, *Breakthrough in Burma*, p. 335.

[33] Guyot, 'Political Impact', pp. 286, 304.

[34] Yoon, 'Japan's Occupation', p. 272.

[35] D.G. Hinners, 'British Policy and the Development of Self-Government in Burma, 1933-1948', Ph.D. thesis, University of Chicago, 1951, p. 173.

unal clashes, giving the Japanese one further reason for its disband-
ment. A more conciliatory approach had followed, and a Karen
battalion was included in the BDA.[36] But Karens, however, formed
2 per cent of the BNA as against 40 per cent of the prewar army.[37]
The British began to recruit Karens in February, and there were
18,000 levies by May.[38] What should their attitude be to the majority Burmans, who had worked with the Japanese? Their cooperation might have a military value. It was the political question that
was more contentious.

Some, like the representatives of Force 136, argued that working with the resistance movement would make future relations
between Britain and Burma much easier, and meanwhile stimulate
similar movements among other peoples. Others – 'Churchillians
and Dorman-Smithians', as Ba Than calls them[39] – thought it would
queer the pitch for Britain in Burma, and spoil the prospects for the
plans for reconstruction developed by the Anglo-Burman government in exile and the Burma Office in London. The latter were
overruled. Slim needed any help he could get in his race to beat the
monsoon to Rangoon. And Mountbatten emphasised the political
advantages in accepting AFPFL/BNA cooperation, as well as the
political disadvantages of refusing it. 'He said that the eyes of the
world would be upon us to see how we handled the first part of the
British Empire to be recovered from the enemy.'

'[W]e should be committing a grave and far-reaching error, now that the
politically active Burmese see that their hopes of the future do not lie along
the road of collaboration with the Japanese if we neglected to make them
feel that co-operation with us is a different matter, and that we are sincere
in our expressed desire to help the Burmese to help themselves.'[40]

The decision speeded the reconquest. It was also of great political advantage to Aung San and the AFPFL. With the uncertainty
over using the Indian army, the restored civil government had no
means of enforcing a political settlement along the lines of the White
Paper of 17 May in which the British had set out their policy, a

[36] Lebra, *Armies*, p. 64.

[37] Guyot, 'Political Impact', p. 327.

[38] R. Taylor, *Marxism and Resistance in Burma*, Athens: Univ. of Ohio Press, 1984,
p. 41.

[39] Ba Than, *The Roots of the Revolution*, Rangoon, 1962, p. 53.

[40] q. N. Tarling, *The Fourth Anglo-Burmese War*, Gaya: Centre for South East
Asian Studies, 1987, p. 124.

policy in any case unsuitable, as Thein Pe Myint put it, for the Burmese who had been 'awakened' by the war.[41] Governor Dorman-Smith was replaced in 1946, and his successor accepted an AFPFL-dominated executive council, which negotiated independence for Burma during a mission to London early in 1947. However, Aung San, assassinated in July, did not live to see it proclaimed on 4 January 1948.

Before the invasion, Burma enjoyed substantial self-government, though not control of foreign affairs or the frontier regions, and had been put on the road to Dominion status. By dislodging the British, the Japanese brought independence into view, though the reality did not live up to the rhetoric. The reconquest gave the Burmese an opportunity to make it a reality, first by offering their military assistance to the British, and then by setting the terms upon which alone they would collaborate politically. The Burmese had scooped independence out of the war, and it was independence outside a Commonwealth that at the time did not accept republican governments.

The Philippines

The Filipinos had failed to scoop independence out of a previous international war. Indeed the American intervention had proved disastrous for the independent republic they had proclaimed, though it averted another possible outcome, the intervention of the Japanese. Under US domestic criticism, however, the venture was rationalised, not as a merely imperialist act, but as a means of preparing the islands for independence. It became a matter of timing, and also of phasing. The Jones Law of 1916 provided for independence when a stable government had been set up, but offered no criteria and no deadline.

The Depression, and the alleged competition of Philippines sugar in a protected market, led to the setting of a deadline, first in the Hare-Hawes-Cutting Act, and then in the definitive Tydings-McDuffie Act. Under that the Philippines was to be given independence after a ten-year interim phase of government by a Commonwealth government with limited powers. Tariff privileges were to end with independence and be reduced meanwhile. American bases might be retained after independence, but meanwhile the US president, with whom the conduct of foreign policy

[41] In Taylor, *Marxism and Resistance*, p. 288.

would continue to rest, was to negotiate with other powers for a treaty neutralising the islands.

Some of these provisions the first Commonwealth president, Manuel L. Quezon, was to find frustrating. In foreign policy, for example, the United States had not made its position clear, but it also denied the Philippines the right to make its own. Throughout their search for independence, Filipino leaders, with Japan's expansion in mind, had also sought security. In the discussions on the Jones Bill, they had looked for neutralisation or a guarantee.[42] In 1933, the year of Manchukuo, Quezon told the newspaper magnate Roy J. Howard that the Americans should either fortify the Philippines and build a navy, or 'leave bag and baggage', or make an 'alliance, or ... partnership in commerce and defense'.[43] A halfway house was insecure. The United States was not clearly binding itself to defend the Philippines if it became a bone of international contention. Nor, however, were the Filipinos themselves in a sufficiently independent position to take alternative steps, such as association with another Western power, neutralisation or accommodation with Japan. The Commonwealth did not solve the dilemma.

The ambivalence that marked the international diplomacy of the Philippines Commonwealth also marked its defence arrangements. 'Self-defense is the supreme right of mankind,' Quezon told the inaugural session of the National Assembly in November 1935.[44] Douglas MacArthur was his choice as military adviser – 'His appointment as Field Marshal of a State and an army, neither of which has, as yet, an independent existence, was more or less ridiculous,' General Pershing commented.[45] A force of 10,000 men was envisaged, about the equivalent of the military strength of the US army in the Philippines at the time, plus a reserve.

Some feared that creating it would only encourage Quezon to act like a dictator. It would not be effective against an invader. Camilo Osias, editor of *Philippine Forum* and member of the

[42] See Wong Kwok Chu, 'The Jones Bills 1912-16', *JSEAS*, 13, 2 (September 1982), pp. 252-69.

[43] q. G.K. Goodman, 'Consistency is the Hobgobin', *JSEAS*, 14, 1 (March 1983), p. 90.

[44] q. A. Gopinath, *Manuel L. Quezon: The Tutelary Democrat*, Quezon City: New Day, 1987, p. 146.

[45] q. Carol M. Petillo, 'Douglas MacArthur: the Philippine Years', Ph.D. thesis, Rutgers Univ., 1979, p. 343.

assembly, argued that, since defence would be inadequate, it would be better to have none, but to have independence earlier, plus neutralisation.[46] Quezon himself wavered. When the Japanese moved on southern Indo-China, however, the Philippine army became part of the US Army Forces in the Far East (USAFFE), and Roosevelt named MacArthur the commander.

Quezon was in fact no dictator, but a masterly manipulator. Spanish rule had in part depended upon, and also helped to build up, a collaborating elite, and the opening of the islands to foreign trade in the nineteenth century had increased its wealth. The collapse of Spanish rule had led elements in it to support the republic, but their fear that political revolution would lead to social revolution helped to prompt their collaboration with the new colonial power. Furthermore its economic policy offered a privileged market, while its policy of political advancement, though expressed in democratic terms, provided the elite with an unprecedented opportunity to apply its wealth and skills at a provincial and national level. They were deployed in a pattern of patron-client relationships that now extended throughout society. 'As Commonwealth President, Quezon was the first Filipino politician with the power to integrate all levels of politics into a single system.' At the provincial level, he sought to 'maintain two equally balanced factions at a peak of conflict that would allow his intervention and manipulation'.[47] 'Ins' were not entirely secure, nor were 'Outs' permanently excluded.

The system was not, however, all-embracing. Not all the earlier revolutionaries had submitted to the Americans, even after a phase in exile on Guam in 1901-2. The great ideologue, Apolinario Mabini, finally took the required oath of allegiance in 1903. Artemio Ricarte never did. Exiled to Hong Kong, he returned to Manila in 1904, hoping to use the Russo-Japanese war as the occasion for a revolt. Imprisoned for conspiracy, he was then banished. He went to Hong Kong, and then to Japan, keeping a coffee-shop in Yokohama, Karihan. He was to be brought back to Cagayan in a Japanese military plane on 19 December 1941.[48]

---

[46] Ibid., p. 293.
[47] A. McCoy in Ruby M. Paredes, ed., *Philippine Colonial Democracy*, New Haven: Yale Univ. Press, 1988, p. 120.
[48] U. Mahajani, *Philippine Nationalism*, St Lucia: Univ. of Queenlsand Press, 1971, pp. 185, 423.

One of his visitors late in 1933 had been a Filipino radical of a later generation, Benigno Ramos. A petty officeholder who had fallen out with the ruling groups, he had founded the *Sakdal* (Accuse) movement, seeking to rally popular support during the Depression. Peasant unrest in Luzon had traditionally taken millennial forms, a rational choice given the lack of any other means of seeking a secure livelihood if the patron-client relationship failed to provide it. The Sakdal movement tested a third alternative, political participation in the democratic structures that were being set up, but it was clear that it had little chance of securing power by those means. In May 1935 it vainly attempted an armed uprising, designed to pre-empt the establishment of a Commonwealth government that, for Ramos, would represent the triumph of the ruling elite and, for the peasants, would mean semi-independence without social change.

At the time Ramos was again in Japan, seen by pan-Asian extremists as a Filipino *shishi*,[49] but unable to secure the effective help he may have led his followers to expect. During his visit to Japan in 1938, Quezon met Ramos and encouraged him to return. The president was looking, as Goodman puts it, for 'an almost mystical "national unity" under his own aegis', and expected Ramos to lead his followers into the fold.[50] In fact he set up a new party, Ganap. By December 1939 he was in jail, where he remained till the Japanese released him on 8 April 1942. Neither he nor Ricarte, however, headed the post-invasion government. The Japanese, as in Burma, preferred more generally accepted figures.

Those could not include the president himself. MacArthur's plan for retreat involved taking Quezon to Corregidor, as he told him on 12 December. He protested: 'I was no American Governor-General, but the Filipino President of the Commonwealth...'[51] MacArthur said it was his duty to prevent Quezon's falling into the hands of the Japanese. 'He was also of the opinion that as long as I was free, the occupation of Manila, or even of the Philippines, by the Japanese Army would not have the same significance under international law as if the Government had been captured or surrendered.'[52]

[49] G.K. Goodman, *Four Aspects of Philippine-Japanese Relations, 1930-1940*, New Haven: Yale Univ. Press, 1967, p. 142.

[50] Ibid., p. 174.

[51] Manuel L. Quezon, *The Good Fight*, New York: Appleton-Century, 1946, p. 194.

[52] Ibid., p. 198.

At a final cabinet meeting on 24 December, he declared he was taking Vice-President Osmena with him, and also Jose Abad Santos, the chief justice. The secretary of justice, Jose Laurel, and the president's executive secretary, Jorge Vargas, were to stay. The latter – Quezon's right-hand man, 'jack of all trades and master of them all'[53] – was made mayor of Manila. MacArthur had declared it a free city, and there was an idea that members of a national government might be arrested by an invader, but not those of a local government.[54] 'You two will ... deal with the Japanese,' Quezon said. What, asked Laurel, should they do and what not do? The president, it seems, was repeating MacArthur's words when he replied that they should do what they thought necessary, but take no oath to the Japanese.[55]

Japanese forces entered Manila, and General Homma's chief of staff, Maeda Masami, sounded out Filipino leaders on the possibilities of cooperation and the formation of an administration. A group of Filipinos met at the home of the Speaker, Jose Yulo. Quintin Paredes and Benigno Aquino suggested working with the Japanese if they offered a republic; Jorge Bocobo and Rafael Alunan rejected a puppet regime, *gobierno muneco*. It was agreed to ask the Japanese to recognise the Commonwealth, with a provisional government.[56] Maeda would have nothing to do with the Commonwealth. A republic might be discussed in future. For now the alternatives were '*un gobierno de hierro respalando por la forza militar*', a government of iron backed by military force, or a *gobierno muneco*.[57]

The group tried in vain to get in touch with Quezon. If they continued to resist the creation of a puppet government, the Japanese might give the opportunity to persons inclined to be 'merce-

---

[53] Gopinath, *Quezon*, p. 67.

[54] A.J. Malay, *Occupied Philippines: The Role of Jorge B. Vargas*, Manila: Filipiniana Book Guild, 1967, p. 14.

[55] Theodore Friend, *Between Two Empires*, New Haven: Yale Univ. Press, 1965, p. 212. David J. Steinberg, *Philippine Collaboration in World War II*, Ann Arbor: Univ. of Michigan Press, 1967, p. 32.

[56] The minutes of the meetings held at Yulo's house from 6 January onwards, kept in Spanish, are printed in M. Garcia, ed., *Documents on the Japanese Occupation of the Philippines*, Manila: Philippine Historical Association, 1965.

[57] Malay, *Occupied Philippines*, pp. 6, 10, 16-17. Friend, *Between Two Empires*, pp. 212-14.

nary, irresponsible and unscrupulous'.[58] They moved towards the puppet solution, minimising alteration in the status quo. And that was convenient to the Japanese, too, for, as was to be the case in Burma, their focus was on meeting their own objectives, and not on revolution. Any idea of using Ricarte was abandoned. Nor, indeed, did the Japanese meet Aquino's wish to be president, though he was strongly pro-Japanese.

It was mainly through Vargas, Quezon's right-hand man, that Maeda had contacted the leading men in Manila, and he convened the meetings that led to the creation of the provisional council of state that, with Japanese approval, the Filipino politicians constituted on 23 January. It did not include Ricarte or Ramos, but it did feature many leading Commonwealth figures, Aquino, Paredes, Laurel, Yulo, Osias and Recto among them, 'no acknowledged Quislings', as the US High Commissioner Paul McNutt was later to put it.[59] The Japanese appointed Vargas chairman of an executive commission and the council became an advisory body.

The politicians' collective letter to Homma had declared that 'in compliance with your advice, and having in mind the great ideals, the freedom, the happiness of our country, we are ready to obey to the best of our ability and within the means at our disposal, the orders issued by the Imperial Japanese Forces for the maintenance of peace and order under the Japanese Military Administration', and were constituting a provisional council of state.[60] The draft had – at Aquino's suggestion – referred to the 'independence' of our country, and also, rather contradictorily, to a 'Commonwealth Council of State'. The words were removed by Maeda.[61]

The draft had been ready by the Japanese deadline of 14 January, but had then been delayed for Tojo's statement of 20 January. Vargas welcomed its conditional promise of the 'honour of independence'. 'It personally ... confirms my confidence and trust in the true and benevolent intentions of the Japanese Imperial Forces and I am glad I have been given the opportunity to co-operate and work with them.'[62] His speeches, however, emphasised the need to limit and repair the ravages of war.

[58] q. Friend, *Between Two Empires*, p. 433.
[59] q. Mahajani, *Nationalism*, p. 426.
[60] Malay, *Occupied Philippines*, pp. 31-2, 19.
[61] Ibid., pp. 60-4.
[62] q. Mahajani, *Nationalism*, p. 426.

Over in Corregidor Quezon, just starting a two-year second term, defended his old associates. The executive commission, he declared, had 'no political significance not only because it is charged merely with purely administrative functions but also because the acquiescence by its members to serve on the Commission was evidently for the purpose of safeguarding the welfare of the civilian population.' He asked MacArthur and, through him, Roosevelt 'whether any government has the right to demand loyalty from its citizens beyond its willingness or ability to render actual protection'. The war, he added, 'is not of our making.'[63]

Roosevelt replied that 'every ship at our disposal is bringing to the southwest Pacific the forces that will ultimately smash the invader and free your country.'[64] Nothing came meanwhile. US broadcasts constantly referred to Britain. '*Que demonio!*' Quezon exploded. 'How typically American to writhe in anguish at the fate of a distant cousin while a daughter is being raped in the back room!'[65]

On 6 February Emilio Aguinaldo, aged ex-leader of the first republic, urged MacArthur to surrender, as he had been ready to negotiate with the United States 'many years before'. He also referred to Tojo's promise. Quezon told MacArthur that he thought of placing himself in the hands of the Japanese 'and defying them, in the belief that such action on my part would solidify the opposition to any Japanese influence'.[66]

Early in January the US government had urged MacArthur to evacuate Quezon to Washington, so that he might function as head of a government-in-exile and 'the symbol of the redemption of the Philippines'.[67] Washington was aware, as Steinberg puts it, of the 'political strain' placed on Quezon by his 'emasculation'. The risk that he might serve a Japanese-sponsored government was 'one which Washington did not dare to gamble on'.[68] MacArthur had then opposed the idea as it would reduce morale. Now he counselled Quezon against his proposal: the Japanese would not make him a martyr, but would speak for him.[69]

[63] Quezon, *The Good Fight*, pp. 258-9.
[64] q. Mahajani, *Nationalism*, pp. 431-2.
[65] q. T.A. Agoncillo, *The Fateful Years*, Quezon City: Garcia, 1965, I, 275.
[66] Quezon, *The Good Fight*, pp. 266-7.
[67] Ibid., p. 236.
[68] Steinberg, *Philippine Collaboration*, p. 39.
[69] Quezon, *The Good Fight*, pp. 237, 268.

Quezon decided to ask Roosevelt's permission to issue a manifesto requesting immediate independence, demobilisation, evacuation and neutralisation, echoing in a sense long-standing aims of the Philippine nationalists. 'The fight between the United States and Japan is not our fight. I want to go back ... and try to protect our own people, Romulo, not America.'[70] He feared that if Japan established an independent government, 'the masses of the people who knew very little of the history of Japan in Manchuria would fall into the trap and our leaders would be powerless in the face of such a situation.' If, on the other hand, Japan rejected the proposal, Tojo's perfidy would be apparent.[71] His cabinet reluctantly agreed.

'After nine weeks of fighting not even a small amount of aid has reached us from the United States,' Quezon wrote to Roosevelt. '.... While perfectly safe itself, the United States has practically doomed the Philippines to almost total destruction to secure a breathing space. You have assured us eventual liberation, but what is needed is present help and preservation.' There was 'no necessity to sacrifice the Filipinos to gain final victory. Officials of your government have asserted again and again that the war against Hitler would be the determining factor in the final outcome of the world conflict.' He offered a 'solution which will spare my native land further destruction as the arena of two mighty nations'. The United States should grant immediate and absolute independence to the Philippines; both it and Japan should withdraw their armed forces and guarantee Philippine neutrality; and the Philippine army should be disbanded.[72] The proposal was, of course, rejected. Roosevelt pledged the United States to drive the invaders from the Philippines and to fulfil its promise of independence. The promises Tojo made were valueless. 'I have only to refer you to the present condition of Korea, Manchukuo, North China, Indo-China, and ... other countries ... to point out the hollow duplicity of such an announcement.'[73] Leaving for Australia, MacArthur asked Quezon to join him there. The president finally left the Philippines on 18 March.

[70] q. Friend, *Between Two Empires*, p. 219.

[71] Quezon, *The Good Fight*, p. 270.

[72] q. Mahajani, *Nationalism*, pp. 432–3.

[73] q. Friend, *Between Two Empires*, p. 222.

The Japanese, it is clear, would have welcomed him in Manila. Only in the course of 1942 did they shift their policy towards him. They had argued that the United States government prevented his return to Manila, then that he was a prisoner in Washington. One reason for installing Vargas was that he was more politically 'neutral' than Aquino or Laurel, and 'would also be, at least temporarily, a stand-in for Manuel Quezon. For there is no question that from the outset the Japanese believed that Quezon himself would be the ideal figure to lead a regime under their aegis.'[74] Naming his alter ego as temporary head of the government, rather than installing a major politico, was designed to encourage his return. Only when it was clear that a return was impossible did the Japanese turn to Laurel, an intimate prewar contact. That was also associated with the move to set up an independent republic. To fulfil that promise, the Japanese were induced, not only, as in the case of Burma, by the deterioration of their overall position and, perhaps, by the existence of government-in-exile, but also, in contrast to Burma, by the presence of guerrilla activity.

The military administration celebrated the first anniversary of the opening of the war with the creation of the Kalibapi, Kapisanan sa Paglilingkod sa Bagong Pilipinas (Association for Service to the New Philippines), a service organisation on the lines of Concordia. On 4 December Vargas duly announced the dissolution of all existing political parties, and on the 6th, in his executive order establishing the Kalibapi, he declared that it was

dedicated to the unification of the Filipinos in order to extend positive cooperation with the Japanese Military Administration and to secure a greater coordination and intensification of all efforts aimed at the rapid reconstruction and progress of the country, the rehabilitation of its people and the establishment of a sound and stable foundation for the New Philippines. One of its immediate objectives is to assist the Filipino in fully comprehending the significance of, and in strengthening his adherence to, the Co-Prosperity Sphere of Greater East Asia by subordinating himself and his interests to those of the Philippines.[75]

Aquino was made director-general. Rizal Day, the anniversary of the execution of the national hero, was chosen for the first mass meeting. He too, Vargas declared, worked for 'the unification of

---

[74] G.K. Goodman, 'The Japanese Occupation of the Philippines: Commonwealth Sustained', *Philippine Studies*, 36 (1988), p. 103.

[75] q. Malay, *Occupied Philippines*, p. 186.

his people, the economic rehabilitation of his country, and the social regeneration of his race'.[76] His Philippines for the Filipinos could now come true, and play an important role in the Sphere.

Vargas welcomed Tojo's speech of January, offering independence 'in the shortest possible time', and pledged to eradicate all connections with the past regime, to bring about economic self-sufficiency, and to work for the reorientation of the people.[77] In a speech at the Luneta he declared that Japan's promise had 'no equal in the entire recorded history of men and nations'. He addressed himself 'more particularly and with all the energy at my command to our brother Filipinos now in hiding in the hills and in the mountains', and said that their 'misdirected activities' were 'hindering and delaying the independence that we so devoutly desire'.[78] To hasten the granting of independence, the commissioners went out on pacification drives.

On 7 May Tojo visited Manila. Consul Kihara gave Vargas instructions for assembling crowds along his route. He himself spoke of 'eternal gratitude', and at a dinner that night spoke of the Sphere as the 'sublime objective' of the war. The following day, the anniversary of the fall of Corregidor, he renewed his appeal to the 'misguided' USAFFE 'remnants'.[79] Back in Tokyo Tojo declared that Philippine independence could be granted within a year. This, Vargas declared, was 'the happiest day in the history of the Filipino people'.[80] A gratitude rally was organised, led by Mayor Guinto.

A delegation invited to Tokyo heard Tojo's speech to the Diet. On 19 June a special convention of the Kalibapi recommended those who should form the preparatory commission for independence. '[R]atified' by acclamation at a Luneta rally,[81] the names were approved by General Kuroda on 20 June. They included Aguinaldo, Aquino, Osias, Paredes, Recto, Vargas, Yulo and Roxas, a released prisoner-of-war. Laurel, though recently wounded by guerrillas, was to be president of the committee, and it was openly expected that he would be president of the republic. So indeed it

[76] q. ibid., p. 195.

[77] q. ibid., p. 113.

[78] q. ibid., pp. 201, 203.

[79] q. ibid., pp. 206, 207-8.

[80] q. ibid., p. 211.

[81] Rafaelita H. Soriano, 'Japanese Occupation of the Philippines', Ph.D. thesis, Univ. of Michigan, 1948, p. 232.

turned out. Apparently Roxas declined, and recommended Aquino, then Laurel. The indignant Vargas, his glutinous speeches unrewarded, was made ambassador to Japan.

During the preparation of the constitution Tojo again visited Manila, and Col. Utsunomiya Naonori, the assistant chief of staff, participated. Like the two constitutions of the 1890s, Laurel indicated on 20 August, it was to be that of a republic: 'no other forms, such as a monarchy, could be established here'. A republic, he explained, was 'a commonwealth where the powers of the state are vested in the representatives who are directly or indirectly elected by the people.'[82] The constitution in fact removed popular suffrage. The president was elected by the national assembly. That was composed of the provincial governors and city mayors and delegates elected every three years, one from each province and city. Within a year after the end of the war, however, a constitutional convention, elected by popular suffrage, was to create a new constitution.

Taken to meet Tojo, though 'ill', Roxas joined a constitutional subcommittee. His aim was to secure a revision of the draft so that it did not commit the Philippines to the Sphere. A bill of rights was also inserted. The constitution was promptly ratified by a convention of the Kalibapi on 6 September, and that was followed by a mass rally. The Kalibapi also quickly produced the elected delegates. In his acceptance speech Laurel declared that he believed 'that every living Filipino, including those from the mountains who still entertain some doubts', would 'come down to help us'.[83]

On 29 September Laurel, Vargas and Aquino, elected Speaker, went to Tokyo. On his return Laurel announced that independence would be proclaimed on 14 October. That day Aguinaldo and Ricarte hoisted the new flag. The Filipino people proclaimed

that they are, as of right they ought to be, a free and independent nation; that they no longer owe allegiance to any foreign nation; that hence forth they shall exercise all the powers and enjoy all the privileges to which they are entitled as a free and independent state; and that for the defense of their territorial integrity and the preservation of their independent existence, they pledge their fortunes, their lives, and their sacred honor.[84]

[82] q. A.V.H. Hartendorp, *The Japanese Occupation of the Philippines*, Manila: Bookmark, 1967, p. 620.
[83] q. ibid., p. 636.
[84] Ibid., p. 650.

The memory of the first republic was invoked. The inaugural address also included another appeal to guerrillas.[85]

A pact of alliance was concluded, but no declaration of war ensued, as in Burma. To that the activities of the guerrillas contributed, the Huks, the left-wing Chinese Hua Zhi[86] and above all those affiliated to USAFFE. 'Even Japanese military observers conceded that pro-American sentiment persisted in the Islands. ... Involvement in the war might further divide opinion and might even bring about a civil war if there were a military draft.'[87] In Tokyo Tojo had sought a declaration. Laurel replied 'that Quezon, Osmena and Roxas were the popular leaders in the Philippines, and not himself; that he could not carry the people, or even maintain a following, with such an unpopular measure; and that it would not be "decent" for the Filipinos to declare war against a benefactor.'[88]

The Japanese took the matter up again in September 1944, when the invasion of the Philippines was imminent. Laurel planned to stick by his refusal and prepared to escape from Manila. Roxas advised compromise, since resistance was impossible: if the Japanese military administration demanded a declaration of war, the republic should consent, but refuse to raise an army. The council of state agreed: 'We will thus save our people from great and heavy sacrifices and the destruction of property,' said Rafael Corpus. 'Would the sufferings of the people be greater if the Americans or [if] the Japanese considered us hostile?' Ramon Fernandez wondered. 'I prefer that the Japanese do not consider us hostile,' Laurel replied.[89] He did, however, adopt a suggestion Recto made, and declared that 'a state of war exists'. He also avoided conscription.[90]

Over Laurel's protest the frustrated Japanese formed 'a volunteer militia of opportunists and Japanophiles',[91] the kind of people the elite had feared when they offered their collaboration in 1942. The Makapili (Kalipunang Makabayan ng mga Pilipino,

[85] q. Benda and Larkin, *World of Southeast Asia*, p. 237.
[86] Li Yuk-wai, 'The Chinese Resistance Movement in the Philippines during the Japanese Occupation', *JSEAS*, 23, 2 (September 1992), p. 313.
[87] Iriye, *Power and Culture*, p. 115.
[88] Friend, *Between Two Empires*, p. 242.
[89] Ibid., pp. 243-4.
[90] Agoncillo, *The Fateful Years*, pp. 829, 831.
[91] Friend, *Between Two Empires*, p. 244.

Patriotic League of Filipinos), which sought to evoke the Katipunan of 1896, was nominally led by Ricarte. Ramos was the executive-general, however, and it drew on the Sakdalistas of the 1930s. Yamashita hoped the Makapili would do the work the republic failed to do. Late in 1944 Muto, his chief of staff, was attracted by Ramos's proposal that all the government except Laurel should be displaced by a coup. 'Others on the staff and in the diplomatic corps objected. They were already thinking of good postwar relations rather than immediate cooperation.'[92] In any case, the extent of Ramos's following was doubtful.

In Washington in January 1943 Quezon had considered asking Roosevelt for immediate independence, so that the US would not appear to be 'plagiarising the magnificent gesture of the Japanese'.[93] In a radio address the following month, he declared that the prospect was a 'Manchukuo': you could not rely on Japan's promise after 'the tragic end of Korea's independence'.[94] Later, however, Commissioner Elizalde approached Senator Tydings, who prepared a bill. Stimson was opposed: it would seem like recognising the puppet republic now clearly under preparation.[95]

In the event Tydings introduced resolutions pledging the US to drive the Japanese out as soon as possible, restore the democratic process and then establish independence, and permitting the US president to declare that independence earlier than 4 July 1946. On 9 December the Senate passed a resolution approving advancement of the independence date.[96]

MacArthur had promised to return, and, more or less winning his argument over strategy, he waded ashore at Leyte in October 1944, together with Osmena, who had taken over as Common-wealth president on Quezon's death in August. The liberated areas were made over to the Commonwealth government, and after the destructive struggle for Manila, he restored full constitutional government to the Filipinos on 27 February. It was clear, however, that MacArthur thought Roxas would be more effective than Osmena. In the islands throughout the war, he had maintained an

[92] Ibid.

[93] Ibid., p. 237.

[94] q. M.P. Onorato, ed., *Origins of the Philippine Republic*, Ithaca, NY: Cornell Univ. Press, 1974, p. 207.

[95] Friend, *Between Two Empires*, p. 237.

[96] Mahajani, *Nationalism*, pp. 442, 443.

association with the puppet government, but also a connection with the Luzon guerrillas, and his popularity was considerable.[97] Indeed, he was to beat Osmena in the presidential elections, and to preside at the inauguration of the republic in 1946. A far more unequivocal collaborator, Laurel himself was soon to return to Philippine politics. He was elected vice-president in 1949.

Collaboration was indeed an issue in the postwar Philippines, and contributed to the creation of a two-party system. It was not, however, the main issue, and the two parties were, in Onofre Corpuz's phrase,[98] only really one and a half. Postwar, as prewar, Philippines politics were a matter of extended faction-struggles. The new prize was the 'rehabilitation' money promised by the United States.

What interregnum? Goodman justifiably asks. The elite that had dominated the Commonwealth continued to dominate the wartime republic and the postwar republic. It had offered collaboration because of its 'intense desire to sustain the political, social and economic status quo as far as possible'.[99] Quezon himself had been a reluctant exile, initially handing over to his right-hand man, not to a major politico. Steinberg suggests that, according to Laurel's reasoning, you could not know when the war would end, or even if it would not end with a deal that left Japan dominant.[100] It was, after all, possible that the United States would not return, as Aquino thought,[101] given the prewar history of its relationship with the Philippines.

Most went along with the new conqueror, as their predecessors had finally done. They took comfort from the instructions Quezon had given and from the sense that they were protecting the Philippines from a harsher government. '[T]hese Filipino "Quislings" were like those Filipino officials appointed by the American Army during the Philippine Insurrection,' as Quezon put it; 'they would do everything in their power to aid their fellow countrymen.'[102] At the same time the elite supported the USAFFE guerrillas. Its

[97] Charles A. Willoughby, comp., *The Guerrilla Resistance Movement in the Philippines, 1941-1945,* New York: Vantage, 1972, pp. 205, 285.

[98] Onofre Corpuz, *The Philippines,* Englewood Cliffs: Prentice-Hall, 1965, p. 95.

[99] Goodman, 'Japanese Occupation', pp. 104, 102.

[100] Steinberg, *Philippine Collaboration,* p. 79.

[101] cf. Friend, *Between Two Empires,* p. 226.

[102] q. Onorato, *Origins,* p. 166.

members were, as Goodman puts it, 'politically astute enough to maintain a foothold among key nonrevolutionary guerrilla organizations and thus protect themselves in the event of a Japanese defeat'.[103] The United States might well return, as MacArthur insisted they would. Each faction in Iloilo, as Al McCoy has shown, maintained representation in both government and guerrilla organisations.[104] Wholly identifying with either side might risk complete destruction.

In the event MacArthur pointed to a compromise figure, sufficiently pro-Allied to be acceptable to the Americans, and sufficiently involved with the Laurel government not to alarm the collaborationists. Osmena was expected to be harder on collaborationists. He sought to reach an intra-elite deal and avoid a party struggle, but in vain, and lost the 1946 election.

The elite saw itself as not merely preserving its own position, but affording protection to other Filipinos. Was that so? It certainly achieved the former. By cooperating, it had been told, it would avoid the threat of a harsher military government. That might well have been one still led by Filipinos, but more radical right-wing ones, like Ramos, the long-time opponent of the establishment. The elite was also apprehensive about the pro-communist guerrillas, the Hukbalahap, who took control in parts of rural Luzon during the occupation, and there were clashes between them and the USAFFE guerrillas, some of whom were condemned by Luis Taruc, the Huk leader, as bandits, '*tulisaffe*'.[105]

The elite managed to avoid both these extremes and emerged from the occupation scarcely divided. At the same time, the Vargas commission had 'tempered the rigors of marital law',[106] and the Laurel government avoided conscription. Indeed its strong position was one of the reasons that the Japanese had at times to compromise. It could not avoid the destruction of Manila. There was, however, some truth in its claim that it protected the Filipinos, even though that had to be at the price of avoiding social revolution.

The elite found the political structures the conquerors set up not without their relevance or appeal, designed, as they were, to

[103] Goodman, 'Japanese Occupation', p. 103.

[104] 'Politics by other means' in A. McCoy, ed., *Southeast Asia under the Japanese Occupation*, New Haven: Yale Univ. Press, 1980, pp. 191-245.

[105] Agoncillo, *The Fateful Years*, p. 762.

[106] q. Willoughby, *Guerrilla Resistance*, p. 283.

mobilise but control the population. The district and neighbourhood associations, DANAS, created by Vargas's executive order of
August 1942 on the *tonarigumi* model, yet had some features, like
mutual help, that were familiar to Filipinos. People were aware,
however, that 'the real purpose ... was to apprehend guerrillas', and
shunned their 'constabulary functions'.[107] It was not unsatisfactory
for the elite postwar to revert to its older methods, more democratic in form, little changed in practice.

Netherlands India

In Burma and the Philippines the Japanese encountered political
regimes already well advanced beyond the colonial pattern. Anxious to complete their conquest and simplify their administrative
tasks, the army authorities tended to deal with the most influential
local leaders who were prepared to collaborate with them. To
facilitate that Tojo held out promises of independence. As the war
situation deteriorated, those promises were carried out, though
the new regimes were not only required to collaborate but had to
act under Japanese advice. The impact of the Japanese measures
was limited by their opportunism and by their half-heartedness.

It was also limited by the presence of indigenous armed forces.
In Burma what became the BNA had been created by the
Japanese, as part of a policy that was concerned with the Burma
Road, and predated the determination to invade Southeast Asia.
When the time came to invade Burma itself, it was more of an
embarrassment than a help. When the fortunes of war changed,
moreover, it changed sides. In the Philippines, despite criticism,
Quezon had created an army. In July 1941 it was absorbed in
USAFFE, fighting on Bataan, pursuing guerrilla activity. Its pre-
sence helped to persuade the Japanese to offer independence. It
also give the elite a reason for not organising a pro-Japanese army.

In Netherlands India none of these political and military conditions prevailed. The Dutch had offered only limited political
participation and did not contemplate independence. An army
existed, but one that under-represented the Javanese majority. In
the Indies, as in Burma and the Philippines, the mere overthrow
of Western rule would, of course, have a dramatic effect. But there
the Japanese had the opportunity of making a much greater

---

[107] Agoncillo, *The Fateful Years*, pp. 356, 357.

impact than in Burma or the Philippines. Offering independence and creating a national army would be revolutionary changes.

There was, however, another contrast. The resources of Netherlands India were far more important to the Japanese than those of Burma and the Philippines. Indeed the oil of Borneo and Sumatra was a prime reason for the determination to invade Southeast Asia. The Philippines was invaded not for its own sake, but because it was on the way. Burma was not initially seen as being part of the Sphere at all. In the Indies there was a still greater premium on the official policy of acquiring resources and maintaining the status quo. It was not till the crisis of 1944 that the Japanese got round to speaking of independence, and, partly because of the reluctance of the subordinate commands, it had not been proclaimed when they surrendered on 15 August.

Such an approach was dictated not only by the opportunism that prevailed in Japanese policy but produced differential effects. It was also encouraged by their racial attitudes. While the Japanese claimed equality with other nations, they did not regard other nations as their equal. Their attitude was at best paternal. Within the Sphere Japan had thus a tutelary role. In Southeast Asia, they repeated the attitudes of Europeans who saw the inhabitants as 'lazy natives'. The rhetoric they used in Burma and the Philippines reflects those attitudes, and it was echoed by their collaborators. In Netherlands India, they believed, the natives were even more backward.

Unlike Burma and the Philippines, Netherlands India was not in the hands of a major power. Well before the nineteenth century the Dutch had lost their primacy in the trade between Europe and Asia, and in that century the prosperity of their kingdom came to be in some measure dependent on mobilising the resources of their empire in the Indies. They retained it partly through their relationship with the British, consolidated by offering them a commercial open door, extended to other powers, including Japan, in the later nineteenth and early twentieth centuries. They also retained it by pursuing within the Indies a policy of 'peace and order', based on an alliance with the *priyayi* elite in Java and traditional chiefs elsewhere. At the end of the nineteenth century, however, that had been challenged, in part by the rise of Islam within the Indies, and in part by a growing concern for a more 'ethical' colonial policy.

The answer the scholar-official Christiaan Snouck Hurgronje offered was 'associationist' in tone: 'the creation of a Netherlands nation consisting of two parts widely separated geographically but spiritually closely united'.[108] The development of the political relationship was, however, unclear. The spread of education, economic changes, knowledge of Japan's achievements, particularly its victory over Russia, the penetration of Marxism from the Netherlands, all conduced to a partial politicisation of Indonesian life, to which the Dutch reacted ambivalently: was it a welcome step towards a lasting association or an alarming lurch towards a breakaway? A moderate nationalism might be acceptable, but not an independence movement. Governor-General van Limburg Stirum sought at the end of 1918 to enhance the powers of the recently created Volksraad, but his superiors disapproved. Amid the unrest of the 1920s Governor-General De Graeff was unable to create 'trust', as he put it.[109]

Under his successor, B.C. De Jonge, nationalists like Sukarno, Hatta and Sjahrir were sent into internal exile. Within the Volksraad, there were, however, 'collaborating nationalists', like those of Parindra, founded in 1935, and nationalist-oriented officials, like Soetardjo. The Dutch, however, did not collaborate with them. Parindra, they exaggeratedly suspected, was under Japanese influence. The Philippines example, which influenced Soetardjo, was unwelcome. Quezon, who visited Surabaya in 1934, they thought subversive. The Soetardjo petition of 1936, which called for a ten-year transition to autonomy within the Dutch constitutional framework, they finally rejected in 1938. No concessions were offered even in 1940, when the majority of the nationalist groups declared their loyalty to the cause of the Western democracies. The Dutch, said M.H. Thamrin, were 'practising exactly the kind of totalitarianism they criticize'.[110] In June 1941 Governor-General Tjarda said there would be a conference on constitutional changes when the Netherlands was liberated.[111] Soetardjo got an evasive answer when he asked about

[108] q. C.L.M. Penders, ed., *Indonesia Selected Documents on Colonialism and Nationalism*, St Lucia: Univ. of Queensland Press, 1977, p. 159.

[109] q. John Ingleson, *Road to Exile*, Singapore: Heinemann, 1979, p. 40.

[110] q. Goto, '*Returning to Asia*', p. 373.

[111] S. Abeyasekere, *One Hand Clapping*, Monash Univ., 1976, p. 62.

the Atlantic Charter.[112] Only in January 1942, when the Japanese were conquering Malaya, did Governor-General Tjarda agree to a conference in the Indies.

To the end of their regime, therefore, the Dutch continued to rely on a European bureaucracy, the BB; on a traditional elite, largely bureaucratised, the *pangreh praja*; and on a military force, the KNIL, 'originally designed for internal security purposes only',[113] but with the growing threat from the Japanese beginning to retrain for external defence as well. A number of Indonesians were now admitted to the new military cadet school in Bandung. But like other colonial armies, the KNIL avoided a national focus, and it also depended on an ethnic mix. A disproportionate number were recruited in Maluku. The regime distrusted the nationalist groups, though its policies had helped to create them, and offered little even to those who wished to collaborate. It also distrusted the *santri*, those who focused their life on Islam and its teachings. Their influence, indeed, it had been one of Snouck's purposes to diminish, but though themselves divided between traditionalists and modernists, they had been able to offer alternative forms of leadership in times of great change.

In many respects, it could be argued, the Japanese in Java maximised their effect by putting Dutch policies into reverse: involving the non-collaborating nationalists, promoting mobilisation, creating a majority-dominated army, renewing the political role of Islam. That, indeed, could also be regarded, not simply as a pragmatic way of gaining support, but also as a step towards creating a new state within the co-prosperity sphere.

The reality was, however, rather different. The Japanese regime in Java, like its predecessor, relied very largely on the *pangreh praja*. Its priorities did not lie with the creation of a new nation, but with the maintenance of order and the extraction of goods and labour. Sumatra, indeed, was placed under a separate military administration, that of the Twenty Fifth Army, and initially linked with Malaya, and Maluku was put under the navy. Japanese policies in Java cannot be described, as the late Harry Benda suggested, in terms of divide-and-rule. Insofar as they were not pragmatic and

---

[112] B. Dahm, *History of Indonesia in the Twentieth Century*, London: Pall Mall Press, 1971, p. 81.

[113] U. Sundhaussen, *The Road to Power*, Kuala Lumpur: Oxford Univ. Press, 1982, p.1.

opportunist, they were concerned to bring people together. Nor was the separation of the administration of Java from other parts on the Indies a matter of divide-and-rule. It was more a matter of military convenience and inter-service agreement.

Except in Aceh – where Fujiwara organised a clandestine operation by Acehnese who offered support after the fall of Penang – there was little anti-Dutch activity during the invasion. On their arrival, however, the Japanese were widely welcomed, and Dutch attempts at guerrilla warfare, lacking popular support, were futile. Nationalists were put on peace preservation committees. Some formed national committees, with a view to taking over the administration, and a Muslim leader, Abikoesno Tjokrosoejoso, even hoped to form a puppet government. Once it was clear that their victory would be prompt, the Japanese had no need, however, to flirt with the nationalists. On 20 March the military authorities in Java decreed the dissolution of all political parties, a ban on the use of the national flag and an end to all political activity.

The official guidelines indeed called for the use of existing administrative machinery. At first, it seems, General Imamura Hitoshi was disposed to use Dutch officials, provided that they 'submit to us as imperial subjects'.[114] They had indeed been instructed by the governor-general to cooperate and continue their work in the interests of the people.[115] Their eagerness to surrender, according to Kahin, proved to educated Indonesians the truth of 'strong rumors that they wished to make a deal with the Japanese such as the Vichy French had done in Indo-China'.[116] A pledge of loyalty stood in their way, however. In any case, there were complaints of General Imamura Hitoshi's mildness,[117] and more hardline officers on his staff were determined to displace them. In April about 2,000 of the 15,000 Dutch officials were interned, and more followed. The Japanese were short of administrative staff, though large contingents of *gunzoku* (civilians employed

[114] q. Sato Shigeru, *War, Nationalsim and Peasants*, Sydney: Allen & Unwin, 1994, p. 23.

[115] Ibid., p. 23.

[116] G. McT. Kahin, *Nationalism and Revolution in Indonesia*, Ithaca, NY: Cornell Univ. Press, 1952, p. 102.

[117] Nakamura Mitsuo, 'General Imamura and the Early Period of Japanese Occupation', *Indonesia*, 10 (1970), pp. 13-14.

by the military) began to arrive in May. The gap was filled, for the most part not by nationalists, but by the *pangreh praja*.

Despite their disappointment nationalists were ready to cooperate with the Japanese. They were victorious, and a working relationship might yet advance the nationalist cause. No government-in-exile offered an alternative focus, nor had the Dutch made any explicit promises. Sjahrir and Tjipto Mangoenkoesomo kept apart, but the underground movement that Sjahrir eventually organised was far from being a guerrilla organisation. The only underground movement with any continuity was that led by the communist Amir Sjarifuddin, to whom the Dutch had given 25,000 guilders in 1942 in the hope of keeping some kind of resistance going.[118] It was all it could do to survive. 'Actually, what was done against the Japanese was precisely resisting destruction, or trying to do so.'[119]

For their part the Japanese looked for nationalist help initially on the propaganda front. The Tiga-A movement, which began in late March, was thus fostered by the *senden-han* (propaganda section). The Parindra members who predominated in the central leadership were looking, however, towards the creation of a political movement, to function when a definite military government had been set up. Its expansion aroused distrust among the Japanese, therefore, and the administrative staff, and the *kempeitai*, criticised Shimizu Hitoshi and the propaganda staff. The failure to involve the former non-collaborators was another weakness, exposing the movement to their criticism also. Allowed back into Java only early in July, Sukarno outwardly endorsed the movement, but behind the scenes apparently sought its dissolution. A new organisation was set up after the military government was organised.

That took place in August 1942, when the Sixteenth Army set up a military government, *gunseikanbu*, in Java, headed by a *gunseikan*. The provincial structure of latter-day Dutch Java was abolished. The residencies were revived, called *shu*, headed by *shuchokan*, usually Japanese. Beneath them were the regency, *ken*, headed by *kencho*, a Javanese; the district, *gun*, headed by *guncho*; the sub-district, *son*, headed by *soncho*; and the village, headed by *kucho*.

---

[118] Kahin, *Nationalism and Revolution*, pp. 111-12.

[119] Jacques Leclerc in A. Lucas, ed., *Local Opposition and Underground Resistance to the Japanese in Java 1942-1945*, Monash Uni., 1986, p. 344.

A single pyramid thus replaced the double Dutch–native pyramid of the Dutch period.

'If we were to avoid the errors committed in occupied China, we had to secure popular support', declared Gen. Okazaki Seizaburo.[120] To secure the cooperation of the formerly non-cooperating nationalists, the army created two institutions. One was a research council on traditional customs and institutions, announced in September 1942. Its object was declared to be 'the research and study of traditional customs and institutions with a view to providing reference material for the administration of Java'. Among its ten Indonesian members were Hatta, Soetardjo, Sukarno, K.H. Mansur (Muhammadiyah), Wondoamiseno (MIAI), Djajadiningrat, Supomo and Ki Hadjar Dewantoro. There were also 14 Japanese members. The meetings began in November, and continued till October 1943. It was more a sounding board than a research group.[121]

The second step was the creation of a mass movement under the leadership of the nationalists in the council. An announcement concerning 'a people's new organisation or movement' was made on 20 November, but it was not possible to inaugurate it, as planned, on the first anniversary of Pearl Harbor.[122] That day, indeed, Sukarno alluded to it in a speech, but in fact the Japanese and the nationalists were not agreed about its nature. The *gunsei* representatives preferred a Japanese-sponsored mass organisation, like Concordia. To that Sukarno and Hatta assented.

They wanted, however, to use the word 'Indonesia' in the name of the organisation, to use the nationalist flag and anthem, to admit only indigenous Indonesians and to allow officials to take part. The military rejected the use of word, flag and anthem: the Sixteenth Army administered only Java; and in any case Tokyo had yet to decide its future. No concessions were offered. Indeed the *kempeitai* were critical: they arrested Sjarifuddin, a member of the preparatory committee. Other Japanese were concerned at the impact on the *pangreh praja*.

The organisation was finally announced on 9 March, the anniversary of the surrender of Java. It was called the Movement for the Total Mobilisation of the People or Movement for the

[120] q. Kanahele, 'Japanese Occupation', p. 66.
[121] Sato, War, pp. 50-1. Kanahele, 'Japanese Occupation', p. 67.
[122] Sato, War, p. 51.

Concentration of the People's Total Energy (Minshu Soryoku Kesshu Undo) or Pusat Tenaga Rakyat (Putera – Centre of People's Power). Its objective, its constitution declared, was 'to create a powerful new Java as a link in the Greater East Asia Co-Prosperity Sphere by extending aid and cooperation to Greater Japan for the purposes of securing the ultimate victory in the Greater East Asia war and harmonizing the operations of military government'.[123]

Sukarno and his ex-non-collaborationist colleagues were rid of their Parindra rivals, but they were no more independent of the Japanese. As the war position deteriorated, Burma and the Philippines had been given new assurances of independence. Nothing of that kind was on offer in Java: 'I heard that the nationalists had organised this movement with a great expectation to make it the kernel of the independence campaign', General Yamamoto Moichiro later declared. 'However, ... the Sixteenth Army had no plan on this question at that time. ... I demanded them to lead this movement more spiritually so as to combine all powers of the inhabitants in directions of the Japanese administration.'[124] Instead of offering independence the Japanese sought to win support by pro-Japanese and pro-Sphere propaganda. Out of this the nationalists could hope to gain only indirectly, and at some risk, short and long term. They could gain prominence, but only by endorsing Japanese propaganda campaigns, such as the Destroy the Americans and English Movement, inaugurated on 29 April, the emperor's birthday. They could seek to twist those campaigns to nationalist purpose, but they could not go far without increasing the doubts the military regime already felt. Promoting the nationalist cause was in a sense a by-product.

The Japanese administration indeed continued to rely above all on the *pangreh praja*. Perhaps, indeed, that reliance increased as the number of civilians in the military administration increased, and the traditional elite showed its reliability. An *ad hoc* relationship was consolidated, rather than displaced, as the war went on. The Putera constitution provided for local leaders at the residency, regency and district levels, but itself declared there should be none below that. Hatakeda, of the interior department, indicated that the Putera leaders should not interfere with the work of the *pangreh praja*, nor contend with it. By January 1944 there were only nine

[123] q. Benda *et al.*, *Japanese Military Administration*, p. 136.
[124] q. Sato, *War*, p. 53.

Putera branches at the residency level, and none below that level. The organisation developed in Batavia and in some of the cities, but not in the countryside. There above all the traditional elite could, as Kurasawa puts it, use 'indirect and subtle compulsion in leading people towards government's intentions'.[125] The Japanese thus followed Dutch practice.

The youth organisation the Japanese created in 1943 again had important long-term effects, but they were by-products, as far as the original intention was concerned. The emperor's birthday was also chosen to inaugurate the *seinendan*, the youth corps, Barisan Pemoeda, copying a Japanese organisation. 'In order to convince the youth of Java to work actively with the government and to support the construction of the Co-Prosperity Sphere in Greater Asia, it is necessary that they be given guidance and instruction.'[126] The Japanese ensured that it had no ties with Putera, though some nationalists were involved at the centre, and some took part in local activities. Here again the *pangreh praja* were expected to exercise a controlling influence: the aim was 'mobilization without politicization'.[127] Though nationalists were concerned at the schism between their movement and the *pangreh praja*,[128] it was not a question of divide-and-rule. The 'basic desire' of the Japanese, Kurasawa stresses, 'was to reconcile the hostility among the different social groups and, by so doing, to consolidate public opinion under one common direction'.[129] The same was true in respect of Islam.

The principles governing military administration in occupied areas of March 1942 envisaged 'grasping people's minds', as part of *senbu kosaku*, the propaganda and taming operations.[130] In Java Islam, identified as opposed to the West, was bound to be a focus, and an independent department, Shumubu, was set up to handle religious affairs. Initially, it seems, the Japanese wished to form 'an all-embracing Muslim body', which would be part of the Tiga-A movement. That would displace the MIAI, the Islamic

[125] Kurasawa Aiko, 'Mobilization and Control: A Study of Social Change in Rural Java', Ph.D. thesis, Cornell Univ., 1988, p. 546.
[126] q. ibid., p. 478.
[127] Ibid., p. 483.
[128] Sato, *War*, p. 55.
[129] Kurasawa, 'Mobilization and Control', p. 578.
[130] Ibid., p. 382.

federation that had in 1937 brought together the two major move-ments, the Nahdlatul Ulama and the Muhammadiyah, joined in 1939 by the PSII.

The Japanese wanted an organisation that brought mass support through the more direct participation of the *kiyayi* and *ulama*. They turned first, however, to Abikoesno Tjokrosoejoso, the PSII chairman, who sought to make up for his disappointment over a puppet government. The Muslim conference of August 1942, though testifying to the importance of Islam in the eyes of the new rulers, did not, however, set up the new organisation they sought. MIAI was re-established.

The Japanese administration demonstrated its interest in the *ulama*, however, by itself holding a reception for thirty-two of them from all over Java on the first anniversary of Pearl Harbor: Okasaki Seizaburo welcomed the guests as 'the leaders of religion, who are honored by the people'.[131] Their role was to 'imbibe ... the quin-tessence of Nippon's culture', and 'then educate the youth, and make them willing to work for a Greater East Asia'.[132] The first training course began in July 1943. Affiliates of the NU (Nahdlatul Ulama) predominated among the trainees, a sign that the Japanese favoured the orthodox. They also expected the *pangreh praja* to guide the *ulama*.[133] Most of the lecturers were *priyayi*. The first non-Japanese head of the religious affairs office, appointed in October 1943, was a member of the *priyayi* elite, Dr Hoesein Djajadiningrat.[134]

By this time, indeed, the Japanese were moving towards the greater 'political participation', *seiji sanyo*, that Tojo promised in his speech on 18 June and on his visit to Jakarta on 7 July. That was, however, very much directed towards mobilisation, for, as the situation deteriorated, the Imperial government had determined to make Java the main fortress and supply base in the south. The initial step was the creation of advisory councils at the centre and in the *shu*. Announced by General Harada on 1 August, it was implemented in September and October. The membership at the *shu* level favoured local officials and Muslim leaders, rather

---

[131] q. H.J. Benda, *The Crescent and the Rising Sun*, The Hague and Bandung: Van Hoeve, 1958, p. 119.

[132] q. ibid., p. 133.

[133] Kurasawa, 'Mobilization and Control', pp. 441, 460.

[134] Benda, *Crescent and Rising Sun*, p. 136.

than nationalists. At the centre, the nationalists were more strongly represented.

The council was, however, strictly advisory. The question on the agenda for the first session was 'What are the practical ways to strengthen the local people's cooperation in the Greater East Asia War?', and the subsequent sessions had a similar focus.[135] The chairman, Sukarno, led a delegation to Tokyo in November. But no Indonesian representatives were invited to the Greater East Asia Conference, 'which had conveniently adjourned upon Soekarno's arrival'. Nor was he allowed to meet any of the delegates.[136] The changes in Japanese policy had done little to enhance the role of the nationalists, or to promote their cause.

In the context of the deteriorating war situation – which, among other things, denuded Java of Japanese troops – and the renewed stress on the importance of a Java as base for the future struggle, the Japanese did, however, take a step that was to have long-term consequences: the creation of an army. Late in 1942, it seems, an operations officer in the war ministry, Nishiura Susumu, had advocated the extended use of indigenous troops in the empire, pointing to France's successful use of Moroccans.[137] The *heiho* or auxiliary soldier system had been introduced in the Indies in May. General Inada, chief of military operations of Seventh Area Army, was taken with the idea of going further when he visited in June, and learned of the Youth Training Centre which the counter-intelligence unit, Beppan, had set up in Tanggerang. Tojo assented on his visit in July.

Fear of arming indigenous soldiers persisted, and the Beppan was instructed not to involve Sukarno and Hatta. A pro-Japanese nationalist, Gatot Mangkupradja, was chosen to make the suggestion, and Beppan used Islamic leaders to find officer recruits. On 3 October 1943 Harada formally established Peta (Pembela Tanah Air), Defender of the Fatherland. Its senior officer was Kasman Singodimedjo, a Muhammadiyah leader, who swore the corps' oath of allegiance to Japan on 8 February 1944. Its flag was not that of nationalism: it displayed the Islamic Crescent superimposed on the Rising Sun. In December, however, the nationalists

---

[135] Sato, *War*, p. 62.

[136] Kanahele, 'Japanese Occupation' p. 108.

[137] Nugroho Notususanto in W.H. Newell, ed., *Japan in Asia, 1942-1945*, Singapore University Press, 1981, p. 33.

were brought closer to Peta, without being given any control, through the creation of the Badan Pembantu Peradjurit, an assistance association for Peta and Heiho.

The restructuring that increased 'participation' involved was completed by the final establishment of a new overall Muslim organisation, and the displacement of Putera. Masjumi (Madjlis Sjuro Muslimin Indonesia, Consultative Council of Indonesian Muslims) was set up in October, with the object of 'strengthening the unity of all Islamic organizations' and 'aiding Dai Nippon in the interests of Greater East Asia',[138] and was open, with the approval of the *shumubu*, to individual *kiyayi* and *ulama*, as well as to approved organisations, like NU and Muhammadiyah.

The long-standing doubts about Putera were resolved by the creation of a new people's organisation, announced by Harada on 8 January 1944. A preparatory committee was set up, though the Japanese had already settled the main points: it was to be an all-inclusive mass organisation similar to Concordia and the Imperial Rule Assistance Association. The name was disputed. Indonesian members of the committee wanted to use the word 'Indonesia', as indeed Masjumi did. All that the Japanese would concede was an alternative title, Himpunan Kebaktian Rakyat (People's Loyalty Association).[139] It was generally called by its Japanese name Djawa Hokokai, Java Service Organisation.

Putera was formally dissolved on 29 February 1944. The new organisation was announced the following day, the anniversary of the entry of the Imperial forces into Java. 'With the establishment of the Java Service Association', proclaimed the *gunseikan* as president, 'the all-out forward surge of the fifty million people of Java, who are in the decisive battle arena of the Greater East Asia war, has been immeasurably strengthened and perfected.' The association was, he added, 'inseparably one with the various organizations of the Military Administration'.[140] Ha Ch'iao Tsung Hui, which had been formed to group the Chinese associations together, was also absorbed.[141]

The platform pledged 'to maintain the spirit of service and to

---

[138] Benda, *Crescent and Rising Sun*, p. 150.
[139] Sato, *War*, p. 71.
[140] q. Benda *et al.*, *Japanese Military Administration*, p. 145.
[141] Charles A. Coppel in J.A.C. Mackie, ed., *The Chinese in Indonesia*, Honolulu: Univ. of Hawaii Press, 1976, p. 38.

make selfless efforts for the permeation of military government'. 'The Greater East Asia War is a Sacred War based on Divine Will and Dictate for the liberation of Greater East Asia from the fetters of the devilish Americans, British, and Dutch, and for the establishment of a New Order based on morality.' For its 'successful completion', the people of Java had 'to take the initiative in the defense of the home land against the external enemy and to undertake the fulfillment of the various policies of the Military Administration within our villages'. In Java, as in Greater East Asia as a whole, 'the peoples shall be harmoniously united around the nucleus of the officials and the army'.[142]

The top leadership was Japanese, and the *priyayi* were used on the widest scale. The involvement of the nationalists did not go below the residency level. The object, however, was not to divide and rule, as Benda says and Harada denied, but to secure the collaboration of the peoples of Java with the military administration.[143] Masjumi was also associated with the new organisation, both at the central and at the local levels.

Simultaneously the military authorities introduced *tonarigumi* or neighbourhood associations, which at the village level were interlinked with branches of the service organisation. Based on the practice of the homeland, they were also presented as consonant with *gotong royong*, the practice of mutual help, upon which the 1942 committee on traditions and customs had reported. The influence of the lower-level *priyayi* and the *lurah* or village heads was enhanced. At the same time, the Japanese obtained Islamic sanction for what they were doing. Indeed, they were anxious that the growing peasant unrest, caused by food shortages and requisitions, should not find Islamic leadership. The lesson of Dutch experience was underlined by a *kiyayi*-led outbreak near Tasikmalaya in February 1944. The Japanese administration, as Kurasawa puts it, 'never relaxed its caution towards Moslem leaders'.[144]

While the aim of the Japanese was to unite and secure support, rather than to divide and rule, their methods had, of course, outcomes or by-products other than those they anticipated. The

[142] q. Benda *et al.*, *Japanese Military Administration*, p. 147.
[143] Benda, *Crescent and Rising Sun*, pp. 156-7. Kanahele, 'Japanese Occupation', p. 142. Kurasawa, 'Mobilization and Control', pp. 499, 501-2.
[144] Kurusawa, 'Mobilization and Control', p. 473.

changes they made to their system early in 1944 reduced the role of the nationalists, if not of the Muslim leaders, and enhanced that of the *priyayi* elite, the main pillar of their rule. Sukarno was director of the secretariat of the Hokokai, Hatta vice-chairman of its central council. They were, however, mere functionaries. 'Under Poetera', as Hatta put it, 'the nationalists actively guided the people; now under the *Djawa Hookookai* [*sic*] they sit idly by in their Jakarta offices.'[145] Yet identification with the regime, as it became more exacting, and as the economic situation deteriorated, was, in the longer term, damaging for the *priyayi* and, in a negative sense at least, helpful for its rivals. The prospects for the nationalists became more positive with the moves towards independence that followed the Koiso statement of September 1944.

In March, a few weeks after the Tasikmalaya disturbances, Hayashi Kyujiro had put up a plan for the governance of Java. The US and the UK were trying 'to force a decisive battle before we can perfect our national defense structure which depends on the utilization of the resources in our occupied territories'. Fully utilising those resources required 'peace and order' in the occupied territories. Yet in Java, 'with the passing of time and confronted with the hardships of daily living arising from shortages of food and clothing, an increasing number of natives have become disillusioned.'

It was impossible to rely only on the new Djawa Hokokai 'for the cooperation of the Javanese public'. Nor had Japan publicly endorsed the hopes of 'liberation'. Indeed, 'with the passing of time Japan differentiated in her treatment of Burma, the Philippines, and Java; thus there is now a trend toward increased suspicion that Japan may assume direct control of Java together with the Malay Peninsula.'

In order to enable the fifty million people of Java to further endure the deprivation of clothing, to deliver foodstuffs while bearing hardships, and to cooperate with the military administration in all aspects, the best policy is to clearly indicate to them that they shall be granted independence when their preparatory education for the postwar future has been completed.

That independence would cover Java: though it was a misinterpretation to suggest that the administrative divisions the military had adopted were designed to prevent independence, the question of the outer islands should be deferred.[146]

---

[145] q. Kanahele, 'Japanese Occupation', p. 143.
[146] q. Benda *et al.*, *Japanese Military Administration*, pp. 244-6.

The proposal made no progress under Tojo, but the question was reappraised in August. In Sumatra the military authorities had questioned the policies pursued in Java, the Putera-type organisation set up in East Sumatra was exceptional, and the word 'independence' was virtually taboo. In the navy area, it was out of the question, though some months after the promise of 'political participation', two nationalists, Ratulangie and Tadjoeddin Noor, had been appointed advisers. In the Tokyo meetings, the ministry of Greater East Asia argued for a federal Indonesia, of which Java would be the first part to become independent. This the army did not care for. Its own proposal, however, the ministry of foreign affairs considered lacked a concrete programme for implementation. A second army proposal thus included the organisation of a preparatory committee. The officials' report did not, however, explicitly cover that. It 'expected' that the territory would include all Netherlands India, except New Guinea, but noted that the navy reserved its position.[147]

No further deliberation among the officials followed, and on 4 September the supreme council only discussed the planned declaration in the Diet. The army took it back to the council on the 6th, when 'there was general agreement that the measures in the Proposal of the Officials of the Ministries Concerned should at least be implemented in Java and Sumatra'.[148] The Koiso speech of 7 September promised independence for the East Indies in the future, omitting the 'near' that the supreme council had been ready to include.[149] No deadlines were mentioned. But the use of the nationalist flag was permitted, and the singing of 'Indonesia Raya'. And the nationalists were able to give an Indonesian tone to the Barisan Pelopor (Pioneer Corps or Suishintai), a militia that, already planned, was now set up. Above all, they could make propaganda for their cause, though it had always to be coupled with propaganda for the Japanese cause.

While the military administration in Java was indeed slow to act on the proclamation, it did increase the role of the nationalists: they predominated among the additional advisers or *sanyo* who

---

[147] q. Ibid., pp. 260-1.

[148] q. Benda *et al.*, *Japanese Military Administration*, p. 262. But contrast Kanahele, 'Japanese Occupation', p. 162.

[149] q. Benda *et al.*, *Japanese Military Administration*, p. 259. Kanahele, 'Japanese Occupation', p. 162.

were appointed, and among the members added to an expanded central advisory council, though the Japanese also added a Chinese, two Arabs, an Ambonese and a Menadonese. Outside Java, the Japanese were slower still. With the arrival of Shibata Yaichiro as commander of the Southwestern Fleet in January, however, the navy shifted away from its 'permanent possession' line.[150] In Sumatra the Twenty-Fifth Army did not set up a central advisory council till May.

The delay in Java may be attributed to the lack of orders from Tokyo, itself the result of continued differences and disagreements as well as preoccupations. Meanwhile, the island was increasingly isolated and vulnerable, and the revolt of Peta units at Blitar on 14 February aroused the worst fears of the occupying power. At a meeting of the central advisory council a week later, the nationalists were bolder than usual, and Hatta demanded the end of *romusha* recruitment. On 1 March Harada announced the formation of a committee to investigate preparations for independence. Then in late March he had to persuade his colleagues in Sumatra and his superiors. Tokyo, which had meanwhile offered independence to Cambodia and Vietnam, also assented. A list of members was announced on 29 April. Nationalists predominated over *priyayi* officials and Muslim representatives. A conference in Singapore on 20 May approved convening the first meeting. That took place at the end of May.

Its most famous event was Sukarno's enunciation of the five principles of the Indonesian state, the *pantja sila*. One was nationalism, the 'unity between men and place', the 'entire archipelago ... from the northern tip of Sumatra to Papua'. Another was internationalism. 'We should not only establish the state of Free Indonesia, but we should also aim at making one family of all nations.' The third principle was democracy, 'representative government'. The fourth was 'social justice'. What was called democracy in the West was merely political, and that was not enough. The final principle was belief in God: 'every Indonesian should believe in *his own* particular God'. Sukarno concluded by invoking *gotong royong*, mutual cooperation.[151]

What he did not invoke was any of the Japanese ideology. The committee did, however, conclude by reaffirming support for

[150] Kanahele, 'Japanese Occupation', pp. 177-8.

[151] Ibid., pp. 197-9; Kahin, *Nationalism and Revolution*, pp. 122-7.

the Japanese war effort; by denouncing the setting-up of a Dutch administration in Morotai and Papua, and by objecting to the decision of the San Francisco conference to impose 'mandate' status. A subcommittee discussed the role of Islam, and produced the compromise 'Jakarta Charter'.

The second session began on 10 July. One issue, the form of the state, was decisively disposed of: only six voted for a monarchy; fifty-five voted for a republic. The extent of the territory to be covered was the subject of sharper debate. Should it include the former Netherlands India, with or without New Guinea? or should it also include Malaya, northern Borneo and Portuguese Timor? Mohammad Yamin argued for the latter, and so did Sukarno, alluding to an appeal from Malay nationalists. Indeed, he confessed to a dream of 'pan-Indonesia', but recognised that the independence of the Philippines had to be respected.[152] The Yamin-Sukarno proposition received the support of the majority. A people's deliberative body, meeting at least once in five years, was to set policy and elect the president. He had extensive powers, but could enact legislation only with the approval of the people's representative council. The models were Western and Indonesian, says Kanahele,[153] not Japanese.

Officials in Tokyo had been deliberating simultaneously, and on 17 July the supreme war council approved independence for 'the former Dutch East Indies' 'at the earliest possible moment'. It was to be proclaimed when preparations were complete 'in the major regions', those areas where they were not complete being transferred when they were ready.[154] A conference in Singapore on 29 July decided that the independence of Java would be announced in early September, and other areas would follow. A committee for the preparation of independence would be set up.

Terauchi's HQ in Saigon suggested 7 September as the date of independence, the anniversary of the Koiso declaration. It proposed that the new state should immediately declare war on the United States, Britain and the Netherlands. The officials in Tokyo were less insistent: 'The new nation shall be so guided, with due consideration of public opinion, to take an opportune and affir-

---

[152] J.D. Legge, *Sukarno*, Harmondsworth: Penguin, 1973, p. 190.

[153] Kanahele, 'Japanese Occupation', p. 214.

[154] q. Benda *et al.*, *Japanese Military Administration*, p. 274.

mative posture in the war situation relative to the United States, Britain, and the Netherlands.'[155]

On 7 August Terauchi approved setting up the committee to prepare independence, and, in a supplementary announcement, the *gunseikan*, General Yamamoto, said it would cover all Indonesia.[156] Sukarno, Hatta and Radjiman, chairman of the previous investigatory committee, were flown to meet Terauchi in Dalat on 11 August. They flew back to Singapore on the 13th and to Jakarta next day. The members of the committee for preparing independence were named that day, and the first meeting, with Sukarno as chairman, was scheduled for the 18th.

Japan, however, surrendered on 14 August. That confronted the nationalists with a new problem. Should they proclaim independence? If they sought Japanese approval, their government might seem to the victorious allies but another puppet. But if they did not, the Japanese might feel bound, under the terms of the surrender, to suppress it. Aroused youth leaders tried to enforce a demand for bold action by kidnapping Sukarno and Hatta. In the event, while the naval liaison officer in Jakarta, Admiral Maeda, agreed to persuade his army colleagues to turn a blind eye, a brief statement was made on 17 August in the courtyard of Sukarno's house.[157] 'We, the people of Indonesia, hereby declare Indonesia's independence. Matters concerning the transfer of power and other matters will be executed in an orderly manner and in the shortest possible time.'[158] The words 'transfer of power' replaced a bolder reference to the seizure of administrative control by the people.[159]

The Japanese had offered their support for independence only belatedly. The nationalist leadership were making a bid for it after the eleventh hour. What the Japanese had done had enlarged their chances, but also aroused their rivals:'To proclaim Independence is easy,' Sukarno said on 23 August.

To make a Constitution is not difficult. To elect a President and a Vice-President is easier still. But to form the bodies and the posts of authority

[155] q. ibid., pp. 275-6, 277.

[156] B.R.O'G. Anderson, *Some Aspects of Indonesian Politics under the Japanese Occupation: 1944-1945*, Ithaca, NY: Cornell Univ. Press, 1961, p. 60.

[157] Mavis Rose, *Indonesia Free*, Ithaka, NY: Cornell Univ. Press, 1987, p. 120.

[158] q. Legge, *Sukarto*, p. 201.

[159] Nishijima Shigetada in A. Reid and Akira Oki, eds, *The Japanese Experience in Indonesia*, Athens: Univ. of Ohio Press, 1986, pp. 322-3.

and administration of the State as well as to seek international recognition, especially under conditions such as the present, where the Japanese Government is still obliged by the international *status quo* to remain in this country to run the administration and maintain public order – these tasks are not easy![160]

To make good their bid for independence was to require of the Indonesians great courage and skilful leadership. It was also to require the support of the United States and Britain. Like the Burmese, the Indonesians had determined to secure their independence, if not out of the Japanese, then out of the international crisis they had created. Unlike them, they were not faced with a colonial power that had driven out the Japanese. Unlike the Filipinos, they were not faced with a colonial power committed to granting independence.

Borneo

In May 1945 Tokyo officials suggested that whether northern Borneo should be included in an independent Indonesian state should be 'separately determined after considering the desires of the natives and the disposition of Malaya'.[161] It was included in the Indonesia Raya that Sukarno and Yamin advocated in June 1945, but not within the boundaries the Japanese finally settled on, nor within the state the independence of which was proclaimed on 17 August.

The position of the area is indeed ambivalent. In many respects akin to Indonesia, it is also oriented to the north. It is strategically significant for the command of the South China Sea, and for the control of the southern Philippines. That had influenced the policies of the British during their nineteenth-century primacy. In the twentieth century the oil of Sarawak and Brunei had given those states an additional significance. The Japanese naturally took account of both factors.

The Dutch had never established themselves in northern Borneo. Under the Anglo-Dutch treaty of 1824, which marked Britain's determination not to set up a rival empire in the archipelago, the British had probably expected them to do so. A change of policy followed in the 1830s and 1840s. That resulted partly from a dispute with the Dutch over commercial access to Java and the outer islands, and partly from the increase in the strat-

[160] q. Anderson, *Aspects*, p. 117.

[161] q. Benda *et al.*, *Japanese Military Administration*, p. 267.

egic importance of the region with the opening-up of the China trade and the British acquisition of Hong Kong. It also resulted from the initiative of a gentleman-adventurer, James Brooke. Initially he hoped to reverse Britain's policy on empire in the archipelago by establishing a reformist British influence in the sultanate of Brunei, which then comprised all northern Borneo. Although it made Labuan into a colony in 1848, the British government would not go so far.

Increasingly Brooke claimed that Sarawak and the neighbouring rivers, the government of which the Sultan of Brunei had granted him, formed an independent state. The British government was unwilling to recognise that, unwilling, too, to condone the further extension of Sarawak's 'frontiers', but also concerned, particularly after the French intervened in Vietnam in 1858, lest another power should step in. One answer was to support the enterprise of other adventurers to the north of Brunei, and to charter the British North Borneo Company in 1881. Another was to extend British protection over all three territories, Sarawak, Brunei and North Borneo, in 1888. In 1905 the British placed a Resident in the now greatly truncated state of Brunei. But, though that was intended as a step towards drawing all the territories of 'British Borneo' together, no further step was taken. The protected states remained separate. Nor, of course, were they effectively protected.

Japanese policy was to govern all the territories as one entity, Boruneo Kita, Northern Borneo in Japanese, 'Our Borneo' in Malay. It was divided into five *shu* or provinces. Kuching-shu covered the First and Second Divisions of Brooke Sarawak, the Natuna islands and Pontianak, part of the Dutch territory. Sibu-shu comprised the Third Division. Miri-shu included the Fourth and Fifth Divisions and the Sultanate. North Borneo included Seikai-shu, the West Coast and Labuan, which was to be renamed Maedashima after the first commander of the Borneo Defence Force, Maeda Toshinari, lost his life in air-crash there; and Tokai-shu, the East Coast, including Sandakan, curiously given back the name its English founder had given it, Elopura.[162] Under the provinces were prefectures or *ken*. The oilfields area, Miri in Sarawak and Seria in Brunei, remained, however, the direct responsibility of Tokyo HQ.

---

[162] Reece, *Masa Jepun*, p. 54. Stephen R. Evans, *Sabah (North Borneo) under the Rising Sun Government*, Singapore: printed by Tropical Press, 1991, p. 30.

The most significant figure in the military administration up to March 1945 was the chief of staff, General Manaki Yoshinobu. He worked with Yamada Setsuo, seconded from Internal Affairs to head the intelligence division, and later governor of Kuching. 'His suggestions', Manaki said,

concentrated on the maintenance of the status quo ante as far as possible, at least for a time, so that the new administration could minimise the local people's confusion. His purpose was to bring peace of mind to the people and to ensure that they were co-operative towards the new administration.[163]

The political participation envisaged by Tojo in his speech of June 1943 should, the Borneo Defence Force thought, be 'minimised', since 'the local people have not been sufficiently educated and are not interested in participating in political matters.'[164] However, the military administration issued a decree on 1 October, setting up prefectoral advisory councils, *ken-sanji-kai*, throughout northern Borneo. The membership of that in Kuching reflected Yamada's orientation to the *status quo*, as well as the attempt at comprehensiveness, that also marked Japanese policy in Java and elsewhere. It included leading members of the Malay elite, on which the Brooke regime so largely relied, several prominent Chinese and two Iban. They were installed in December and the first meeting was held in February. Other *ken-sanji-kai* also met in 1944, advising on padi-growing, self-sufficiency, the war effort.

The *kempeitai* were most active as the war situation deteriorated and their suspicions became more paranoid. Supplementing it was the *jikeidan*, self-protection corps, sustaining a version of the *tonarigumi*: 'a vigilante system which divided all areas of concentrated population into units of approximately thirty houses each with leaders responsible to the police for what happened in their division'.[165] The network facilitated surveillance and community control. It also facilitated the mobilisation of forced labour and the collection of 'subscriptions'. The system 'came into its own' in the first half of 1945 'when the authority of the administration was sorely strained by air raids, currency collapse and other signs of Japan's increasing weakness'.[166]

In October 1943 the Borneo Defence Force was instructed to

---

[163] q. Reece, *Masa Jepun*, p. 63.
[164] q. ibid.
[165] R. Reece, *The Name of Brooke*, Kuala Lumpur: Oxford Univ. Press, 1982, p. 146.
[166] Reece, *Masa Jepun*, pp. 80-1.

recruit and train a North Borneo Volunteer Corps or militia. The object was to free regular troops from tasks like guarding strategic installations or supervising forced labour, and to permit their relocation elsewhere. Officially a *giyugun*, or volunteer army, in Sarawak the body was known as *kyodo-hei*, local militia. In this body – unlike the advisory councils – there were to be no Chinese. The NCOs were drawn from elite Malay families. Most of the rank-and-file were Iban from the 2nd Division, though some were recruited in the 3rd Division and in North Borneo. They were men of a warrior culture, and other opportunities for the traditional *bejalai*, wandering in search of cash and adventure, were no longer available. The Bidayuh had to be conscripted.

No prospect of independence was held out. 'There was never the slightest suggestion that Boruneo Kita would ever be anything other than a colonial dependency of Japan.'[167] No public reference was to be made to Japan's recognition of independence movements elsewhere in Southeast Asia. Talk of preparing the people for independence would only encourage the Chinese and others to resist the Japanese army, said Yano Tsuneo, an influential staff officer.[168]

The regime remained oriented to the status quo, even to divide-and rule. Involving the Iban in the *kyodo-hei* in a measure replicated the raj's use of them. Again, like the Brookes, the regime recognised the *penghulu*, although it also won the support of the mission-educated Iban by opening up administrative posts that the raj had denied them. It utilised the traditional Sarawak Malay elite, though it did not encourage the Sarawak Malay National Union, formed in 1939 to give expression to non-elite apprehension that the Malays were falling behind, nor did it allow any contact with nationalists in Malaya or Indonesia.

The regime's distrust of the Chinese, however, clearly exceeded that of its Brooke predecessor, and also that of the Japanese military administration in Java. Organisers of the China Relief Fund were treated harshly. The object was partly punitive, partly, somewhat paradoxically, also designed to secure cooperation through the Kakeo Kokokai, the United Overseas Chinese Association. One object of that was in turn, however, to secure payment of the *shu-jin*, the life-redeeming money or blood debt required of the Chinese for supporting Chiang Kai-shek.

[167] Ibid., p. 105.
[168] Ibid.

The major guerrilla exploit in Boruneo Kita was organised by Albert Kwok (Guo Hengnan), a Chinese born in Kuching, educated in Shanghai. He set up a medical practice in Jesselton (Kota Kinabalu) in 1940, as a cover for his work as a KMT intelligence agent. Early in 1943 he made contact with the anti-Japanese guerrilla movement in Tawi-Tawi in the southern Philippines, and in July he was given an American commission. He began to organise a guerrilla force based at Menggatal, including Chinese, but also Suluks and Bajaus, Sikh ex-policemen, and ex-volunteers, like Jules Stephens, but not Dusun farmers, nor interior Muruts.[169] He was prompted to act when the Japanese revealed their intention to conscript 3,000 Chinese for their militia.[170]

On 9 October the small force successfully attacked the Japanese police at Tuaran and Menggatal, and it then went on to Jesselton (Api). The Japanese struck back, and no reinforcements came. Kwok surrendered on 19 December. Mass executions and large-scale reprisals followed. In April 1944 the Japanese HQ was moved to Api, where the guerrillas had shown that Japanese control was 'rather tenuous'.[171] Only later in the year, as the war changed the strategic role of northern Borneo, was the Borneo Defence Force put on an operational footing as the Thirty-Seventh Army, and additional troops sent to Boruneo Kita.

Though the Japanese kept northern Borneo apart from Indonesia, and administered it as an entity, they took no steps to promote its political unity, either by reconstructing the sultanate of Brunei or otherwise. Nor did they promote the political advance of the individual territories. Their emphasis at the outset was, as elsewhere, on the *status quo*. They relied on a mix of violence and attempts to secure collaboration by modified forms of divide-and-rule. They made no promises. Their invasion meant that the raj and the company could not return, but new colonial regimes succeeded them. The elites, as Ooi Keat Gin suggests, largely preserved their position.[172] But it had been eroded, and inter-ethnic tension had been aroused.

---

[169] Evans, *Sabah*, p. 52.

[170] Reece, *Masa Japun*, p. 162.

[171] Ibid., p. 164.

[172] *Rising Sun over Borneo*, Basingstoke: Macmillan, 1999, p. 123.

Malaya and Singapore

In Malaya, again, Japanese policy was politically unconstructive, though not without effect. There, too, they saw little need to make promises of an independent future. Indeed they intended to retain Singapore, while they made over the northern states to Thailand. That, and their attitude to the Chinese, helped to intensify the divide-and-rule aspects of their regime. In some sense, again, they supported the *status quo*, while at the same time reshaping it. The inter-ethnic tensions – which had both sustained it and been contained by it – were sharpened by what they did and by the unintended consequences of what they did.

'British Malaya', like 'British Borneo', was a form of words, not an entity. Its political system was a variegated inheritance of the past, and its society a 'plural' one. In order to protect their route to China, and to secure a share in the trade of the archipelago, the British had secured, between 1786 and 1824, the three 'Straits Settlements', Penang, Melaka and Singapore, administered as a colony from 1868. In 1874 they had formalised their intervention in some of the Malay states on the west coast by appointing Residents at the rulers' courts, and in 1895-6 they had pulled the states of Perak, Selangor, Negri Sembilan and Pahang into the Federated Malay States (FMS), in respect of which the governor of the Straits Settlements acted as high commissioner.

In 1909 the Thais transferred their suzerain rights over the northern states, Perlis, Kedah, Kelantan and Trengganu, but neither they, nor Johore, joined the federation. Attempts at rationalisation were half-heartedly pursued. They seemed likely to provoke more problems than they solved, and in the interwar period the British were unwilling to take risks, especially in view of the strategic importance Singapore had acquired, and of the dollar-earning capacity of the Malayan rubber industry.

The issue was also related to the nature of Malayan society. The creation of commercial entrepots, the expansion of tin-mining and the establishment of rubber-growing had led to widespread immigration from India and especially from China. The retention of the Malay states was a guarantee against the political dominance of the Chinese. Drawing them together in an all-Malaya federation might at once preserve the political position of the Malays, while offering the Chinese wider economic opportunity. The British did not get far with the idea. Yet their failure could leave the way open to other more radical solutions. While the Indian and Chinese communities might look to their homelands, the Malay community might look to Indonesia. In 1938 younger educated Malays indeed formed Kesatuan Melayu Muda (KMM), vaguely Marxist, anti-colonial, looking to Indonesia Raya.

The Twenty-Fifth Army was responsible for Malaya following its conquest, and for Sumatra as well, the two areas comprising 'the nuclear zone of the Empire's plans for the Southern area'.[173] It relinquished control of Malaya in April 1943, when the Southern Army HQ was set up in Singapore. A direct connection with that was in turn displaced in January 1944 by the creation of the Twenty-Ninth Army, with its HQ at Taiping. In April that was placed under the new Seventh Area Army, made responsible for defending Singapore.

In Malaya, as elsewhere, peace preservation committees were created as the Japanese came in. Then a more regular military administration took over. 'The fundamental policy is to preserve peace and order', stressed the instructions issued in Selangor. The 'special objective' was to reconstruct 'industrial enterprises' so as 'to increase the power and resources of the strategy of war and also to meet the shortage of public requirements'. The army was to be self-supporting, but its needs had to be balanced against those of the natives. Their customs were to be respected, and 'the remaining administrative organs of the natives ... used to the best of advantage.' 'As for the treatment of American, English and Dutch citizens, it is our principle to instruct them to co-operate with us in executing military administration. However, anyone who disagrees with our policy will not be permitted to remain.'[174]

The FMS was dissolved and the peninsula, officially called Malai from December 1942, was divided into ten provinces or *shu*. Eight were made up of the nine Malay States, Perlis being incorporated in Kedah. The other two were Penang and Melaka. Singapore, renamed Syonan (Brilliant Harmony), became a special municipality under a Japanese mayor.

The provincial governors were Japanese civilians, some from the ministry of home affairs. Senior provincial posts were also held

[173] q. Benda *et al.*, *Japanese Military Administration*, p. 169.

[174] q. P. Kratoska, *The Japanese Occupation of Malaya*, London: Hurst; Sydney: Allen & Unwin, 1998, pp. 55-6.

by Japanese, but there were too few to fill all the positions even in the reduced establishment the Japanese created, and it was necessary to appoint some Malayans. Most of the district officers had been British. At this level the Japanese appointed Malays, generally of aristocratic origin. They continued to supervise. Indeed a new post was created shortly before the occupation ended, the *gun shidokan*, the officer in charge of promoting district administration. Village headmen were made responsible, as in Java, for recruiting forced labour.

Japanese policy towards the sultans themselves varied. In February Yamashita approved a policy document under which they would retain their political status.[175] Formerly a senior member of the Total War Institute, Watanabe Wataru, who became *gunseibusho* in March, wanted to end indirect rule, however, and place the states and settlements under 'unified control and authority of the military'.[176] 'Items concerning the disposition of heads of autonomous areas', a Twenty-Fifth Army document of July 1942, thus took a different line:

Malaya became an integral territory of Japan when it came under Japanese occupation. It is only proper, therefore, that the existence of heads of autonomous areas, who claim personal control of lands and peoples, if only nominally, be eliminated. But it is impractical from the viewpoint of civil administration to dispose of them abruptly by force; hence special plans shall be formulated on the basis of which the heads of autonomous areas shall be induced to surrender voluntarily their political privileges.

In return they would receive annuities, and 'retain their position as religious leaders'.[177]

In the event the proposal – which, as Marquis Tokugawa pointed out, recalled the Meiji treatment of the *daimyo*, and incidentally paralleled the current attitudes of British postwar planners – was not fully carried out. The central authorities opposed their removal, partly because of· its impact on the rulers of the princely states in India.[178] Sultans were to be 'utilized in such a way as to be the central driving force for reconstruction and the leaders

---

[175] Ibid., p. 67.
[176] q. Akashi Yoji in K.S. Sandhu and P. Wheatley, eds, *Melaka: The Transformation of a Malay Capital*, Kuala Lumpur: Oxford Univ. Press, 1983, I, 320.
[177] q. Benda *et al.*, *Japanese Military Administration*, pp. 184-5.
[178] Itagaki Yoichi in K.G. Tregonning, ed., *Papers on Malayan History*, Singapore: JSEAH, 1962, p. 257.

for inspiring an Asian consciousness' ran a document of 28 November 1942.[179]

At a meeting of representatives of the rulers in Singapore in January, the head of military administration indicated that sultans would retain their titles, would be the supreme authority in respect, of Islam, and would receive the same allowances as prewar. In fact, Itagaki Yoichi suggests, the sultans had lost their political authority with the suspension of the state councils of the British phase.[180] In April 1943, however, the sultans became official advisers to the governors. In July, the visiting Tojo acknowledged their help, and enjoined them, as 'accepted leaders of your res- pective places', to guide the people in creating a new order.[181] The sultans were made vice-chairmen of the advisory councils, *sanji kai*, set up in December 1943-January 1944. The *shu-chokan* were, however, chairmen, and the councils had no legislative funct- ion. The military administration convened a major conference of Islamic leaders at Kuala Kangsar in December 1944.[182]

The advisory councils included substantial representation of the Indian and Chinese communities. *Jikeidan* were set up in Septem- ber 1942. The *tonarigumi*, which the Japanese began to set up in October 1943, were based on the place of residence. The object, as the Johore proclamation declared, was that 'all citizens must unite, co-operate and work together by way of assisting in the present war for the benefit of the Greater East Asia Co-Prosperity Sphere.'[183]

Japanese policy towards the Chinese was, as in Borneo, ambi- guous. In one part, it was punitive, aimed at supporters of the Chiang Kai-shek regime, the China Relief Fund and the National Salvation Movement,[184] and of the hastily recruited British-led Dalforce, whose 'fierce fight' against the Japanese was 'neither for- gotten nor forgiven'.[185] In the case of the notorious *sook ching* (purification by elimination) in Singapore, it went much further:

---

[179] q. Kratoska, *Japanese Occupation*, p. 69.

[180] Tregonning, *Papers*, p. 259.

[181] q. Kratoska, *Japanese Occupation*, p. 70.

[182] Abu Talib in P. Kratoska, ed., *Malaya and Singapore during the Japanese Occupa- tion*, Singapore: JSEAS, 1995, p. 30.

[183] q. Kratoska, *Japanese Occupation*, p. 82.

[184] See S. Leong, 'The Malayan Overseas Chinese and the Sino-Japanese War, 1937-1941', *JSEAS*, 10, 2 (September 1979), pp. 296ff.

[185] Cheah Boon Kheng in McCoy, *Southeast Asia*, p. 94.

some 40,000-70,000 were killed.[186] In another part, indeed, it was a policy of intimidation by terror.

Yet at the same time, the Japanese recognised the importance of winning the collaboration of the Chinese, given their leading economic role.

The entire overseas Chinese community which controls a network of commercial influence spanning the Southern area totals approximately 5,000,000 while their capital mobilization amounts to approximately 5,000,000,000 yuan. With the mobilization of these human and financial resources, their activities, which extend through the southern area and all China and even into the Near East and the South Pacific, truly indicate their formidable position. This should be directed toward becoming a basic driving force in Japan's major policy of employing them cooperatively in the administration of the Southern area.[187]

Harshness and intimidation did not consort well with such a policy. In Malaya the Japanese created an Oversea Chinese Association, displacing many of the existing clan and dialect associations. Its first task was to raise a 'voluntary contribution' of $50 million to the military administration. 'Despite intense Japanese pressure the Chinese community raised just $28 million',[188] the balance coming through a loan from the Yokohama Specie Bank.

Indian residents were encouraged to join the Indian Independence League (IIL). The Japanese looked for leadership to the Bengali nationalists, R.B. Bose and later S.C. Bose, but local figures like S.C. Goho, N. Raghavan and K.P.K. Menon were involved. Raghavan was a minister in the Azad Hind government, and J. Thivy an adviser. Locals also joined the reconstituted INA. Between July 1943 and the retreat from Imphal in June 1944, 'there was indeed considerable popular support for the League and the Army, but this support was never universal and was often coerced'. An appearance of communal solidarity was no more than that: the occupation deepened the tension between the mainly Tamil labourers and the mainly Malayalee professional men who headed the IIL.[189]

---

[186] Otabe Yuji, 'Japanese Occupation Policy in Singapore' in P. Lowe and H. Moeshart, eds, *Western Interactions with Japan*, Folkestone: Japan Library, 1990, p. 86.

[187] q. Benda *et al.*, *Japanese Military Administration*, p. 181.

[188] Kratoska, *Japanese Occupation*, p. 102.

[189] M.R. Stenson, *Class, Race and Colonialism in West Malaysia*, St Lucia: Univ. of Queensland Press, p. 93

Chinese formed the main component of the guerrilla movement in Malaya. The Malayan People's Anti-Japanese Army
(MPAJA) was created by the Chinese-dominated Malayan Communist Party and backed by the Malayan People's Anti-Japanese
Union. It suffered a severe setback in September 1942 as a result
of the treachery of its secretary-general, Lai Teck: the Japanese
ambushed a meeting of MCP leaders at Batu Caves. Perak had
the strongest MPAJA force, the 5th Battalion, 800-1,000 men by
August 1945. For the Japanese they were 'an irritating nuisance,
like a bone stuck in the throat'.[190] British intelligence operatives,
Force 136, made contact with the MPAJA from May 1943.

SOE, however, also thought it desirable to create a parallel
Malay organisation. Some Malays had indeed taken part in fighting
during the invasion, as members of the Malay Regiment, created
in 1933, and of the FMS Volunteer Force. Now Force 136 had an
appeal to younger Malays. Some joined armed anti-Japanese
groups like Askar Melayu Setia in Perak and Kedah and Wataniah
in Pahang. Others participated in the less openly anti-Japanese
Saberkas in Kedah.[191]

During the invasion, it appears, Japanese officers had contacted
Malay nationalists, men like Ibrahim Yaacob of the Kesatuan Melayu
Muda (KMM). Once their control was established, the Japanese
looked to more conservative elements, and in June 1942 KMM was
banned. Ibrahim and Ishak Haji Muhammad were, however,
given jobs in the propaganda department. In December 1943-
January 1944 recruitment began for a Malay volunteer army, a
giyugun, called Peta in Malay, and Ibrahim became commander.
No Chinese were recruited to it. It had 2,000 members by April 1944.

The threat of Allied invasion grew as the British advanced in
Burma, and new measures were taken to win support. Following
a conference of the secretaries-general of the military administrations of Java, Sumatra, Celebes and Malaya in Singapore on 2-3
May 1945, the military administration set up a new organisation,
the *hodosho*. It was also designed, Itagaki suggests,[192] to promote
Malayan nationalism. The central *hodosho* opened at Taiping on 3
July 1945. By the end of the month, there was one in each of the
states that remained in Malai.

---

[190] Akashi Yoji in Kratoska, ed., *Malaya and Singapore*, p. 117.
[191] Abu Talib in ibid., pp. 17-18.
[192] Tregonning, *Papers*, p. 262.

The British had been ambivalent, and ultimately inactive, about the future of Malaya: in general they leant towards continuing a Malay Malaya, rather than a trans-communal Malayan Malaya. A somewhat similar problem faced the Japanese as they were forced into taking the political decisions they had so far avoided or taken only implicitly by maintaining the status quo. It presented itself, however, in the contrast between the trans-communal Malaya envisaged by the *hodosho*, and the Indonesia Raya that the Malay radicals saw as the solution of the communal problem.

Initially Malaya and Sumatra were treated as an 'integral territory' of Japan. Even when the Sumatra policy changed, no promises were made about Malaya, either in terms of its independence, or even in terms of its association with Indonesia, the goal of the radicals. Following Koiso's statement of 7 September 1944 the Malays in Singapore sought to hold celebration meetings, and to form an Indonesia association, but that was not permitted.[193] The events of 1945 led to a change in policy. Early in May Itagaki informally told Ibrahim Yaacob to start preparing for the independence of Malaya. He and his colleagues began setting up an organisation called KRIS, Kekuatan Rakya Istimewa (Special Strength of the People) or, according to Ibrahim, Kesatuan Rakyat Indonesia Semenanjung (Union of Peninsular Indonesians).[194]

The second conference of secretaries-general, held on 29 July 1945 to discuss the independence of Indonesia, formally decided to establish KRIS, and that was endorsed by the military administration on 10 August. The object was to appeal to the radical Malays and their wish to be part of Indonesia Raya, and, as Itagaki puts it, the movement had to be 'carried out in close connection with the general activities of the Hodosho', lest it aroused 'misunderstanding and suspicions of other races'.[195] Ibrahim met Sukarno and Hatta at Taiping aerodrome on 12 August. After the surrender, KRIS met 'informally' in Kuala Lumpur on 17 August. Ibrahim, however, was on his way to Java.

The Japanese, Itagaki points out, had lost Malay support, not only because of war conditions, but also because of the transfer of

[193] Ibid., p. 263.
[194] Cheah Boon Kheng, 'The Japanese Occupation of Malaya, 1941-45: Ibrahim Yaacob and the Struggle for Indonesia Raya', *Indonesia*, 28 October 1979, pp. 110-11.
[195] Tregonning, *Papers*, p. 263.

the northern states to Thailand in October 1943. In what remained of Malai, the Chinese thus became relatively even more significant, and the radicals' case for joining Indonesia even more urgent. Further concessions to Thai nationalism had indeed taken priority over any attempt to develop Malai. Regarded as imperial territory, it could be disposed of in an imperialist manner. Southern Malaya would be retained as a protection for Syonan. The occupation's main political legacy to Malaya was its worsened inter-communal relations. They were to defeat the new plan for a trans-communal Malaya upon which the British had finally resolved.

Thailand

The occupation was initially oriented to the maintenance of the political status quo in Southeast Asia. Indeed, it remained so, even after the fortunes of war compelled the Japanese to mobilise support in new ways, and in some measure to expand the idealism of the Sphere. In Burma and the Philippines, it was possible for the two strategies to be more consistent than in Indonesia, let alone Malaya. They were already substantially self-governing, and at the outset the Japanese could scarcely offer less than the fulfilment of their independence, an undertaking they carried out, though only as their position deteriorated, during 1943.

Under the Dutch, by contrast, Indonesia had scarcely the rudiments of self-government. Like them, the Japanese depended above all on the existing elite, endeavouring to ensure their predominance in the organisations that they set up to mobilise support. Only in the last months of the occupation was independence promised, and the nationalists offered a larger political role. The last-minute gesture in Malaya envisaged associating its remnant with Indonesia Raya.

The response the Japanese gestures secured also differed from territory to territory, and their impact varied. The offers of independence could hardly be refused. It so happened, however, that the two countries to which they were first made were not only the most politically 'advanced', but also those which were to be fought over a second time. That made it hard for the ruling elites to preserve their unity.

For both Burma and the Philippines, moreover, there were governments-in-exile, a testimony to prewar political advance, but also an alternative focus of loyalty. That in Washington was more

effective than that in Simla. The British, moreover, recruited mi-
nority elements in their guerrilla warfare rather than Burmans. By
contrast USAFFE guerrillas were a constant irritation to the Japanese and to the Laurel regime, and a factor which the elite families
had to bear in mind. By changing sides at the right moment, the
Thakins were able to maintain their power, and, for a while at
least, their unity. The elite in the Philippines sustained its continuity, though only at the cost of some division. The Indonesians'
declaration of independence came after the Japanese surrender.
To make it good, they were to emphasise both that they could
maintain order and that they were not merely Japanese puppets.

The case of Thailand, of course, differed again. Though it had
lost territory it claimed to the colonial powers, and had made unequal treaties, it had not lost its political independence. For the
Japanese, therefore, there were two possibilities. Thailand could
be treated as a full member of the Co-Prosperity Sphere, and the
relationship used as a positive demonstration to others of what
that meant. Thailand could also be won over by concessions to its
'pan-Thai' ambitions, and to its wish to regain the territories of
the suzerainty over which they had been deprived by the intervention of the colonial powers. The Japanese, in other words,
could expand the policy begun by Matsuoka's one-sided
mediation at the expense of French Indo-China by altering
the territorial frontiers of British Burma and British Malaya.
Characteristically, the Japanese took advantage of the second opportunity more fully than the first. In turn, of course, the arbitrary
treatment of the old frontiers could only alienate the Burmans and
the Malays.

In their response, the Thai elite had, like the elites elsewhere,
especially in the Philippines and Burma, to bear the future in
mind. Was it a future of continued Japanese dominance, or would
the Allies prove victorious? If, as seemed increasingly likely, the
latter was the case, it would be desirable, if possible, to play off the
Americans against the British. There was a substantial measure of
agreement among the ruling oligarchy of Thailand, as there was
among the ruling oligarchy in the Philippines. There were also
rivalries. In both cases the main objective was attained, but at the
cost of some polarisation within the elite.

The extent to which the Thai elite was already divided before
the war has been the subject of some controversy. In 1932 the

absolute monarchy had been overthrown by a small group of military and civilian leaders, organised as the People's Party, alienated by the new king's reliance on princely advisers and by the measures his government had adopted to deal with the Depression. The leading civilian figure among the 'Promoters' was a French-educated lawyer, Luang Pradit (Pridi Phanomyong). His radical proposals for internal reform were not, however, accepted, and the military figures became increasingly predominant, and among them above all Luang Pibun. A new nationalist ideology was articulated, its proponent, Luang Vichit, citing Goebbels, though also echoing King Vachiravudh.[196]

Even so too rigid a distinction between the civilians and the military cannot be readily sustained. Pridi, for example, had taken a lead in the renegotiation of the unequal treaties in 1937-8. In the occupation, on the other hand, Pibun became concerned over Manchukuoification. Japan's policies towards Thailand were not in fact unlike those it was to pursue towards Burma and the Philippines, but Ambassador Tsubokami Teiji certainly cited Manchuria as a model.[197]

The creation of the ministry of Greater East Asia caused concern in Bangkok, as it did in Nanking. Vichit, now foreign minister, called on the Japanese ambassador on 3 September 1942 to express the Thai government's 'deep concern'.[198] In Tokyo Direck complained to Tojo himself. The liaison conference of 29 September nevertheless insisted on the need for 'a close and unbreakable unity with Thailand in military affairs, political affairs, and economics for the sake of the self-sufficiency and self-defense of the empire'. Japan was to 'guide or take control of those aspects of the Thai economy which are essential to the prosecution of the Greater East Asian War and those related to the fundamental economy of East Asia'.[199]

A Japan-Thailand cultural treaty was concluded in October, and early in 1943 the Japanese Cultural Institute was set up in Bangkok. Pibun had set up a national cultural institute in Sept-

[196] Stowe, *Siam Becomes Thailand*, pp. 102-3.

[197] Reynolds, 'Aftermath of Alliance', p. 136.

[198] q. ibid., p. 133.

[199] q. ibid., pp. 134, 135. See also William L. Swan, 'Japan's Intentions for its Greater East Asia Co-Prosperity Sphere as Indicated in its Policy Plans for Thailand', *JSEAS*, 27, 1 March 1996), pp. 140-3, 147-9.

ember 1942.[200] He was later to claim that his Thai nationalism was designed to avoid Japanisation.[201]

In 1943 the Japanese changed their attitude to Thailand, as to China. 'Our economic policy', Aoki Kazuo, the Greater East Asia minister, declared in March, 'should be to keep to a minimum our demands, even for goods which are absolutely necessary for the prosecution of the war.' Visiting Bangkok in April, he emphasised that 'although Japan would extend her cooperation and assistance ... it was not her intention to interfere in internal affairs.'[202] Aoki also took up the promise of 'lost territory'. That was to include not only the Shan States of Mongpan and Kengtung, into which the Japanese had allowed Thai troops to penetrate, but also the northern Malay States, a claim Vichit had raised.[203] Tojo told the imperial conference on 31 May:

Due to the enemy strategy of seizing upon the people's lack of freedom due to the pro-Japanese policy of the Phibun regime, the presence of the Japanese army, and the activities of antigovernment bad elements, feelings toward Japan are certainly not satisfactory. Because of the troubled position of the Phibun regime and the psychological tendencies of the people, based upon the Japanese-Thai alliance, we will return lost territories in Malaya from the area we have occupied.'[204]

Tojo went to Bangkok to announce the decision. 'When Tojo's proclamation reached the cession of the six states – and one would have to say that Phibun was being more and more favoured – he displayed a joyful countenance,' the commander of the Garrison Army, Nakamura Aketo, recalled. 'But it was not to the point of a broad smile.'[205] Nor did the final transfer in October produce the desired effect. Pibun declined to attend the Greater East Asia conference in November. Prince Wan attended in his place.

In the meantime Pridi, who had been made one of the regents for the young king, had been making contacts with the Allies. In

---

[200] E.B. Reynolds in G.K. Goodman, ed., *Japanese Cultural Policies in Southeast Asia during World War II*, Basingstoke: Macmillan, 1991, p. 107.

[201] Thamsook Numnonda, *Thailand and the Japanese Presence, 1941-45*, Singapore: ISEAS, 1977, pp. 38-9.

[202] q. Reynolds, *Southern Advance*, p. 153.

[203] Kobkua Suwannathat-pian, *Thailand's Durable Premier*, Kuala Lumpur: Oxford Univ. Press, 1995, p. 265.

[204] q. Reynolds, *Southern Advance*, p. 155.

[205] q. ibid., p. 158.

a broadcast of February 1943 Chiang Kai-shek declared that the Chinese attributed Thailand's alliance with Japan and declarations of war to coercion, and themselves had no design on Thailand, nor any desire that might impair its independence. President Roosevelt 'fully endorsed the statement as of great value',[206] though the British made no statement, partly because they believed it might be necessary to secure Kra.

Just before the Chiang broadcast, Pridi had sent a young intellectual, Chamkat Phalangkun, to Chungking, to tell the Allies that he wished to escape from Thailand and set up a government-in-exile. No such step was taken. The United States was, however, supportive of the Free Siamese Movement led by the ambassador in Washington, Seni Pramoj, and while the British were less able than the Americans to disregard the declaration of war, they supported a contingent of Free Siamese in India. The first SOE-trained agents were dropped in north-central Thailand on 15 March 1944.

Pibun himself seems to have made contact with the Chinese as well. Arguably his plan to move the capital to Phetchabun, announced in October 1943, was designed as a means of relocating his headquarters. There he might watch events and determine the right moment to turn against the Japanese, and he might also more readily link up with the Chinese. A news article in May 1944 described the move as 'a matter closely connected with the preservation and development of national strength which is absolutely necessary for the achievement of our final victory in the war'.[207]

While adding to the growing Japanese distrust of Pibun, these moves also gave the Thai opposition an opportunity. That it took shortly after the fall of Saipan had led to Tojo's own resignation. The assembly rejected bills authorising the capital city project. Instead of ignoring it or dissolving it, Pibun resigned, and Pridi and his fellow regent, Prince Athit, accepted the resignation. On 29 July the assembly voted for Khuang Aphaiwong as prime minister. Pridi favoured him, but Athit did not. On 31 July, however, he resigned, and Pridi became sole regent. He advised Khuang to form a new cabinet.

At this point Pibun was still supreme commander. He expressed

[206] q. N. Tarling, 'Atonement before Absolution: British Policy towards Thailand during World War II', *Journal of the Siam Society*, 66, 1 (January 1978), p. 30.
[207] q. Reynolds, *Southern Advance*, p. 171.

his determination to stay on and fight the Japanese. CID Division Chief Chalo Sisarakon asked him:

What kind of fight could you engage in since you have never contacted the United States and Britain? How could you manage successfully alone? Before, you ordered the people to stop fighting, but if you want to fight again, you should first contact other countries. ... Fighting against the Japanese alone is like clapping one hand. How can you make a noise?[208]

On 24 August the government abolished the post of supreme commander and gave Pibun a merely titular advisory post.

The Japanese did not intervene. 'If there is a government which cooperates with Japan, based on the Japanese-Thai alliance, whoever is prime minister, we will not interfere,' Nakamura had declared.[209] They did not trust the opposition any more than they now trusted Pibun. A showdown, however, would have meant taking much-needed troops from Burma. Allowing a change of government also demonstrated the flexibility of the Sphere. The Koiso government sent a new ambassador, Yamamoto Kuma'ichi.

The Khuang government had the difficult task of reassuring the Japanese, while allowing or facilitating contacts with the Allies. Khuang's famous charm helped. So did his offer of a supplementary military assistance loan, and his readiness to attend the second Greater East Asia conference. In fact, of course, the Japanese knew of the Allied contacts. They did not, however, wish to make things worse, provoking open guerrilla war and demanding additional military commitments. Nakamura did not realise who 'Ruth', the British contact, was. He thought it was Police General Adun. In fact it was Pridi himself.[210]

When the Japanese finally overthrew the Vichy regime in March, the foreign ministry instructed Yamamoto to assure Khuang of support for his government and for Thai independence. Some Southern Army staff officers argued for a takeover in Thailand as well. Nakamura, commanding what had now become the 39th Army, opposed it, as did Yamamoto. In French Indo-China, the latter reminded Tokyo on 24 May, the Japanese had only to deal 'with a few thousand Frenchmen who didn't have the cooperation

---

[208] q. Ibid., p. 196.

[209] q. Ibid., p. 193.

[210] Ichizawa Kenjiro K.M. de Silva *et al.*, eds, *Asian Panorama*, New Delhi: Vikas, 1990, p. 463.

of 26 million colonials'. In Thailand, 'we must expect that 16 million Thai, inflamed with traditional pride, would all resist desperately.' That would divert Imperial troops from their main task. Moreover, 'based on our war aims and the ideals of the Greater East Asia Declaration, we should avoid with all our might having to infringe on the independence and sovereignty of an allied country because of operational necessity.'[211]

In May 1945 Pridi surprised the Allies by proposing a Free Thai uprising. A further Japanese loan-request was the ostensible cause of the 'crisis' to which he referred. His main concern, however, was international. No government-in-exile had been set up, and the British had been particularly reserved about Thailand's future. A rising at that point did not fit in with Mountbatten's plans, and it was discouraged. That meant, however, that Pridi had established something of an obligation towards Thailand without having had to take action. When the Japanese surrendered, he stated that the declaration of war had been unconstitutional, and renounced the territorial acquisitions of 1943.[212]

Yamamoto admired the Thais' performance:

It must be said that Thailand's scheme for managing the end of the war by separating from the Japanese camp without irritating the feelings of allied Japan and without causing her loss of face, and by becoming a semi-ally of the Allies, had been executed with extreme skill. Accordingly, it can be forecast that the Allied side will be more liberal than expected toward Thailand.[213]

Though they made no territorial demand on Kra, the British were indeed to have great difficulty in enforcing their main demand, a free delivery of rice. That, and the retrocession of the 1940-1 acquisitions, weakened Pridi, however, and promoted the military comeback in 1947.

Indo-China

In Indo-China the Japanese were present both longer and shorter than elsewhere in Southeast Asia. Their troops moved into northern Vietnam in September 1940. It was not, however, till March

---

[211] q. Reynolds, *Southern Advance*, pp. 207-8.

[212] N. Tarling, 'Rice and Reconciliation: The Anglo-Thai Peace Nogotiations of 1945', *Journal of the Siam Society*, 66, 2 (July 1978), p. 69.

[213] q. Reynolds, *Southern Advance*, p. 230.

1945 that they turned out the French. Their emphasis on continuity was thus at its greatest where they found the colonial regime the most collaborative. After the coup they encouraged the setting-up of independent regimes without any of the preparatory steps they had pursued elsewhere. There was, indeed, little time for them to establish themselves.

Nor was it clear who would or could lead them. The French had kept the monarchies, but confined their role. Prewar they had also repressed the nationalists. In the Vichy phase they had belatedly sought to mobilise support in order to pre-empt the Japanese, as Pibun claimed he was doing. The major political force at the end of the war was, however, the Vietnamese communist movement, which took advantage of the north's unique proximity to China, and which neither the French nor the Japanese were able to eliminate.

Though they established a federal structure in what they called Indo-China – effecting it in 1897, two years after the creation of the FMS – the French had acquired the territories piecemeal and dealt with them differently. Their first major step was a war with Vietnam in 1858. That had resulted in the acquisition of Saigon and in the creation out of six provinces of southern Vietnam of a colony called Cochinchina. Further conflict with Vietnam and with China in 1883-5 led to the assumption of control over the rest of Vietnam. It was not, however, formally made into a colony. Instead it was in effect divided into two protectorates, one, Tonkin, ruled more directly than the other, Annam, ostensibly on behalf of the Nguyen emperor at Hue.

The other two constituents of the five-part federation were Cambodia and Laos. Over them both Nguyen Vietnam and Siam had claimed suzerainty. Making the kingdom of Cambodia a protectorate in 1863 was a first step in fending off the claims of the Thais, though it left the Khmers exposed to the Vietnamese without a balance but for the French. The position of Laos was yet more equivocal. Though their expansion led the French into a confrontation with the Thais – marked by the Paknam incident of 1893 – they did not acquire the whole of Laos, much of which was incorporated into Siam. Nor did the Lao kingdom they protected control the whole of French Laos.

The earliest nationalist movements were directly connected with the mandarin loyalists who resisted 'pacification' in Tonkin in the 1880s. Initially they proposed to restore the monarchy and looked to Japan. Following his expulsion from Japan, however, Phan Boi Chau turned to revolutionary China and the KMT model. Another nationalist, Phan Chu Trinh, sought concessions from the protecting power by invoking the principles of its own revolution of 1789. The response was entirely negative: the French would not go even as far as the Dutch.

In the colony of Cochinchina nationalism emerged rather later and as a result of substantial economic and social changes. Again, however, the French offered its moderate elements little or nothing. Nguyen An Ninh, an admirer of the French, told a demonstration in 1926: 'There is no collaboration possible between French and Annamites. The French have nothing more to do here. Let them give us back the land of our ancestors.'[214] In 1930 the French reacted to the Yen Bay mutiny, and to the peasant unrest in Nghe An and Ha Tinh that drew in the newly formed Indo-Chinese Communist Party (ICP), with a policy of 'frightfulness'. 'Really, we should do something else here than repress,' wrote Grandjean, the secretary to the Résident Supérieur Annam in January 1931.[215] The Popular Front government of 1936 promised a commission of inquiry, but did not fulfil its promise.

The undeclared war led the ICP to call on the Popular Front government to grant democratic concessions and to be ready to distribute weapons widely. That was not done, and the Trotskyists 'openly predicted that French imperialists and Japanese fascists would get into bed with each other.'[216] The pretender Cuong De, allowed to slip back into Japan in 1915, moved to Shanghai in early 1939, and formed the Viet Nam Phuc Quoc Dong Minh Hoi (Vietnamese National Restoration League). Within Vietnam some groups responded to his pro-Japanese propaganda. In the south the Cao Dai sect supported the League, and a pro-Japanese Dai Viet (Greater Vietnam) party was set up in the north.

Restoration League auxiliaries took part in the Langson clash of 22 September 1940. After the Trotskyist prediction had proved accurate, some stayed on, and were joined by local ICP cadres in

---

[214] q. William J. Duiker, *The Rise of Nationalism in Vietnam*, Ithaca, NY: Cornell Univ. Press, 1976, p. 148.

[215] q. Hue-Tam Ho Tai, *Radicalism and the Origins of the Philippine Revolution*, Cambridge, MA: Harvard Univ. Press, 1992, p. 248.

[216] Marr in McCoy, *Southeast Asia*, p. 130.

what the ICP called the Bac Son uprising. The French reoccupied Langson in a particularly brutal manner. Up to 1,000 of the League men struggled back into KMT China. Cuong De, meanwhile, had been escorted back to Tokyo.

Isolated from France, the Vichy regime took steps to win support, in so doing at once pre-empting the Japanese and taking steps like those they took elsewhere, with results that were again unpredictable. More Vietnamese were promoted to the middle and upper echelons of the administration: the number doubled between 1940 and 1944. Decoux sought to evoke loyalty to an 'Indochinese nation', and to emphasise Pétainist values: family, work, country. Such values had their appeal, though the colonial office was optimistic in declaring: 'The marshal's cult is spreading among the Annamites ... the ideas of Labor Family and Country parallel the Confucian ideas at the base of Annamite civilization.'[217]

The youth organisations, *Sports et Jeunesses*, set up by Decoux's assistant, the naval officer Maurice Ducoroy, to distract attention from Japanese propaganda had perhaps 200,000 participants by late 1943. But, as Marr puts it, 'from March 1945 the French would have no control over the uses to which these young minds and bodies would be put.'[218] '[M]ore Viet-Minh company commanders were to graduate from that Petainist youth corps than from all the Viet-Minh Communist cadre schools.'[219]

While the Japanese did not support Cuong De, many of those in Indo-China sympathised with non-communist groups who wished to eject the French. The groups were, however, 'quite unable to build themselves to a point where they represented any serious threat to French rule'.[220] The Japanese protected the Cao Dai leaders, and also those of the Buddhist Hoa Hao sect. In May 1943 they sponsored a revival of the Restoration League, including Cao Dai, Hoa Hao and Dai Viet leaders. When, however, the French broke it up, they did not resist. Neither Vietnam nor Indo-China was on the agenda of the Greater East Asia conference in November.

The communists, learning from the Bac Son episode and from

[217] q. Bruce M. Lockhart, *The End of the Vietnamese Monarchy*, New Haven: Yale Univ. Press, 1993, p. 121.

[218] Marr McCoy, *Southeast Asia*, p. 137.

[219] Bernard B. Fall, *The Two Viet-Nams*, New York: Praeger, 1963, p. 48.

[220] Marr in McCoy, *Southeast Asia*, p. 139.

the ICP-led uprising in Cochinchina that Decoux had savagely put down in November 1940, worked out ways in which to benefit from the crisis of authority. It was necessary, they realised, both to create a guerrilla force and to win mass backing. While Chinese support was important, that had, moreover, to be done within Vietnam, so that the movement could at the critical moment offer something to the Allies in their struggle with the Japanese. With the coup of 9 March and the elimination of the Free French network, the Viet Minh or Independence League, which had been founded by the ICP in 1940-1, indeed became more important to the Allies. It was not, however, the moment to seize power, the ICP concluded. The communists should prepare for a general insurrection, 'for example when the Japanese Army surrenders to the Allies or when the Allies are decisively engaged in Indochina'.[221]

Other Vietnamese meanwhile welcomed the independence the Japanese offered. It was, however, a limited offer, a 'fake', as some saw it. The Japanese commander told the emperor, Bao Dai: 'We would like to avoid the changes and disturbances which would harm security and order. For that reason, we would like that, with regard to the political and administrative aspects, reforms be effected only within the most necessary limits of the strategic arrangements.'[222] The Japanese army, it was announced, would

support any endeavour to satisfy the eager desire for independence, so dear to all the peoples of Indo-China. It declares at the same time that it is its firm intention to fulfil the duties incumbent upon it for the defence of Indo-China, in collaboration with the above mentioned peoples and to help their sincere national movement in conformity with the fundamental principles of the declaration of Greater East Asia.[223]

Yokoyama Masayuki, supreme adviser to Bao Dai, urged him to proclaim the independence of his kingdom. In the proclamation of 11 March he unilaterally abrogated the protectorate treaty of 1884. Tran Trong Kim, a retired school inspector and respected writer who had been protected by the Japanese, formed a cabinet in April. Asserting the unity of the kingdom was not easy, let alone taking over control. In June, Phan Ke Toai, the imperial delegate

[221] q. Marr in ibid., p. 145.
[222] q. Huynh Kim Khanh, 'The Vietnamese August Revolution Reinterpreted', *JAS*, 30, 4 (August 1971), p. 765.
[223] q. Nitz, 'Japanese Military Policy', pp. 345-6.

in Tonkin (Bac Ky), was made responsible to the imperial government in Hué instead of the governor-general, General Tsuchihashi Yuki, commander of the 38th Army. Only in August, however, did Tsuchihashi agree to the transfer of Cochinchina, pointing to the emergence of Cambodian claims. No real authority was granted in defence, internal security, foreign affairs or communications. The surrender of the Japanese thus offered Ho Chi Minh his opportunity.

In contact with the OSS, he was probably informed promptly of the bombs and the Soviet entry. On 12 August he ordered the general uprising. It became clear that the Japanese would not resist the takeover of Hanoi, effected on 19 August. Ho telegraphed OSS:

We were fighting Japs on the side of the United Nations. Now Japs surrendered. We beg United Nations to realize their solemn promise that all nationalities will be given democracy and independence. If United Nations forget their solemn promise and don't grant independence, we will keep fighting until we get it.[224]

Bao Dai tried to save his government by offering Viet Minh participation, and by appeals to world leaders, then abdicated on 25 August. A week later Ho proclaimed independence. He evoked the US Declaration of Independence and the Rights of Man. 'All the peoples on the earth are equal from birth, all the peoples have a right to live, be happy and free.'[225]

The struggle was to be a long one. That was not so much because the French were wrong in their prediction that, once its continuity was broken, their rule would be difficult to resume. Much more it was the result of their negative policy towards Vietnamese nationalism, which enabled the communists to take the lead, and involved the Vietnamese nationalist struggle with the Cold War. In the few months that remained to them after the coup, the Japanese had done little to build up the non-communist nationalists. Nor were the Americans to succeed.

If not for the coup, Marr suggests, 'Decoux almost surely could have kept the colonial system intact, quelled any disturbances at the end of the war, and delivered Indochina back to the French government of the day.' If the Japanese and the imperial Vietnam-

[224] q. Marr in McCoy, *Southeast Asia*, p. 147.
[225] q. Allen B. Cole, ed., *Conflict in Indo-China and International Repercussions*, Ithaca, NY: Cornell Univ. Press, 1956, p. 19.

ese government had been given several years to devise alternatives to the colonial system, then 'Vietnam's fate might have been very different'.[226]

In Cambodia prewar nationalism was limited. In 1942, one of its representatives, Pach Choeun, was arrested for his role in an anti-French demonstration, and another, Son Ngoc Thanh, fled the country. With the coup independence had 'fallen out of the sky',[227] and in May Son Ngoc Thanh, brought back by the Japanese, became King Sihanouk's foreign minister. In July the Japanese encouraged the organisation of a militia, the Green Shirts, and on 10 August some broke into the palace and demanded that the king change his cabinet.

On 15 August, the day of the surrender, Son Ngoc Thanh became prime minister. He vainly sought an end to French protection, appealing both to the Viet Minh and to Pridi. Sihanouk reluctantly welcomed the French back – they promised to regain the lost territories – and a new agreement was signed. In the subsequent years, however, Sihanouk put himself at the head of the struggle for independence. His success abroad created a dangerous monopoly of power at home.

In Laos the loss of territory to Thailand in 1941 had prompted the Vichy regime to implement a policy of Lao Nhay (Lao Renovation). It also allowed Luang Prabang to extend its authority over Xieng Khouang, Vientiane and Nam Ta. Sports et Jeunesses was active, and more schools were built than in the whole of the period since 1893. Crown Prince Savang responded to the coup by assuming power and relegating the prime minister, Prince Phetsarath. That was done perhaps with Free French connivance.

The royal family were pro-French, as the Free French promised to restore the lost territory. On the arrival of the Japanese troops, however, the king declared the independence of Luang Prabang on 8 April, and Phetsarat resumed his post. Some, like Katay Don Sasorith, saw little option but to collaborate with the Japanese in face of the Vietnamese threat.[228] No one knew when the war would end. On the Japanese surrender Phetsarath reaffirmed

---

[226] Marr, *Vietnam 1945*, pp. 149-50.

[227] q. D. Chandler, 'The Kingdom of Kampuchea', *JSEAS*, 17, 1 (March 1986), p. 92.

[228] C.J. Christie, 'Marxism and the History of the Nationalist Movements in Laos', *JSEAS*, 10, 1 (March 1979), p. 149.

independence, and declared Laos a unitary state. The French were, however, able to secure the lost provinces and re-establish their relations with Laos.

The prime factor in the policy of Laos, as of Cambodia, was its relationship with its larger neighbours. In this sense the Japanese were to be seen as protectors, in succession to the French. The return of the French brought the return of the territories of which the Japanese had earlier deprived Cambodia and Laos for the benefit of the Thais. But it was in the coming years to engulf them in the war in Vietnam, and that all but destroyed them.

6

DEMAND AND SUPPLY

Disruption and inflation

The ideology of the Greater East Asia Co-Prosperity Sphere was, as its name suggests, not only political but economic in content. Politically it sought to place itself both in the tradition of right-wing expansion and also in a more modern form that strove to transcend imperialism through an association of nations with Japan at the head. Economically it again emphasised Japan's leadership, grounded in this case on its industrial transformation. Again it modified the Western model, inasmuch as it was more prepared to promote industrialisation in its dependencies, at least in Korea and Manchuria.

The concept of co-existence and co-prosperity arose from the recognition that Japan's future, like its past, must in large measure be related to China, and its development into the concept of a Sphere was part of an attempt to place that long-standing relationship in a new context. The Sphere concept was also developed, however, in a larger context, promoted by the encompassing growth of the superpowers, particularly the United States, and by the onset of the Depression. In a competitive world, where political power was more likely than ever to back up economic objectives, security, economic as well as political, might be found in breaking the world into more or less autarkic spheres.

The general viability of the concept was doubtful. It might rather be seen as an argument in economic diplomacy, a 'weapon' in trade war. Certainly the general internationalisation of trade was so far advanced as to ensure that dividing the world into economic spheres would be extraordinarily disruptive, and more likely to ensure the continuance of the Depression than to find a way out of it. Most of Japan's cotton, for example, came from outside the putative Sphere, from India and the United States. As a temporary and partial device, however, it might offer some advantages that could be turned to account when world trading

218

patterns renewed the expansion that had marked them for over a century before the Great Depression. But it was no basis for 'co-prosperity'.

Invading Southeast Asia was in itself to be destructive, particularly where, as in the Philippines, Malaya and Burma, there were substantial military struggles, and where the colonial powers engaged in scorched earth policies. The Japanese armies, moreover, were instructed to live off the land, and their food demands were burdensome. The occupation also made extended use of forced labour, drawing not only, as is well known, on prisoners of war, but also, perhaps less known, on the villages of Burma, Java and Malaya. The practice was indeed traditional in Southeast Asia, and it had continued to be used particularly by the French in the infrastructural projects. But the scale – and the ruthlessness – of its revival were dislocating. Much of it in the latter year or so went, too, on defence measures that proved worthless. At the same time, the Allies destroyed Japanese shipping, and intra-regional trade and trade with Japan itself collapsed.

Inflation hit all the occupied territories. The minister of finance had been clear that it would do so, as he had told the imperial conference on 1 December 1941:

In the past the southern areas that will be the scene of military operations imported a considerable quantity of goods; when we occupy these areas the imports will cease. Accordingly, to enable their economies to function smoothly, we should provide them with goods; but our country does not have enough reserve capacity to do this. Hence for quite a long time it will not be possible for us to be concerned with the livelihood of the peoples in these areas. It must be said that even if we issue military scrip and other kinds of currency to secure goods and labor in these areas, it will be difficult to maintain their value. That is, it will be necessary for us to adopt a policy of self-sufficiency in these areas as much as possible, to keep the shipments from our country to the minimum amount necessary to maintain peace and order and to secure labour services there, and to disregard the decline in the value of paper money and the economic dislocation that will result from it.[1]

Inflation indeed worsened during the occupation, damaging Japan's rice policies, sharpening social tensions, alienating the masses. By late August 1942 the military administration had issued 40m. pesos, 20m. Straits dollars, 40m. Burma rupees and 10m. guilders. By March 1943, the figures were 172m. pesos, 303m.

---

[1] q. Ike, *Japan's Decision*, p. 275.

Straits dollars, 270m. rupees and 353m. guilders. From April 1943 Southern Development Bank notes were put into circulation. In the Indies the circulation rose to 674m. in December 1943, and 3,153m. at the end of the war. During the occupation of Malaya, the Japanese issued 4,000m. dollars in currency, eighteen times the amount circulating prewar.[2]

Even apart from the destruction that accompanied the invasion of Southeast Asia, the Japanese concept was, as the minister had recognised, destructive in itself, as far as the economy was concerned. There were meaningful economic ties with the core part of the empire, partly, of course, forced on it by the policies Japan pursued in Taiwan, Korea and Manchuria. There was also meaning, however controverted, in the concept of co-existence and co-prosperity with China. Not much meaning lay behind the Sphere as it extended south.

Southeast Asia had become very much part of the wider international patterns which the Sphere would disrupt. To those the trade within the region, in rice in particular, was linked: moreover, it used gunnies from India. The economic policies the ruling colonial powers pursued had recognised these international and regional links, and they had also shaped them by the state-building activities in which they engaged, by their infrastructural endeavours, and, in so far as they existed before the depression, by their protectionist or preferential measures.

Earlier patterns

This pattern had emerged only during the nineteenth and early twentieth centuries. Southeast Asia had, however, been involved in international trade for many centuries before that. It had as a result been linked with China and with India and, beyond that, with Europe well before the Europeans themselves arrived in the early sixteenth century. The 'age of commerce' of which Tony Reid has comprehensively written began in the mid-fifteenth century and lasted into the seventeenth century. The recession of its middle decades encouraged the Dutch East India Company in its monopoly policies. By the end of the century, however, their English rivals were establishing new links with India and China, in which maritime Southeast Asia could not but be involved.

[2] P. Kratoska, 'Banana Money: Consequences of the Demonetization of Wartime Japanese Currency in British Malaya', *JSEAS*, 23, 2 (September 1992), p. 326.

Those preceded the larger changes that the industrial revolution brought. A pattern of largely intra-Asian trade was now overlaid by a pattern of colonial and international trade, tied more closely to European markets by the opening of the Suez Canal in 1869. Netherlands India produced coffee, sugar and later tobacco for world markets. Under Spanish rule the Philippines put sugar and hemp on international markets and came to import rice and textiles. Under American rule, it gained a protected sugar market. Malaya sent its tin to the West, as it had traditionally sent it to China. Introduced into Malaya, rubber became Britain's dollar-earner in the early twentieth century, when the automobile industry was created. Like lower Burma and Siam, Cochinchina became a major rice producer, important for the international market, but also for other parts of the region that became dependent on imports. Major Western companies exploited the oil of Burma, of southern Sumatra, of southeastern, and northwestern Borneo. At first an entrepot for the trade within Asia, Singapore came to fill a larger role, attracting, indeed, much of the trade of Netherlands India as well as British Malaya.

The seventeenth-century recession had affected the trade of Southeast Asia. The depression after 1929 had a dramatic impact. It struck a devastating blow at the Java sugar industry. It prompted restriction schemes for producers of natural rubber that in the longer term conduced to the production of a synthetic substitute. It also prompted protectionist measures in Netherlands India, and some industrialisation developed behind them. It did not, however, produce a fundamental change in the pattern.

In all these phases the Japanese had played some part. Japanese silver contributed to the expansion of the sixteenth century, and Japanese traders were active in the mainland states before the Tokugawa seclusion. They reappeared after the Meiji Restoration, even the prostitutes contributing to the overseas earnings that modernisation required.[3] The 1920s had prompted a rationalisation of Japanese manufacturing,[4] and in the 1930s Japanese traders benefited from the relative cheapness of Japanese goods.

[3] cf. James F. Warren, *Ah Ku and Karayuki-san*, Singapore: Oxford Univ. Press, 1993, pp. 7-9, 85.

[4] P. Post, 'Japan and the Integration of the Netherlands East Indies into the World Economy, 1868-1942', *Review of Indonesian and Malaysian Affairs*, 27 (1993), p. 135.

It was also, of course, in that decade that the Japanese government began to take a more definite interest in the area. National
policy companies, *kokosaku kaisha*, were formed on the model of
the Toyo Takushoku Kabushiki Kaisha (Oriental Colonisation
Company), formed to exploit Korea in 1908. Both Nanyo Takushoka
KK (South Sea Colonisation Company), established on a colonial
ministry initiative for Micronesia in 1936, and Taiwan Takushoku,
established the same year, concerned themselves with Southeast
Asia as well. The South Seas Association (Nanyo Kyokai), founded
by government and business interests in 1915 after the occupation
of the German Pacific islands, had also become involved with the
'South Seas areas', and the Nanyo Kohatsu KK (South Seas Development Company), established in 1921 to develop what had become the mandates, became identified with the government and
turned to the Indies. Ishihara Hiroichiro, 'the single most prominent Japanese business figure in Southeast Asia before the Pacific
War',[5] was both backed and checked by the government when he
competed with Dutch shipping.[6] The great *zaibatsu*, Mitsui and
Mitsubishi, also increasingly involved themselves in Southeast
Asia. They were to do well in the occupation.

The relationship of economic and political activities among
the Europeans had been diverse. The East India companies had
been squarely backed by their respective states, though often able
to operate with a large degree of autonomy. The more complex
relationships of the nineteenth century had produced a more differentiated approach. The creation of colonial regimes was rarely
the direct result of economic interests, and the Colonial Office in
London took a hands-off view. Once established, however, the
colonial administrations developed closer relationships with the
enterprises established in their territories, though their objectives
were even so not always identical.

Within Japan the networks that sought to influence policy were
perhaps more elaborate and more effective. When the prospect of
adding to the empire emerged, those networks became especially
active. There were still tensions, however. The government saw
itself as acting in the interests of the homeland in broad strategic
and economic terms. It did not see itself as backing commercial

[5] Peattie in Duus *et al.*, *Japanese Wartime Empire*, p. 202.
[6] H. Dick, 'Japan's Economic Expansion in the Netherlands Indies between
the First and Second World Wars', *JSEAS*, 20, 2 (September 1989), p. 256.

interests in particular, still less particular commercial interests. In April 1941 a retired colonel, Sugano Kengo, who had spent several months in the Indies, suggested that the Japanese residents could play only a limited role in Japan's Heaven-sent task: 'They are the so-called trading class, imbued with a mercenary spirit that has no intention of working for the extension of national power based on a broader viewpoint. There is no hope of increasing Japanese influence through them.'[7]

The army planners adopted something of the same view. Former Japanese residents – who had gone to Japan as war loomed and might now return – might be used if suitable as guides, interpreters or advisers, or in some cases as managers of enterprises. 'Japanese nationals wishing to enter the occupied areas after the start of military preparations', declared the principles of 20 November 1941, 'shall be carefully screened beforehand, and preference shall be given to former residents now residing in Japan and desiring to return to these areas.'[8] The navy's outline on the conduct of military administration in occupied areas, dated 14 March 1942, declared that Japanese nationals wishing to enter the territories would be 'rigorously screened'. They had to be 'guided and educated to a firm realization of and the necessary temperament of their role as the leading people, so as to gain the devotion and respect of the local residents through proper leadership'.[9]

Only in 1943, as Japan's position deteriorated, did the military authorities in Java begin to make effective use of the returnees. 'Allocation of the returnees in various fields was undertaken in order to have them work in the production and distribution of resources and materials', the military, however, insisted, 'and we are not thinking of giving any new rights to the returnees'.[10] The *zaibatsu* and other large companies benefited most from the policies the army and navy pursued.

Wartime patterns

The main principles for economic policies in the southern areas were decided by the sixth committee of the planning board on 11

[7] q. Goto, '*Returning to Asia*', p. 255.
[8] q. Benda *et al.*, *Japanese Military Administration*, p. 2.
[9] q. Ibid., p. 30.
[10] q. Goto, '*Returning to Asia*', p. 269.

December 1941, and ratified by the relevant ministers the following day. The main objectives – to apply in French Indo-China and
Thailand as well as the other territories – were 'to contribute to the
war effort by developing important resources and building up
the self-sufficiency of the Japanese empire'.[11] The production of
petroleum, seen, of course, as particularly important, was to be
expanded by the army and navy, with the assistance of Japanese
petroleum companies. Other minerals the planning board emphasised were nickel, copper, bauxite, chrome, manganese, mica,
phosphate, metals necessary for special steel manufacturing, and
non-ferrous metals, not tin.

It formulated criteria for selecting the companies to be involved:
they should have sufficient experience and capacity. A single
company should develop a resource in a particular region, but two
or more should be involved in developing the same resource
across the region. '[N]ewcomers in the sectors of agriculture, forestry and fisheries should be curbed.' The government had 'no
intention of promoting manufacturing in the areas, with the
exception of shipbuilding and the repair of equipment needed
for development'.[12] The planning board, and later the first section
of the liaison committee of the ministry of Greater East Asia,
decided on the companies that would take part.

The deterioration in Japan's position led the liaison committee
to revise the criteria on 29 May 1943. The loss of convoys led to an
emphasis on self-sufficiency, and that changed the attitude to
manufacturing. 'Japanese authorities should promote local manufacturing industries judged to be crucial', including 'the production of everyday requirements, especially textiles, for the sake of
self-sufficiency'. 'Japanese middle and small-scale manufacturers
should be utilized in suitable industries.'[13]

Hikita Yasuyuki's research group has shown that Indonesia was
the most important area and that the big businesses, *zaibatsu* and
others, played the largest role. 'They received 69.2% of all orders:
the zaibatsu 45.8%, and other big companies 23.4%.' The *zaibatsu*
were especially dominant in army areas, while state and local
companies had a much larger role in navy areas. 'In the main, Japan's

---

[11] q. Hikita Yasuyuki in Peter Post and Elly Touwen-Bouwsma, eds, *Japan, Indonesia and the War*, Leiden: KITLV P, 1997, p. 138.

[12] q. Ibid., p. 139.

[13] q. Ibid.

economic rule in Indonesia depended on private big businesses.'[14] Mitsubishi monopolised soap, cigarettes, soya beans and inter-island trade. Mitsui monopolised coconut oil.[15]

The trade between the occupied areas and the homeland involved many medium-scale and local companies as well as *zaibatsu* companies. Many of the former were linked to the control agencies, which were the core of the Japanese trading network. The large companies traded through the agencies and also between branches and main offices. The *zaibatsu* companies formed the 'sub-core' of the network. The network was in turn connected with local distributing and producing networks, official or black market. Each kind of business had its *kumiai*, Japanese-led inter-ethnic groups of businessmen brought together to provide a means of control. In Java, for example, commercial *kumiai* obtained food-stuffs from the army administration and distributed them to the public. Industrial *kumiai* obtained raw materials from Japanese organisations and supplied finished products.

The Japanese companies 'investigated local resources enthusiastically'.[16] In that, of course, they were continuing a long-standing activity that the colonial powers had viewed with some suspicion and increasingly sought to impede. Now the barriers they imposed were removed. The investigation team the government sent to French Indo-China in June 1941 was 'the first of many'.[17] The immediate aim was to contribute to the war effort, but the information was to be put to good use after the war.

The same was true of the Chinese trading networks. '[I]n Indonesia ... the Japanese must shake hands with the Chinese,' Ide Iwata of the Taiwan governor-general's office had written, 'and expand our mutual economic influence through division of work. We can utilize their distinctive distributive network for the development of a New World.'[18] The relationship with the Chinese in the occupation was ambivalent. But they were used for 'Southern construction', while at the same time they found new opportunities in smuggling and the black market, created by controls and

---

[14] Ibid., p. 138.

[15] Twang Peck Yang, *The Chinese Business Elite in Indonesia and the Transition to Independence 1940-1950*, Kuala Lumpur: Oxford Univ. Press, 1998, pp. 79-80.

[16] Hikita in Post and Bouwsma, *Japan, Indonesia and the War*, p. 149.

[17] Ibid., p. 150.

[18] q. Goto, '*Returning to Asia*', p. 413.

shortages, and established new networks, like that centred on Karimun, 'little Syonan'.[19]

The failure of Japanese economic policy was not merely the result of wartime conditions alone. It was also a result of misconception. Only a long-term occupation, and the kind of ruthless assimilationism adopted in Korea, could have worked the change it sought. Whatever its source, however, the failure of co-prosperity was a factor, along with the overall deterioration of Japan's strategic position, in prompting the political concessions that began to give a more liberal meaning to the political implications of the Sphere.

The leaders of colonial Southeast Asia were offered a greater measure of independence, at the same time as the economic position of the masses in what the journalist Kuroda called the Co-Poverty Sphere[20] deteriorated. They could hardly be expected to decline what was offered. For most of them, it was indeed a step towards independence postwar. They had to seek it, however, amid harsh conditions, deep resentments and high expectations. It was only with their political success, however, that a real break in the colonial economic patterns could be brought about. To that, of course, the Japanese and the Chinese networks were to be substantial contributors, and they were also to be substantial beneficiaries.

Netherlands India

The Dutch had expanded Java's production of coffee and sugar in the nineteenth century, initially through the 'cultivation system', and then through private, though still state-supported, enterprise. In the late nineteenth and early twentieth centuries the Outer Islands had become mere significant exporters. That was the result of the production not only of oil but also of copra, coffee and rubber. The Japanese were involved as traders, retailers and investors.

The First World War had provided Japan with an opportunity in Netherlands India as elsewhere in East and Southeast Asia. It disrupted existing patterns of shipping and trade, particularly, after the Germans resorted to unrestricted submarine warfare, the connection with Europe. European firms in the East ordered

[19] Twang, *Chinese Business Elite*, pp. 90-5.
[20] q. Nakamura, 'General Imamura', p. 26.

industrial goods from Japan. Japanese shipping also competed with Dutch shipping, impeded by requisitions by the Allied powers. With the end of the war and the worldwide recession, imports of Japanese goods fell away, and the Japanese flag all but disappeared from the feeder services it had penetrated.

The rationalisation of Japanese manufacturing in the 1920s laid the basis for the rapid development of Japan's trade in the 1930s. The Japanese community – 7,195 (including Taiwanese) in 1930 – was the largest of the groups classified as European. It was mainly engaged in retailing and the service sector. 'Japanese shops were the last link in a direct Japanese-controlled chain from the Japanese producer to the Indies consumer.'[21] Unpegging the yen from the gold standard at the end of 1931 gave Japan a major advantage in world markets, particularly for textiles and light manufactures. It was particularly successful in the Indies textile market, promoting the Dutch to introduce quota restrictions under the Crisis Import Ordinance of 1933. The small Japanese retailers and import houses competed with *zaibatsu* firms and those sponsored by Nanyo Kyokai. The trend was against the former group, and the typical Toko Jepang was challenged by *zaibatsu*-owned retail stores by the late 1930s.[22]

Japanese investment also grew in the interwar period. The main foci were rubber and copra plantations and fisheries, timber, mining and oil. The involvement in the Indies of the *kokosaku kaisha* was limited. The Dutch, however, reluctantly permitted Nanyo Kohatsu KK to develop cotton plantations in Dutch New Guinea. Among the *zaibatsu* Mitsui and Mitsubishi were very active, and from 1917 Nomura became something of a specialist in Indies investment. It was also interested in rubber in south Kalimantan. Timber companies were also involved in that region, demand having expanded after the earthquake. Nanyo Ringyo Kabushiki, a subsidiary of Toyo Takushoku, was active in Kutai.

Japanese business success, the consul at Surabaya declared in January 1929, resulted from 'the untiring efforts and thoughtful activities of the individuals concerned', 'made possible by their living in a paradise under the good administration of the Netherlands East Indies government'. His successor took a somewhat

---

[21] Dick, 'Japan's Economic Expansion', p. 250.

[22] P. Post in J. Th. Lindblad, ed., *Historical Foundations of a National Economy in Indonesia*, Amsterdam: North-Holland, 1996, pp. 302, 308-9.

different line ten years later: 'The greatest gift to our brave men in the battlefield would be to tell them that their compatriots in the South Seas are desperately sustaining their commercial front despite various restrictions, making great strides forward together with the warriors on the China front.'[23] The contrast suggested the growing polarisation among the Japanese even before the war, between the more settled group of traders and retailers and the migrant group serving the *zaibatsu*, banks and consulates, often adherents of southern policy. The policies of the occupation sustained, even expanded, the differences.

In Java sugar agriculture, struck a major blow by the Depression, had by 1941 regained some 50 per cent of its 1930 peak. The Taiwan sugar industry, however, had made the Japanese self-sufficient by 1928, and they had no use for the Java product: by 1945 production was .018 per cent of its level in 1930. The Japanese – like the Dutch under the cultivation system – sought to establish new export crops, in particular cotton. It was started in 1943, using seed and credit provided by Mitsui or Mitsubishi companies, who also bought the crop. Labour was mobilised by the village, and proceeds went to the peasants, to the village or to the headmen. Peasants were also forced to cultivate jarak, the castor oil plant, used as an aircraft lubricant. Sisal was also grown and hand-woven into gunny sacks.

Java's main product was, of course, rice, largely intended to meet the needs of its own population. In the occupation phase it failed to do so, and, though the reasons for that have been controverted, it is clear that the hunger and famine conditions must largely be blamed on Japanese policies. The additional demands made by the occupying army do not appear to have been the main cause. Nor was the recruitment of *romusha*, either in the sense that it affected the supply of agricultural labour or that it created an additional demand.

The objectives of the policy were, indeed, sound enough. They were, by securing the rice surplus of the villages, to prevent war profiteering and secure equitable distribution at stable prices. The concept was, however, more relevant to the relatively simple structure of the rice industry in the homeland than to the complex position in Java,[24] and its implementation was badly managed.

[23] q. Goto '*Returning to Asia*', pp. 223, 228.

[24] Sato, War, pp. 113-14.

Prices were set too low, and a black market emerged. Of this not all could take advantage: those who had been wage labourers on plantations or in factories were particularly badly off.[25]

In their attempts to secure the surplus, the Japanese once more relied on the village officials. Their tasks, under the Japanese as under the Dutch, were at once invidious and profitable. Enforced complicity contributed to 'the secular decline in the prestige and authority' of officials, politicians and businessmen, as Ben Anderson puts it.[26] 'The reputation of the leaders is ruined in the eyes of the people,' Ki Hadjar Dewantoro complained.[27] Usually not only the government's agents but also the main producers of the surplus, village officials manipulated the allocation of the quotas to their benefit.[28] At the same time, they also increased the quotas so that they might take advantage of the black market that developed as the fixed price became increasingly inadequate. The overall effect was to diminish rice production. It fell 35 per cent between 1942 and 1945.[29]

The effect of that was worsened by deficiencies in distribution. The residencies into which the Japanese had broken down the administration began to pursue self-sufficiency policies of their own, inhibiting the free flow of rice within the residency, and yet more crucially among residencies. The controls tightened as compulsory low-price deliveries were pursued. '[A]ll private food transmission has been forbidden', Van der Plas wrote in December 1944, 'which has created a desperate situation in regions with an habitual food shortage as for instance Madura. ... Several people have reported from Madura that they have seen people dying on the roads.'[30] In 1944, in all residencies except Jakarta and Priangan, the death rate exceeded the birth rate.[31]

The native officials also had the unenviable task of recruiting

---

[25] P. van der Eng in P. Kratoska, ed., *Food Supplies and the Japanese Occupation in South-East Asia*, Basingstoke: Macmillan, 1998, p. 201.

[26] B.R.O'G. Anderson, *Java in a Time of Revolution*, Ithaca, NY: Cornell Univ. Press, 1972, p. 14.

[27] q. Reid in McCoy, *Southeast Asia*, p. 21.

[28] Sato, *War*, pp. 130-1.

[29] P. van der Eng, *Food Supply in Java during War and Decolonisation*, Hull Univ., 1994, p. 17.

[30] q. Sato, *War*, p. 133.

[31] Kurasawa, '*Mobilization and Control*', p. 171.

romusha, meaning 'physical labourer', in fact describing impressed labour or forced labour. In traditional Southeast Asia, its effects had been modified by a widespread sense of mutual obligation and a recognition that labour was in short supply. In colonial Southeast Asia it had been largely displaced by contract and wage labour. The Japanese, however, saw *romusha* as 'expendable'. They had 'no notion of preserving and maintaining manpower so as to ensure its long term and constant supply'.[32]

Java was seen as a pool of labour, and many Javanese *romusha* were employed within Java as well as in other parts of the Indies and overseas. The initial tasks were to restore the infrastructure destroyed by Dutch scorched-earth policies. The labour demands, not unduly heavy, could be met more readily because the closure of Dutch estates led to unemployment. In the latter part of 1943, however, the defence build-up in the 'sphere to be absolutely defended' greatly expanded the demand for labour.

A meeting of labour managers for the southern regions met in Singapore in October, and between November and March 1944 labour recruitment agencies were established in most parts of Java. By November 1944, 2,623,691 *romusha* were employed in Java alone. Probably the whole of the mobilisable work force – 12.5 million – worked as *romusha* at one time or another, engaging in defence works, but also in often ill-conceived construction projects, designed to build a 'New Java'. Perhaps some 160,000 were sent outside Java, the numbers limited by the collapse of shipping facilities. Of these about 135,000 may have returned to Java after the war.[33] Before late 1943 *romusha* had been recruited on an *ad hoc* basis through the local *pangreh praja*. After the setting-up of the recruitment agencies, quotas were set at various levels, and the village head became 'finally responsible', having to decide 'who should be the victims'.[34] Through the central advisory council nationalist leaders sought to press for improved conditions, and the Body to Assist Working Soldiers (Badan Pembantu Perajurit Pekerja) was set up. But Sukarno and others made propaganda for the scheme, doing a week's service in September 1944 to show that labour was noble.

The cause of Indonesia's independence was advanced by the

[32] Ibid., pp. 220, 232.
[33] Sato, *War*, pp. 156-60.
[34] Kurasawa, 'Mobilization and Control', p. 243.

occupation, though that was not squarely the aim or the achievement of the Japanese. It exacted a heavy price, particularly from the landless labourers and the smallholders, 'coerced to sell their labour and rice to the occupation government', receiving in return military currency of little value. 'As a consequence of Japanese misrule numerous people suffered and died in their villages, at their work places, or on road sides; many without ever seeing a Japanese.'[35]

Malaya and Singapore

Malaya and Singapore had assumed a significant role in Britain's economy as a result of the development of the rubber industry. Initially Britain's economic interest in the peninsula was limited. The three Straits Settlements, founded partly for strategic reasons, tended to focus on external trade, and Singapore became a major entrepot, serving the archipelago as well as the peninsula. The peninsula was indeed thinly populated before the British intervention of the 1870s. Its main contribution to international trade was tin, mainly found on the west coast, which for centuries had been taken to China, and which in the nineteenth century, with the creation of the canning industry and the exhaustion of the Cornish mines, increasingly interested the British.

The disruption that the expansion of tin-mining caused – stimulating rivalry among the Malay chiefs and disputes among the immigrant Chinese – indeed helped to account for the establishment of the resident system in Perak, Selangor and Negri Sembilan. The subsequent infrastructure development in those states located the rubber industry when it was established after the turn of the century. The rise of the US automobile industry gave Malaya a new importance in British eyes: its rubber became a major dollar-earner.

At the same time, Singapore acquired a new importance, too. It benefited from the expansion of the Malayan economy, though without losing its status as an entrepot and a service centre for the maritime region as a whole. But it also acquired a new strategic importance with the decision to set up there the base that the British navy would need at a time of crisis. The Japanese conquest that demonstrated the failure of that strategy had a drastic effect on

---

[35] Sato, *War*, p. 200.

Malaya's economy. It offered little that Japan needed, while its chances of self-sufficiency were limited.

Before the war the most important Japanese investments were in rubber and iron-mining. The rubber boom of 1909-10 had prompted the Japanese to acquire rubber estates, and a Japanese Planters' Association was founded in Singapore in 1912.[36] By 1917 the Japanese had 130,000 acres, mainly in Johore.[37] The Rubber Lands (Restriction) Enactments of that year cut it back, but planting resumed when it was repealed after the war, with large Japan-based companies playing a bigger role. The production control schemes introduced in the recession of the 1920s and the depression of the 1930s were, however, discouraging, and the Japanese plantations never played a major role in supplying Japanese industry.

In this respect the prewar iron-mining enterprises in Malaya were more significant. The pioneer of Malaya's iron-mining was Ishihara Hiroichiro. The quality of the ores was poor, and they were of little interest except to the Japanese, who had few alternative sources. The main focus was in Johore and in other Unfederated States, Trengganu and Kelantan, where British administrators were ready to welcome investment. In 1928 Malaya provided about 40 per cent of Japan's iron consumption, and in 1937 the three Malayan states were producing about half of its ore imports.[38] Bauxite was also found in Johore.

While tin-mining and, in particular, the rubber industry had made Malaya important to the British, they did not interest their Japanese successors:

Malaya played almost no role in supplying raw materials because, with the exception of bauxite, the peninsula produced very little that Japan needed to prosecute the war. The primary economic advantage Japan won with the conquest of Malaya was that the resources of the peninsula were no longer available to the Allies, but in other respects Malaya was far more of a burden than an asset.[39]

[36] Yuen Choy Leng, 'Japanese Rubber and Iron Investments in Malaya, 1900-1941', *JSEAS*, 5, 1 (March 1974), p. 18.

[37] Yuen Choy Leng, 'The Japanese Community in Malaya before the Pacific War', JSEAS, 9, 2 (September 1978), p. 169.

[38] Yuen, 'Japanese Rubber', p. 33. Kratoska, *Japanese Occupation*, p. 243, says one-third.

[39] Kratoska, *Japanese Occupation*, p. 154.

In some sense the peninsula reverted to the position it had occupied before the British intervention, important only because of the existence of external interests. Singapore, indeed, lost its worldwide significance under the Japanese. It remained, however, a strategic centre of their empire in the south, and its facilities made it useful. The big shipyard had been granted to Mitsubishi even before the attack.

Encouraged by wartime purchasing, Malaya produced 547,000 tons of rubber in 1940. Japan's wartime requirements were 70,000-80,000 tons a year, and it had seized about 150,000 tons during its advance into the region. In 1944 its requirements were 35,000 tons, and some of that came from Indo-China and Thailand. Not much got to Germany. Only Japanese companies that had been involved in the industry prewar were allowed to handle rubber in the occupation, and they took over the operation of the enemy estates. Smallholders found it impossible to continue, and all the producers suffered from a severe shortage of the acid required as a coagulant for raw latex. Singapore rubber industries revived, but operated at a loss.

With the introduction of dredges, tin-mining had increasingly come into the hands of European enterprises, Britain's scorched-earth policy had targeted the dredges. It was hard to secure materials for restoring them, and hard to find lubricants to keep them going when restored. In any case, Malaya's tin production far exceeded Japan's requirements, and there were alternative sources in Thailand and Indo-China. Production fell during the occupation, and idle machinery was transferred to other industries or broken up.

The iron mines largely escaped the scorched-earth policy, and iron was mined during the occupation by private firms under the control of the military administration. Lacking equipment and labour, the mines did not work at full capacity, and shipments to Japan fell far short of expectations. Priority was given to the extraction of bauxite, found in Johore, and also in Bintan, where Furukawa took over the Dutch mines. In 1944 Johore and Bintan supplied Japan with 650,000 tons of bauxite, 80 per cent of its total supply. In 1945, however, Allied attacks made its shipment impossible.

Self-sufficiency, another goal of the invaders, was hard to secure. Before the war, Malaya had imported about two-thirds of its rice requirements from the major rice exporters of the region, Burma, Thailand and Indo-China. Most was needed in Perak and Selangor, but by the 1930s even the east coast states required imports, and only Kedah and Perlis produced a surplus. In Burma the infrastructure had been damaged by scorched-earth policies and by the fighting, but the rice export industries in Cochinchina and Thailand were 'unscathed', and they were unable to sell to India and to Europe. What prevented their supplying Malaya was the shortage of transport and fuel. Production declined, and the trading networks ceased to operate or became part of a black market. That was operated by small-scale suppliers from Burma, Thailand or the Indies. It was also operated within Malaya, since, as in Java, the quest for self-sufficiency extended downwards, to the state and even the district level.

Needing food for their personnel and for the population, the Japanese attempted both to implement an effective rationing system and to expand local production. 'You already know that to increase the production of foodstuffs is the primary function of the state,' the governor of Perak told his district officers in July 1943. 'It is the most important problem for assuring the people's living and securing of public peace.' If production did not increase, supply would be reduced. 'If we still go on supplying those idlers with food, that means we encourage them to idle away their time and retain their British and American corruptive thoughts. The only consequence will be that our fighting strength will be impaired.'[40]

The Japanese mixed threat and inducement. They released land from forest reserves, authorised tree cutting on rubber estates, and in some cases instructed smallholders to drop rubber and plant food products. They also allowed non-Malays to occupy land in Malay Reservations, though the policy was strongly opposed by Malay officials. Yet overall the size of the Malayan rice crop fell during the occupation. Low prices and the fear of confiscation played their part. So did the inadequate maintenance of irrigation schemes and the requisitioning of labour.

Initially the collapse of the estates and mines created unemployment, and the Japanese urged even the teachers and clerks to grow food. Increasingly, however, the Japanese recruited labour for military construction projects in Malaya and elsewhere, and by

[40] q. ibid., p. 265.

1944 there was a labour shortage. Quotas were assigned at the district level, and workers sent to work, for example, on the Kedah airport and the Dungun iron mines. European prisoners of war were sent to work on Burma-Thailand railway, but the Japanese made extensive use of conscripted Malayan labour, too. Some 75,000 workers, mostly Malay and Indian, were sent to Thailand: the death rate was 38 per cent.[41] Labourers were also sent to build a trans-Sumatra railway and an airfield in Borneo.

'The Kumiais ... helped Black Market activities by creating the maximum of inconvenience, difficulties and hardships for the public, by their sloppy and tyrannical methods of distribution of commodities,' wrote Chin Kee Onn. 'Many Kumiai-officials were themselves Black Market kings.'[42]

Borneo

British Borneo, unlike British Malaya, was not a major field of foreign economic enterprise. The Brooke raj had been ambivalent about 'development', while the Company found North Borneo unattractive to capitalists. In the interwar period oil gave Sarawak and Brunei a new importance. By 1941 production in Sarawak had declined, and the Sarawak Oilfields Company was concentrating on the richer field at Seria in the neighbouring sultanate.

Japanese first came to British Borneo in the 1880s. In Kuching they were petty traders and hawkers. Early in the new century, they took up rubber cultivation and market gardening on the fringes of the town, and in the town they were doctors, dentists, photographers and prostitutes. In the 1930s there was some tension between the fiscal interests of the raj and the security concerns of the British government. The former wanted revenue, and the latter recognised both the strategic significance of Borneo because of its proximity to Singapore, and the importance of its oilfields.

The issue was raised in 1937 by the possibility that the Nissa Shokai, prospecting for coal since 1924, might be given a lease in the Belaga area. Raja Vyner, however, told Colonial Office officials that the only Japanese concession was a rubber plantation in Kuching, and assured them that he was 'not in the least anxious to

[41] Ibid., p. 184.
[42] Chin Kee Onn, *Malaya Upside Down*, Singapore, Kuala Lumpur and Hong Kong: Federal, 1976, p. 35.

encourage penetration in Sarawak of Japanese, nor the development by them of an important commercial interest in that area'.
Over any substantial concession he would consult the Colonial
Office beforehand, so that it might examine the question and consider 'the safeguards considered desirable from the defence
aspect'. It is clearly *most undesirable to* have the Japanese in Sarawak,'
wrote the under-secretary at the Colonial Office. 'They would
inevitably make any place they get there a further advance base in
their Imperialist designs.'[43]

To the north the Company was more disposed to encourage
the Japanese and the government just as concerned, if not more so.
In 1916 the Company granted land for rubber-growing at Tawao
to Kuhara Funosuke, owner of Kuhara Mining Co., later called
Nissan, and the Mitsubishi group opened the Kubota Estate
(Tawau Estate Ltd). In 1926 the ministry of foreign affairs commis-
sioned Orita Ichiji, a member of the Taiwan secretariat, to undertake a 'trial immigration project'.[44] Cautioned by the British
government over previous migration plans, the Chartered Company was prepared to welcome a small-scale venture, but it did
not succeed. Orita had more success with the Borneo Fisheries
Company, with its fishing base at Si-Amil, purchased by Nissan in
December 1933. In 1937 the Japanese government began to assist
Nissan to set up abaca plantations. The Company also gave Nissan
and Mitsubishi companies concessions to export timber.

By the time war broke out there were 1,175 Japanese workers in
Tawau, 308 of them at Si-Amil. Migration had, however, been
stopped early in 1941 for security reasons. For the same reasons,
too, Tawau had been closed to foreign trade. Policing there was
improved, in case of a coup by the '600 able-bodied Japanese'.[45]
'Moreover the important Dutch oilfields lie on the Borneo coast
southward of Tawao and the Dutch authorities have expressed to
H.M.G. their anxiety about our arrangements for control of the
Japanese in North Borneo.'[46]

---

[43] Minutes by Gent, 15 September 1937; Ormsby-Gore, 5 October. CO 531/
27(53038), Public Record Office, London.

[44] Sabibah Osman, 'Japanese Economic Activities in Sabah from the 1890s until
1941', *JSEAS*, 29, 1 (March 1998), pp. 27-9.

[45] Gent, q. in Osman, 'Japanese Economic Activities', p. 41.

[46] CO Memorandum, 'Closing of North Borneo Ports', 3 March 1941. FO 371/
27814.

In occupied British Borneo, as elsewhere, the Japanese were concerned to secure the commodities they needed, and to promote self-sufficiency. Among the former, as in Dutch Borneo, oil was, of course, the most important. A refinery at Lutong had processed the production from both fields, using gas from Seria as fuel, and the production was taken off by tanker from long sea-lines. The technical staff and the Punjabi garrison carried out a denial operation immediately the war began. '[T]here were moments when I could reflect on the pitiful nature of our work,' the engineer recalled. 'The labour of years destroyed in a few hours.'[47]

With the help of skilled non-European Shell employees, the Japanese were, however, quickly able to get the two fields going again at about half capacity, and, concentrating on Seria, they surpassed prewar crude oil production during 1944. The Lutong refinery did not recover, and much of the oil was shipped unprocessed, either through the repaired sea-lines, or along a pipeline that carried it 120 miles to jetties at Muara, built largely by Javanese *romusha*. Heavy Allied bombing of Balikpapan from August 1944 made the Miri–Seria area even more important, but bombing there began in November. The Japanese denial exercise, begun on 10 June, was more effective than that of the British.

Sarawak had also exported rubber and pepper, and imported not only manufactures but also over half of the rice it needed. With the occupation, the market for Sarawak's exports, other than oil, collapsed, and the Japanese made self-sufficiency in food a priority. The Japanese took up the schemes to expand wet-rice growing that the raj had begun in the 1930s. They 'succeeded where the Brookes had failed', Ooi tells us;[48] but they used different methods, conscripting Chinese and Malays for the purpose.[49] The 'achievement' was 'the very antithesis of economic development. It was dependent on the collapse of the export economy, a reversion to subsistence agriculture..., and the emigration of over half the urban population to the countryside.'[50]

The economy also had to meet the needs of the occupation force. That was feasible while it stood at some 3,000 troops. When in September 1944 the Borneo Defence Force became the 37th

[47] q. Reece, *Masa Japun*, p. 27.
[48] Ooi, *Rising Sun*, p. 77.
[49] Reece, *Masa Japun*, p. 142.
[50] Robert Cramb in Kratoska, ed., *Food Supplies*, p. 159.

Army, another 17,000 troops had to be fed. The methods used to obtain rice became more ruthless.

Zaibatsu companies were given the monopoly of wholesaling and retailing basic commodities. Mitsui agents were responsible for the purchase and distribution of rice and food crops, and also for the padi-planting schemes. The exception was sago flour, monopolised by Mitsubishi's North Borneo offshoot. The inequity and inefficiency of the Mitsui monopoly led to concealment, barter trading and smuggling along the coasts and across the Sambas border. Mitsubishi and Nissan took over the British and the Japanese companies in North Borneo. The Kapit coal, discovered by Nissa Shokai, was not exploited.

Conscript labour, required for road and airfield building, and recruited through the ethnic organisations and the *jikeidan* structure, toiled under conditions 'scarcely better than those experienced by European and Indian prisoners of war assigned to similar tasks'.[51] At the end of 1943 the defence force sponsored the formation of the North Borneo Labour Business Society, Kita Boruneo Romukyokai, the main task of which was to obtain workers from Java. Some 12,000 *romusha* were brought in, to work at the Miri oilfield, on military works in North Borneo, on plantations and road-building. They were badly treated, and thousands died in the last months of the occupation, when they were more or less left to fend for themselves.[52]

The Philippines

In the Philippines, by contrast to Indonesia and Borneo, the conquerors had no major economic interest. It had been conquered because it was, of course, strategically important. The takeover disrupted its economic ties with the rest of the world. Those had been built up since its Spanish rulers opened its ports to foreign commerce, first Manila in the 1830s, then Sual, Iloilo and Zamboanga in the 1850s. The Spaniards promoted tobacco exports. It was foreigners, working with the native elite, who expanded hemp production in the Bikol lands, and above all sugar in the Visayas, while rice, initially also an export, had to be imported.

The American takeover in 1898 was followed by the creation

[51] Reece, *Masa Japun*, p. 149.
[52] Ibid., p. 150.

of a privileged market for Philippines produce, tobacco and especially sugar, in the United States. American involvement remained limited, partly because domestic beet and cane sugar interests supported a law that limited the land leases and purchases that corporations might secure. 'By preventing large-scale American investment in Philippine agriculture and extractive industries, [Congress] effectively frustrated American exploitation of the islands.'[53] Only a few US companies had sizable investments in the Philippines, like Dole Pineapple and Benguet Consolidated Mining. Otherwise, as under the Spaniards, the Filipino elite continued to benefit.

The move towards independence was promoted by the US sugar interests, and the programme was accompanied by a staged reduction of protection. At its conclusion the elite would need to seek not only political guarantees for an independent Philippines but alternative means of sustaining the export economy.

Japanese trade and investment began under the Spaniards. The first consul was appointed in 1888, and in 1898 the first retail store was opened in Manila.[54] The Americans put few obstacles in the way: they had no major economic interests themselves; and they did not wish to worsen their relations with the Japanese. By 1934 200 Japanese firms were operating in the Philippines, 139 local, and 61 branches of Japan-based concerns, and the Japanese dominated the fishing industry. From 1929 Japan was the Philippines' second-largest trading partner, though far behind the first. For most of the 1930s exports to the Philippines exceeded imports, thanks to the cheapening of Japanese textiles, but purchases of metals, hemp and timber reversed the balance in 1939 and 1940. This was the result of war conditions.

The Japanese had not been slow, however, to point out that, since the Philippines would need to reorient its trade when it became independent, it ought to be preparing the way. In 1933 Watanabe Kaoru, commercial agent in the Philippines for the Japanese ministry of commerce and industry, had urged Filipinos to plan for independence by diversifying their markets, developing their home industries, reducing the import of foodstuffs and plant-

---

[53] Glenn A. May, *Social Engineering in the Philippines*, Westport, CT: Greenwood, 1980, p. 150.
[54] Goodman in N.G. Owen, ed., *The Philippines and the United States: Studies in Past and Resent Interactions*, Ann Arbor: Univ. of Michigan Press, 1983, p. 40.

ing cotton. Later, in an address at the University of the Philippines Consul-General Kimura Atsushi counselled Filipinos not to erect tariff barriers against Japanese goods, and to consider the development of free trade with Japan.[55] In economic as in political matters, Quezon had to balance the demands of the present and the future, the Commonwealth and independence.

Those appeared in relation to immigration, too. Over that the United States became increasingly concerned, particularly because of the concentration of Japanese in Davao. There a Japanese community had been built up as a result of the enterprise of Ota Kyosaburo, a community 'in which, although they were living in a foreign land, the Japanese could strut about as if they owned the place'.[56] In 1939, there some 24,000 Japanese in the Philippines, 19 per cent in Manila, 71 per cent in Davao. Despite the consulate's deployment of funds and persuasion, an Immigration Act was put on the books in 1940, and the Japanese were allocated a quota of only 500.

In conversation with Acting Consul-General Kihara Jitaro, Quezon had implied that he was going along with a policy the United States wanted:

After independence is complete and we undertake large scale irrigation construction, we plan to develop various products with a fairly sizable number of Japanese immigrants, but at present the feeling of the United States toward Japan is rather bad. Until independence it is very difficult to confirm my schemes for Japanese-Philippines cooperation. There is some opposition to independence in the United States, but I want to see independence secure before I retire.[57]

Even before the occupation, indeed even before the creation of the Sphere, the Japanese had hinted at the kind of economic relationship they would have with a Philippines independent of America. The military administration took steps to implement them. The director-general, Wachi Takaji, outlined its policies to the executive commission on 10 August 1942. The United States, he said, had encouraged the sugar industry, despite its lack of natural advantage, and then manoeuvred to close the market by 'the ruse of offering independence'. Now the war had severed the

[55] Ibid., pp. 48-9.
[56] q. Furiya Reiko in Shiraishi Saya and Takashi, eds, *The Japanese in Colonial Southeast Asia*, Ithaca, NY: Cornell Univ. Press, 1993, p. 170.
[57] q. Goodman, *Four Aspects*, p. 38.

market, and the way was open for rationalisation. The solution was a five-year plan, under which sugar should be manufactured for the local market, alcohol and liquid fuel should be made from cane, and cotton, used in the manufacture of explosives as well as clothing, should be grown on the sugar lands not required. 'For the re-orientation of the basic industries of the Philippines, Japan is ready to give necessary aid and guidance in order that this country may perform her mission as a member of the Greater East Asia Co-Prosperity Sphere and enjoy a rightful share of profit and prosperity.'[58]

The Sphere had other sources of sugar, but its cotton supply was cut off. Nine Japanese firms were allocated 1,500 hectares to make a start in 1942, and a Philippine Cotton Association was formed to regulate and coordinate the plans. Production fell below expectations, however, and too few spindles were available. The priority given to military needs meant that little was available to the Filipinos.

The Prime Commodities Distribution Control Association (Primco) was set up by the military administration in July–August 1942. Its board had a Japanese majority, though it was said to be the intention to make over control to Filipinos. Filipino retailers and businessmen had to take shares, equivalent to assessment. 'Under the new plan only members who paid their assessment [i.e. shares] will enjoy the right and privileges of buying controlled commodities from the federation at the lowest possible prices.'[59] Distribution was in the hands of the neighbourhood leaders. Many sold them at black-market prices.[60]

A Foodstuffs Control Association was also set up in August 1942, involving eight Japanese firms and five Filipino. The object was to purchase foodstuffs other than rice from the provinces for the army and the Manilenos, and all foodstuffs brought into the city were to be purchased at four purchasing associations on the outskirts. 'Ultimately the same control will be applied in all the larger cities in the provinces.'[61] The National Rice and Corn Corporation (NARIC), set up in 1935 to deal with a rice crisis by stabilising prices and supplies, continued under Japanese control.

[58] q. Hartendorp, *Japanese Occupation*, I, 208-9.

[59] q. ibid., p. 208.

[60] Agoncillo, *The Fateful Years*, p. 551.

[61] q. Hartendorp, *Japanese Occupation*, I, 208.

Late in 1942 rice producers associations were organised, and in February 1943 a National Rice Growers Cooperative Association was set up. Associations were to function as 'subordinate agencies of the NARIC and of the Food Control Association'.[62] Members were compelled to sell their rice to NARIC at prices determined by the military administration. That led to concealment and profiteering and indeed to non-production.

Taking over, Laurel issued an ordinance on 25 November 1943 that, 'in order to secure an equitable distribution ... as required by the present emergency', fixed the amount each member of a rice and corn growers' cooperative association might keep for home consumption and for seed. Any surplus was to be sold to the association, which was to sell it to the control organisation. 'The maximum selling and reselling prices for every province or municipality shall be fixed by the Minister of Agriculture and Commerce for each crop year at such rates as shall afford the producers a reasonable profit.'[63]

Laurel replaced NARIC by Biba (Bigasang Bayan, National Rice Granary) on 6 January 1944, declaring that NARIC was corrupt and an instrument of the military administration, and Roxas agreed to lead Biba. The army replaced the Foodstuffs Control Association by the Army Administered Foodstuff Company on 1 April.[64] Under its pressure, moreover, Laurel displaced Roxas, whom it found uncooperative, and replaced Biba by the joint Filipino-Japanese Rice and Corn Administration (RICOA), which, it seems, also incorporated the control association. 'Lokoa' it was called (from *loco*, mad).[65]

None of this enhanced production. Indeed the controls, even if driven by equity, were counter-productive. A grower in Kalumpit, Bulakan exclaimed:

What! The rascal is asking us to sell all our stocks to the NARIC so the Jap Army could live off us? How about the prices of other commodities which we need in order to live? Sell all our stocks, *pwe!*[66]

Most of the people of Manila rode on trains in going to and from the provinces. It was quite a sight to see trains packed to capacity, including

[62] q. Ibid., p. 500.
[63] q. Agoncillo, *The Fateful Years*, pp. 543-4.
[64] Hartendorp, *Japanese Occupation*, II, 268.
[65] Jose in Kratoska, ed., *Food Supplies*, p. 542.
[66] q. Agoncillo, *The Fateful Years*, p. 542.

the roofs of coaches where men sat hugging their sacks or bags of rice. The area between the Kalookan Station and Tayuman Street was the scene of smuggling. As the train raced from the Kalookan Station to Manila [where inspection took place], men took a chance with their lives by jumping off the train accompanied by their precious grain. There were successive thuds of falling bodies and sacks of rice, while along the railway tracks men, women, and children, all emaciated, hungry, and pale, watched expectantly for the smuggled rice.[67]

By December 1944 'the dead and dying were common sights on Manila's streets.'[68]

In April 1944 Laurel created the Labor Recruitment Agency, 'which will cooperate with the Japanese circles in meeting the need for labor and relieve unemployment in the country.'[69] A headline on 26 May reported that 25,789 Filipino labourers had been 'drafted by the Labor Recruitment Agency from 13 provinces including Manila for the Imperial Japanese Army and Navy and Japanese firms'.[70] In Manila compulsory labour service was introduced in May. 'Although it is compulsory', said Mayor Guinto, 'it is in fact voluntary inasmuch as it is addressed to our civic consciousness.'[71] By late 1944 the Japanese were pulling people off the streets.[72]

Burma

Unlike Indonesia, Malaya and the Philippines, Burma had become an exporter of rice in the colonial period. That had not been the main British objective in acquiring the kingdom, stage by stage, during the nineteenth century. Indeed, it is arguable that the main concern was strategic rather than economic: the British viewed Burma from an Indian perspective, and saw it more as a border kingdom than a commercial resource. British merchants were, however, interested in its timber resources, and also viewed the country as a means of access to inland China.

Once the British regime was set up, Lower Burma, in particular

[67] Ibid., p. 545.

[68] Ricardo T. Jose, *The Japanese Occupation*, Manila: Asia Publishing Co., 1998, p. 219.

[69] Hartendorp, *Japanese Occupation*, II, 274.

[70] q. Ibid., p. 272.

[71] q. Ibid., p. 276.

[72] Jose, *Japanese Occupation*, p. 198.

the delta, increasingly turned to rice production, supplying at first markets mainly in Europe, then in the twentieth century, particularly after the First World War, markets in Asia. There, compared with the other Southeast Asian rice exporters, Siam and Cochinchina, it enjoyed an advantage in India and Ceylon, while the position was reversed in East Asia.[73] British investment focused on timber, on minerals, such as lead, zinc, nickel and silver from the vast mine at Bawdwin in the Shan States and tungsten from Mawchi in Karenni, and in particular on oil, mostly produced at Yenangyaung and Chauk, and sent by a 300-mile pipeline to refineries at Syriam.

Prewar Japan was an importer of rice only when supplies were insufficient to avoid price increases. Before about 1928, supplies from Korea and Manchuria did not make up the deficit, and rice was imported from Southeast Asia and from California. Imports from outside the empire were rare after 1928. Burma was a source, as also of raw cotton, grown in the dry zone. In return Japan supplied Burma with textiles, cement, hardware, electric goods, drug sundries and fish.

The plans of the Hayashi army group echoed the general emphasis on procuring resources essential for national defence, and on the army's self-sufficiency. They were also to harmonise the economic development of Burma with that of the Sphere as a whole. Agriculture was to be diversified with a view to meeting domestic demand. 'In order to facilitate the self-sufficiency of the Greater East Asia Co-Prosperity Sphere, the production of cotton shall be accelerated while rice crops shall be gradually reduced.' 'Special emphasis shall be placed upon the procuring of aviation gasoline and oil for machinery.' 'Great effort must be made to exploit lead at the Bawdwin mine.' 'Efforts must be made to increase the production of tungsten and limit the production of tin to the needs of Burma.'

The mining of iron was to be halted, and resources transferred to the mining of copper and lead. Light industries were to be sustained, but heavy industries discouraged. The interruption of trade with India 'might cause an extreme economic disruption – a surplus in export goods, shortage of import goods, a fall in the price of native products, a rise in the price of the necessities of life

[73] Cheng Siok-hwa, *The Rice Industry of Burma*, Kuala Lumpur: Univ. of Malaya Press, 1968, ch. 8.

and unrest in the life of the natives.' Hence the need for controls on trade and commodity distribution.

The Japanese who have been residing in the area shall be, when necessary, summoned for cooperation. They may be employed in the Military Administration Department or they may be permitted to continue their business. The group shall, however, not permit them to engage in business beyond their immediate needs.[74]

Rice production in wartime Burma fell dramatically. It lost its markets in the British empire, while Japan drew more on Siam and Indo-China, and after January 1943 the shipping shortage stopped all its imports from Burma. By March 1943, moreover, Allied air raids had immobilised all the major rice mills except one at Moulmein. The shortage of cattle – requisitioned for food, hides and transportation – also cut production. Indian manual labourers had fled, and Burmese labour was diverted to other projects. More than 2 million acres of paddy land turned into jungle during the war.[75] Rice became scarce in the dry zone because of the collapse of transport.[76]

A five-year plan was drawn up for cotton, setting production targets and dividing the cultivation among four Japanese firms with exclusive rights to produce and sell. Success was limited by a shortage of cotton seeds and by drought. The production of jute – hitherto supplied from India – was promoted under a similar system in the delta, but again the output was disappointing. Timber, taken over by a combine including Mitsui and Mitsubishi interests, also fell short of its targets, mainly because of the bombing of mills.

The Japanese were mainly interested in minerals, particularly oil and non-ferrous metals. Mitsui undertook the rehabilitation of the Bawdwin mine, completed in March 1943, but production was kept low by repeated air raids. Mawchi, also put out of action by scorched-earth policies, was partly restored by the Kobayashi Mining Co., but production was limited by a shortage of dynamite. 'The Japanese could not even reach one-fifth of the prewar output.'[77] The oilfields at Yenangyaung and the refineries at Syriam were back in operation in mid-1942, but repeated bom-

[74] q. Trager, Burma, pp. 67–72.
[75] John F. Cady, *Thailand, Burma, Laos and Cambodia*, Englewood Cliffs: Prentice-Hall, 1966, p. 134.
[76] Yoon, 'Japan's Occupation', p. 254.
[77] Ibid., p. 217.

bardment kept their production down. British intelligence estimated production early in 1944 at about 44,000 gallons a day, as against 700,000 prewar. The Japanese were not producing enough for their military needs.

Labour was compulsorily recruited for military and infrastructural work, about 177,000 men in total.[78] Many in the 'Sweat Army' died, 'the truest heroes that Burma produced in that worldwide conflict', as Ba Maw put it.[79] The most notorious of the projects was the construction of the Burma–Thailand railway. Some 85,000 Burmese labourers were used on the Burmese side of the Three Pagodas Pass.[80] On 2 March 1943 the commander of the Hayashi Army Group issued instructions for the creation of a Labour Service Corps, to be raised from 'young and able Burmans in every district throughout Burma'. 'The main task of the corps is to raise the ground level for the railroad.' Members were not to be 'treated as common laborers. The term coolie shall be strictly prohibited.'[81] Commendation and preferred employment opportunities were offered to those who completed their three months' service. 30,000 died.[82]

The Central Labour Service Bureau was headed by Thakin Ba Sein, the minister responsible for transportation and irrigation. He was backed by Ba Maw and the other members of the BCEA, anxious to convince the Japanese that Burma merited independence. The first recruiting campaign exceeded the target of 30,000. Conditions were, however, so bad that by the end of June more than half had died or deserted. Two further recruiting campaigns were needed. The targets could not be met, even though there were rackets and forceful measures were adopted. The AFPFL manifesto of 1944 'listed forced labor as one of the greatest grievances of the Burmese people against the Japanese'.[83]

Thailand

Thailand, though independent, was part of the Sphere. In the imperialist phase, it had, of course, avoided the political fate of

---

[78] Guyot, 'Political Impact', p. 261.

[79] Ba Maw, *Breakthrough in Burma*, p. 297.

[80] Yoon, 'Japan's Occupation', p. 281.

[81] q. Trager, *Burma*, pp. 233–4.

[82] Yoon, 'Japan's Occupation', p. 225.

[83] Ibid., pp. 223, 225.

neighbouring Burma and Vietnam, but economically had been drawn into the new pattern of relationships created by the industrial revolution. In some measure, indeed, that was part of the price it paid, alongside surrendering control or claims over tributary regions, for the retention of independence. Like Netherlands India, it offered economic opportunity first to the major economic power, Britain, and then to the other powers, as a means of limiting their political intervention. In the case of the Thais it took the form of unequal treaties, which, like Japan and China, they sought to undo in the new century.

The development policies of the absolute monarchy remained cautious, but society was transformed by the incorporation of Siam in the new world created by imperialism and the industrial revolution. It remained a primary producer, its main export by far being rice. About 70 per cent of that went to British Malaya. About 70 per cent of its exports as a whole went to British empire ports, and some 37 per cent of its imports came from the British empire.[84] The Bombay-Burmah Company dominated the production of teak in northern Siam, while the British had a large share in the development of tin and rubber in peninsular Siam. The British supplied the government's financial adviser, and the currency reserves were held in sterling. Mercantile activity, however, was dominated by the Chinese community. The civilian-military elite that took over in the 1932 coup were disposed to follow nationalistic policies in the economic as well as the political field.

Japan's economic role increased during the First World War, but remained limited: even in textiles, the Japanese had only 12.5 per cent of the import trade in the 1920s. Only one major company, Mitsui, had a branch in Bangkok, and the lone Bank of Taiwan closed during the scandal of 1927. After the devaluation of the yen in 1931 the Japanese made considerable gains, and their share in imports rose from 15.8 per cent in 1933 to 25.5per cent in 1936. Mitsubishi established a branch in Bangkok in 1935, and the Yokohama Specie Bank in 1936. Independent Siam was 'the only place in Southeast Asia where Japanese companies could compete on an equal footing with their Western rivals'.[85] But the tension between the ideas that were to produce the Sphere, and

[84] Richard J. Aldrich, *The Key to the South*, Kuala Lumpur: Oxford Univ. Press, 1993, p. 7.
[85] Reynolds, *Southern Advance*, p. 13.

the nationalist aspirations of the elites in Southeast Asia, was already apparent in the state that had maintained its independence, rather than having to seek to regain it. That tension was, of course, increased when Thailand was incorporated in the Sphere after 1941.

Thailand's 'basic economic policies' in the war, according to a Japanese report, were 'supplying food to Japan and other areas of Greater East Asia, establishment of a self-sufficient economy, and stabilization of the people's livelihood'. They were, as Batson says, 'remote from reality'.[86] The war drastically changed Thailand's economic position. Japan was the only buyer for its strategic exports, once transport to Germany became impossible, and it had no need of Thailand's tin or rubber once it had secured maritime Southeast Asia. The export of rice also fell away, and production declined. The Japanese military became 'the primary purchaser of Thai agricultural commodities'. The purchases were financed, however, by loans from the Thai government. 'This Japanese ability to extract funds from their ally encouraged a free-spending mentality'[87] and, with the decline in government revenues,[88] forced the Thais to increase their money supply. No longer able, of course, to link the baht with the pound, the Thais were, moreover, pressed into linking it with the yen at an artificial rate. Inflation followed, though it was less drastic than in other parts of Southeast Asia.

The Thais relied on Japan for consumer goods, but it could not meet the demand. Shortages and inflation led to the introduction of price controls. They 'accomplished nothing except to make the black market blacker and to make illegal what might just as well have been done in the open'.[89] Allied bombing and the arrival of additional Japanese troops worsened the position in 1944-5. By April 1945 commodity prices were 46 times the 1937 level. At least the Thais, major rice producers, would not starve, unlike the Javanese. The shortages mainly hit the townsfolk.

Thai loans were also used on the Burma railway, and so was Thai labour, including Chinese labour, recruited by the Chinese

[86] Batson in McCoy, *Southeast Asia*, p. 277.

[87] Reynolds, *Southern Advance*, p. 122.

[88] E.B. Reynolds, 'Aftermath of Alliance: The Wartime Legacy in Thai-Japanese Relations', *JSEAS*, 21, 1 (March 1990), p. 69.

[89] q. Reynolds, *Southern Advance*, p. 123.

chamber of commerce.[90] Considerable tension on the spot flared into violence on 18 December 1942.[91] Pibun's own construction programme – for the creation of a new capital – imitated Japanese methods, however. 'Like the railway labor force, conscripted workers sent to Phetchabun suffered grievously from inadequate supplies and disease.'[92]

Except for those conscripted for national or labour service, however, the rural masses were not greatly affected by the war. 'When one went out into the country', a Japanese officer recalled, 'except for key railway lines, there was no bombing and it was very tranquil. With no newspapers or radio, one could almost forget the war.'[93] The Thai leaders were not only adroit in preserving the independence of their country amid an international crisis. They were also able to insulate the masses of the people from the effects of the war and from contacts with the Japanese. The French in Indo-China were less successful.

Indo-China

The French had come to Indo-China rather for political than economic reasons. Once there, however, they endeavoured to turn its resources to account. The government made substantial use of *corvée* labour in the extensive infrastructural developments it undertook. Besides linking Tonkin and Yunnan by rail, the government sought to draw the territories themselves together economically, even as it kept them apart politically. The colony of Cochinchina had already begun to produce a rice surplus in the later nineteenth century, and, though it could be used to supply Annam and Tonkin, much of it was exported, to Europe, to French colonies, and to other parts of East and Southeast Asia. Rubber was added to Indo-China's exports in the new century, plantations being established in the red lands of the colony and in Cambodia. The core of traditional Vietnam, Tonkin, provided a source of coal, but it did not provide an agricultural surplus. Imports into Indo-China were affected by the highly protectionist policies France pursued in favour of its home industry. Japan imported from Indo-China more that it exported to it. Its imports included

[90] Ibid., p. 177.
[91] Ibid., p. 138.
[92] Ibid., p. 171.
[93] q. Reynolds, 'Aftermath of Alliance', p. 73.

rice, cotton, coal and metal ores, and in particular rubber and vegetable oils.

Other parts of Southeast Asia were subjected to Japan's economic policies in three phases. First, there was a shift from the private and semi-public contacts of the prewar period, placed within the overall context of the colonial and international patterns of Southeast Asian trade and investment. That gave way on the conquest to the policies of the military administrations, as broadly set out late in 1941, and elaborated and pursued within the context of the disruption of the prewar patterns and the needs of the military. A third phase was dictated by the adverse course of the war and the collapse of communications: it emphasised self-sufficiency and preparations for last-ditch resistance. The pattern in Indo-China differed, not simply because European collaborators were retained till the last phase. The shift from the prewar to the wartime phase was taken in two steps.

Before the opening of the war, Indo-China had not only to admit Japanese forces and accept a one-sided mediation: it had also to conclude the economic agreements of 6 May 1941, promising a supply of rice and rubber.[94] 'In regard to rice, aside from price all that we have asked for has been granted,' Matsuoka told the privy council, 'and in other matters it can be said that 80% of our objectives have been achieved.'[95] With the opening of the Pacific war, Indo-China became the main supply base for the southern operations. Like Thailand, it was also to be fitted into the policies of the new empire when it was acquired. 'Once the holy war has been completed', as a report of the ministry of Greater East Asia put it, '...many materials which our Empire had expected to obtain from French Indochina are now not necessarily only obtainable therefrom.'

Big changes needed to be made. Rubber, now available elsewhere, was de-emphasised, and part of the plantation area was to be switched to cotton. Indo-China was also to expand its production of vegetable oils, and to cultivate jute and hemp. At the same time, it was to retain its function as a granary for Japan, for its military, and for other parts of Southeast Asia. '[R]ice', as the report put it, 'will still be the most major item among the materials of which pro-

---

[94] Morley, *Fateful Choice*, p. 149.

[95] Bui Minh Dung, 'Japan's Role in the Vietnamese Starvation of 1944-45', *MAS*, 29, 3 (1995), p. 602.

duction is to be increased in French Indochina in the coming years.'[96]

After the occupation of northern Indo-China, the Japanese had required the French to supply 468,000 tons of rice to Japan in the last three months of 1940, far in excess of prewar amounts. Rice levies continued in the subsequent years: 583,000 tons in 1941, 937,000 in 1942 and 1,008,000 in 1943. Only in 1944-5, when transport collapsed, did Korea replace Indo-China as the major supplier. Rice continued to be levied, however, for the supply of the Japanese armies, the self-subsistence of which was emphasised, and for delivery to other parts of the Sphere. Before they were overthrown, the French, too, had been stockpiling rice.[97] The Japanese exaction of rice continued after the coup, and 61,000 tons had been exported by the end of August.[98]

Yet a major famine was clearly looming in the north. For that various reasons have been offered, among them flooding, the disintegration of the transport system and Allied bombing. More important was the fact that the enforced conversion to other crops, like jute and peanuts for machine oil, was applied not only to southern rubber plantations but also to northern rice agriculture.[99] The area of rice cultivation in Tonkin shrank from 1,487,000 hectares in 1941-2 to 1,386,000 hectares in 1943.[100] That policy was coupled with continued attempts to exact rice at low rates of return, inflation and labour exactions. At least one million Vietnamese died, perhaps as many as two millions.[101] The famine helped the Viet Minh, who began a campaign to destroy the granaries.[102] Hanoi, a foreign observer declared at the end of the war, 'is literally dying of hunger. ... People are dying in the streets every day.'[103] In the hamlets which Motoo Furuta and Van Tao surveyed in 1992-5, the losses in the 1945 famine were greater than in the thirty years of war Vietnam was then about to undergo.[104]

---

[96] q. Ibid., pp. 600-1.

[97] Ibid., pp. 583, 614. Marr, *Vietnam 1945*, p. 97.

[98] Bui Minh Dung, 'Japan's Role', p. 617.

[99] Huynh Kim Khanh, 'Vietnamese August Revolution', p. 768.

[100] Bui Minh Dung, 'Japan's Role', p. 592.

[101] Ibid., pp. 575-6. Sugata Bose, 'Starvation amidst Plenty: The Making of Famine: Bengal, Honan, and Tonkin, 1942-45', *MAS*, 24, 4 (1990), p. 702.

[102] Huynh Kim Khanh, 'Vietnamese August Revolution', p. 776.

[103] q. Nguyen The Anh in Kratoska, ed., *Food Supplies*, p. 221.

[104] Furuta in ibid., p. 237.

7

MEMORY AND LEGACY

Violence

The Second World War was fought with increasing violence. It married the result of advances in weapons technology with mass mobilisation. Its objectives came to be stated in extreme terms, not armistice but surrender, not punishment but extermination. Not surprisingly, the majority of the deaths it caused were civilian not military. Some 55 million lost their lives, perhaps more. Of those, 39 million came from Western Europe and above all the Soviet Union. The rest came from Asia, predominantly from China, but also from Java and from Vietnam, and from Japan itself. The last months of the war saw the conflagration of Dresden and of Tokyo. It concluded with the dropping of bombs of unsurpassed destructive power on Hiroshima and Nagasaki. Against them there could be no resistance, and the emperor could justify surrender without using the word. They ended the war, and in a sense made it the war that ended war.

Amid so much violence, that of the Japanese is still readily recalled: though atrocities were not peculiar to them, theirs still stand out. In part, no doubt, it is a question of perception. The Germans have accepted their defeat in the war, even their responsibility for it, more fully than the Japanese. The holocaust, the climax of Hitler's anti-Semitic policies, helped to bring that about, though also diverting attention from other issues. It has no Japanese equivalent. In Japan there is no clarity about responsibility for the war, nor any official interest in encouraging debate about it. The sense that, without an army and dependent for defence on the United States, Japan is not 'equal' no doubt hampers an appraisal of the past.

Fourteen of the condemned war criminals are in the national shrine at Yasukuni.[1] Such an approach, if the product of resent-

[1] Richard B. Finn, *Winners in Peace: MacArthur, Yoshida and Postwar Japan*, Berkeley: Univ. of California Press, 1992, p. 183.

ment, only fuels the resentment of Japan's critics. Some have bitter memories, some have axes to grind. The economic success of the postwar Japanese, accompanied by a euphoric insensitivity that might be compared with what accompanied the earlier military campaign, could only stir those memories, and give an opportunity, on the one hand, to those who wished for a better deal from them, or, on the other, those who criticised the new collaboration with them.

In such a context, it is difficult to offer a judgment. Yet it is also difficult quite to avoid the conclusion that the Japanese, who indeed saw themselves as different from other peoples, indeed behaved in a different way. The Field Service Code of January 1941 enjoined 'kindness to those who surrender', but while the mortality rate of the American and British prisoners of war who fell into the hands of the Germans and Italians was 4 per cent the percentage for those who fell into the hands of the Japanese was 27 per cent.[2] Their behaviour may have been connected with their belief that surrender was dishonourable, and those who surrendered were therefore an object of contempt. 'There can be no mistaking the Army's belief that death was preferable to capture, or that the Navy had comparable ideas': ships did not carry life-belts.[3]

Though Japan had signed and ratified the 1907 Hague Convention on the treatment of prisoners, it had signed but not ratified the Geneva Convention and the prisoner-of-war convention of 1929. The vice-minister of the navy, recommending against ratification, had argued that, as Japanese servicemen had no concept of being taken as prisoner, the obligations would be one-sided. The guarantees would be a disadvantage. 'For instance, if an enemy airman planned an air raid expecting to be taken prisoner after accomplishing his mission, he could double his flying range.' The provisions for punishment were more liberal than those in the Imperial forces, he added.

In 1942 the Allies indicated that they would apply the 1929 provisions. The *gaimusho* replied that Japan was not bound to do the same, but rather obscurely added that it would observe them *mutatis mutandis*.[4] Ignoring the provisions of the Geneva and

[2] Dower, *War without Mercy*, pp. 26, 48.

[3] Marder *et al.*, *Old Friends*, II, 579.

[4] Oba Sadao, *The 'Japanese' War*, trans. Anne Kareko, Sandgate: Japan Library, 1995, pp. 64-6.

Hague Conventions was, however, a deliberate policy, favoured by Tojo in order to demonstrate the superiority of the Japanese to the whites: it was, he said, a racial war.[5]

In Southeast Asia the treatment of Europeans can indeed be explained in part by the Japanese wish to destroy not only their empire, but the prestige on which it was based. Their treatment of the Chinese in Southeast Asia may be related to the struggles in China itself, which the overseas Chinese sought to keep going. What is less easy to explain is the violence with which they treated the other peoples of Southeast Asia, even though they were avow-edly being drawn into a co-prosperity sphere. Their arbitrariness and their use of terror alienated those whose support they needed, and their exploitation of labour was as ruthless as it was inefficient.

Japan was a late-comer to the colonial scene. That had two implications. One was that the concept of empire was already changing when it launched its venture in the 1890s. The kind of policy it adopted in Korea and Manchuria, it might be said, was only an updated version of the policies that European powers had adopted in the outside world. Yet its very updating showed it was outdated. It was a question, too, of empire in a hurry, and that was also bound to make for a ruthless policy. Most colonial powers have based themselves on a mixture of collaboration and the sel-ective application of force, deployed to convince and bolster the collaborators. The Japanese seldom got the mixture right.

In Southeast Asia, that was still more difficult. First of all, its hasty acquisition was not originally intended. The military oper-ation was brilliantly carried out, though admittedly against poorly prepared and distracted opponents, with a success that bred eup-horia. The civilian planning was much less complete. Indeed, the Japanese were not well informed about the peoples and cultures of Southeast Asia, whatever information they had secured about its politics, its strategic resources and its military capabilities. Nor did it make good use of what it had. Civilians, driven out in the last months before the war, were used by the army planners without enthusiasm. In the occupation the army looked to the *zaibatsu* more than to the 'local' firms. There was a tendency, too, to fall back on devices derived from Manchurian experience and from the Manchuria-influenced wartime measures adopted in the homeland itself. That applied to the structures of political control

[5] Nakamura, 'General Imamura', p. 16.

and mobilisation and to the interventionist approach to the economy.

Second, the new imperial venture was permanently under war conditions. Though development plans were drawn up, their implementation was not only undermined by their irrelevance and by the tendency to adopt command approaches. It was also overtaken by the collapse of transport within the Sphere, and by the increasing need to provide for defence and military and regional self-sufficiency. That involved ever harsher attempts to impress labour, ever greater shortages, ever more grotesque levels of inflation, and ever more counter-productive attempts to control food supplies.

These two factors added to the impact of a third one. The tradition, recruitment and training of the Japanese army made it an effective instrument of war, but a blunt instrument of occupation. It was an army that selectively built upon Japanese traditions, with a view to enhancing the effectiveness of a newcomer among modern states. As it expanded, it reflected, as well as reinforced, the hierarchical values of the Japanese village community.[6] 'The "toughness" of the Japanese military ... actually came from the poverty of rural Japan ... rooted in privation, obedience to authority, and brutality.'[7] Its training was brutalising. 'Having been subjected to cruel and irrational punishments we were trained to act without thinking in response to orders,' declared a soldier beaten 264 times during his military service.[8] Sent into foreign lands, the army fought desperately, but it also engaged in rape, massacre and looting, alarming even to its commanders from Port Arthur onwards.

In occupation it engaged in a high level of everyday violence. Officers like Suzuki and Fujiwara, who earned respect, were outnumbered by those who relied on fear. To make their men effective as builders of empire required more time, and probably more inclination, than was available in 1941, or later, when the demands of the war led to ever wider recruitment. The soldiers drawn from the core colonial areas, Taiwan and Korea, were, not surprisingly, even more brutal. They were 'prone to kick out against the local population to

---

[6] R. J. Smethurst, *A Social Basis for Prewar Japanese Militarism*, Berkeley: Univ. of California Press, 1974, p. 182.

[7] Ienaga Saburo, *Japan's Last War*, Oxford: Blackwell, 1979, p. 54.

[8] Iritani, *Group Psychology*, p. 191.

compensate for their own lowly status'.[9] The Koreans were 'the worst of all'.[10] The *kempeitai* – all the harsher, perhaps, for their relatively small numbers[11] – were notorious. Among them the Koreans were again especially brutal.[12] Frei seeks to 'liberate the discussion from its black-and-white fetters' by analysing military behaviour elsewhere: deadening fear and acts of bravery are mixed, atrocities and looting not uncommon.[13] But that hardly covers the occupation, whatever explanation or palliation it offers of the conduct of combat soldiers, and whatever the stress of war conditions.

The end of imperialism

The behaviour of their forces made the attempts of the Japanese to win support at once more necessary and more fruitless. The attempts were designed to win over an elite that would in turn win popular support. In that sense, it might help Japan to sustain the war, and secure a less than totally unfavourable outcome through the long but vaguely contemplated negotiated peace. At the same time, it could convince conservative opinion in the homeland that the war would not have been in vain, since the return of the colonial powers would have been made more unlikely.

The ideology of the Sphere had little to offer the Southeast Asian elites except insofar as it took a liberationist form. Independence was more welcome. At the outset of the war that had been held out only to Burma and the Philippines, already the most autonomous of the imperial regimes. When finally granted in 1943, it was still hedged about by Japanese controls. No more steps, moreover, were taken till 1945, when the French were overthrown, and last-minute moves made to implement a promise to Indonesia.

Though these moves were taken pragmatically and reluctantly, they represent perhaps Japan's major achievement in Southeast Asia. '[N]othing can ever obliterate the role Japan has played in bringing liberation to countless colonial peoples,' Ba Maw wrote. Its victories 'really marked the beginning of the end of all imperialism and colonialism'.[14] Even so, it cannot be said that the South-

[9] Reece, *Masa Jepun*, p. 91.

[10] Lai Ping Khiong, q. Kratoska, *Japanese Occupation*, p. 46.

[11] Kurasawa, 'Mobilisation and Control', p. 29.

[12] Syjuco, *The Kempei Tai*, p. 9.

[13] In Kratoska, *Malaya and Singapore*, pp. 166-7.

[14] Ba Maw, *Breakthrough in Burma*, pp. 185-6.

east Asian states owe their independence to the Japanese. Breaking the colonial continuity meant, as the French saw, that it would be difficult to return. Securing independence out of the international situation at the end of the war was, however, very much the work of the Southeast Asian elites themselves.

'Japanese military occupation temporarily severed Western control and weakened the former rulers,' wrote Ienaga Saburo. 'But this was merely an incidental consequence: Japan did not liberate Asia.'[15] Louis Allen put it differently: 'Japan liberated Southeast Asia in the perspective of its own defeat, rather than as a set policy from the start.'[16] Again differently, and perhaps most persuasively, Joyce Lebra argued that the Japanese army did not have 'basically revolutionary goals', but that the occupation 'stimulated many endemic revolutionary forces. Part of this was inadvertent, but part of it also derived from the Japanese political goal of encouraging anti-colonial independence movements.'[17]

The elites had been helped by the Japanese, but also hindered, since the main aim had been mobilisation, not the creation of a new state. They now faced the victorious Allies, the colonial powers in somewhat equivocal relationship with the triumphant US. Only the Vietnamese – caught up in a new war, though a cold one – were unable to secure independence for their country. The victory in this war was the victory of the Southeast Asian elites, though they had been fought over more than they had fought. As Lee Kuan Yew was to put it:

My colleagues and I are of that generation who went through the Second World War and the Japanese occupation and became determined that no one – neither the Japanese nor the British – had the right to push and kick us around. We were determined that we could govern ourselves and bring up our children in a country where we could be self-respecting people.[18]

It remained to be seen whether the elite could redeem the suffering and meet the expectations of the masses for whom they now became directly responsible.

[15] Ienaga, *Japan's Last War*, pp. 179-80.
[16] Allen, in Newell, *Japan in Asia*, p. 98.
[17] Lebra, *Armies*, p. 181.
[18] q. Otabe Yuji in Lowe and Moeshart, *Western Interactions*, p. 89.

Reparations

In the task of development they were to look for Japanese help, even to borrow Japanese models, and the Japanese responded. The onset of the Cold War had encouraged the United States to change its attitude to Japan, and under the 'reverse course', the *zaibatsu* and the wartime planners were recruited for the restoration and expansion of the economy. Unable in the Korean War to look to China, Japan looked to Southeast Asia. One month before the truce, Prime Minister Yoshida remarked:

I do not think it is necessary to dwell upon the importance of our relations with Southeast Asia, since we cannot expect much from our relations with China. The government desires to extend every possible cooperation for the prosperity of the countries of Southeast Asia in the form of capital, technique, service or otherwise, in order thus to advance further the relations of reciprocal benefit and common prosperity.[19]

Hence what Shigemitsu, back as foreign minister, called 'economic diplomacy'.

The payment of reparations, organised on a bilateral basis after the peace treaty, was a means of re-entry into the Southeast Asian economies. The knowledge of the resources acquired in the war was turned to account, and so, too, the Chinese commercial networks. 'Japan's so-called reparations programme was invented by business, and run by business, exclusively as a self-serving plan.'[20] 'Reparations were not a serious burden upon Japan at any time.'[21]

Becoming a worldwide economic power, Japan still played a major economic role in Southeast Asia in the 1960s. Indeed its 'over-presence' produced a reaction, as Prime Minister Tanaka found on his 1974 tour. Fukuda enunciated a different approach in 1977:

Diplomacy towards Southeast Asia until now was contact through money and goods. It was not contact based on the policy of good friends acting for mutual benefit. Even when viewed from our country there was an impression of economic aggression and arrogant manners, and it was a situation which was symbolized by the expression 'economic animal'.[22]

[19] q. Chaivat in Chaivat Khamchoo and E.B. Reynolds, eds, *Thai-Japanese Relations in Historical Perspecite*, Bangkok: Innomedia, 1988, p. 239.

[20] Jon Halliday and Gavan McComack, *Japanese Imperialism Today*, Harmondsworth: Penguin, 1973, p. 21.

[21] L. Olson, *Japan in Postwar Asia*, London: Pall Mall Press, 1970, p. 26.

[22] q. Sudo Sueo, *The Fukuda Doctrine and ASEAN*, Singapore: ISEAS, 1992, p. 158.

The new co-prosperity was concerned with the security of the Straits, now the route of Japan's oil supply, and the redistribution of some of the homeland's industrial activities.

Continuities can be found in this activity, as in the rhetoric. In some sense the Japanese were back on the track that Ashton-Gwatkin had pictured their taking in the 1920s. The continuities are, however, combined with discontinuities. In the expansive conditions of recent decades, globalism prevails over regionalism, and Japan's interests are global not regional. Southeast Asia is not part of a Sphere. But the Japanese invasion, and the subsequent creation of independent states, removed it from the economic and political framework of the colonial period, and opened it to the wider world.

Like the 'reverse course', the 'Green Revolution' was a product of the Cold War. The term, apparently invented by William S. Gaud, a USAID administrator, covered the development and application of a 'new technology' that would increase rice production, banish hunger and avoid 'Red Revolution'.[23] It involved the development of new strains and the application of fertilisers, and got under way in the 1960. The Japanese had attempted to introduce Northeast Asian strains and seed fertiliser techniques during the occupation.[24] In Java they characteristically acted in their 'command' style, neglecting local factors in their top-down approach.[25] Their methods cancelled out their objectives, but in different circumstances their concepts were to be realised. Is it too fanciful to draw a comparison between these endeavours and those in the economic and political fields?

Malaya, Singapore and Borneo

The extent of Japanese non-combat violence varied from territory to territory and from phase to phase. In some cases it was measured by economic or political requirements. Even then it might get out of hand. The devolution of power, as well as the lack of discipline or training for an occupation, indeed made that probable. In territories where a local elite remained in control, and the Japanese wished to conciliate it, the extent of their violence might be curbed.

[23] B.H. Farmer, 'Perspectives on the "Green Revolution" in South Asia', *MAS*, 20, 1 (February 1986), p. 176.

[24] Kratoska, *Occupation*, p. 271. Sato, *War*, p. 177. Jose, *Japanese Occupation*, p. 211.

[25] Van der Eng in Kratoska, ed., *Food Supplies*, p. 21.

Where they were dealing with a displaced colonial population, or with Chinese, the reverse would be true. The indigenous population was likely still, however, to be subjected to an everyday level of violence that could only alienate it.

In Singapore the prisoners of war were interned at Changi, the military prisoners at Selarang and the civilians in Changi gaol – their march out there led by the governor, but not jeered at, as the Japanese hoped[26] – and then at Sime Road. Initially conditions were tolerable, partly because Asahi, in charge, was a considerate man.[27] Life was harsher under his successor, Tominaga, and hunger, disease and hard manual work took their toll. Following a sabotage exploit in Syonan harbour – with which in fact the internees were not connected – the *kempeitai* raided the goal on 10 October. One suspect was executed and of the fifty-seven arrested fourteen died as a result of their treatment.[28]

The conditions at Changi became yet more rigorous, but those who stayed there or at Sime Road were better off than those in camps in Malaya and Netherlands India. Military prisoners were sent off to work on the Burma railway, however, and more than a third perished. Late in 1943, the Japanese decided to build an airport at Changi, using military prisoners, some 12,000 of whom were eventually crowded into the goal.[29] It was completed in May 1945.

The Chinese in Malaya and Singapore were 'treated more harshly than their countrymen in any other part of South-East Asia'.[30] The initial massacres in Singapore could not be forgotten. Worried lest his under-strength Twenty-Fifth Army could not maintain the security of Malaya and Singapore, and apprehensive lest it face the kind of guerrilla warfare the Japanese faced in China itself, Yamashita ordered the 'severe punishment of hostile Chinese'. The result, however, was the *sook ching* or purification by purge. A loosely worded instruction was made over to the *kempeitai*, which proceeded with 'severe and prompt punishment'. 'Many soldiers who had built up animosity towards the Chinese interpreted the term as a summary execution or abused the order,

[26] Montgomery, *Shenton of Singapore*, p. 149.

[27] Turnbull, *History of Singapore*, p. 197.

[28] Joseph Kennedy, *British Civilians and the Japanese War in Malaya and Singapore*, Basingstoke: Macmillan, 1987, pp. 96, 148-9.

[29] Turnbull, *History of Singapore*, pp. 209-11.

[30] Ibid., p. 202.

committing themselves to atrocities.'[31] Plenty of 'undesirables' could be found, and others were 'dobbed in'.

To pick out the wanted men spies, 'bad hats', the riff-raff of society, detectives, informers, ex-convicts just freed from jail were hastily summoned. A volunteer chief, a N.C.O. and three others were used to pick out their colleagues, a Chinese Community leader to rope in all other influential merchants, and communists to identify other communists and even anti-Japanese men to catch their anti friends.[32]

'Some were taken to prison, but most were roped together and either taken out in boats and dumped overboard off Blakang Mati or herded into the sea off Changi and Siglap and machine gunned to death.'[33] It was not only a crime, but a blunder. The *sook ching* was one of the 'most serious stumbling blocks for establishing good relations between Japanese and Chinese', the Syonan police chief found.[34]

'[W]hat was it that men feared most? Ghosts? Sook-chingas? Kidnappings? Blackmail? The Police-lockup? No. It was the fear of being taken to MP-headquarters.' The kempeitai 'by their arrogance, high-handedness and flagrant abuse of power, played a large part in making the occupation period the saddest and darkest epoch in the history of Malaya.'[35]

In Borneo some Europeans attempted to escape the Japanese by fleeing to the interior. In some cases they met their death at the hands of headhunters. One of the 'most horrific'[36] events of the occupation was, however, the massacre of forty-one European men, women and children at Long Nawang in Dutch Borneo in August-September 1942. That was carried out by a party of Japanese marines. According to a Kenyah witness, 'the children suffered the most cruel deaths: forced to climb arecanut palms, they were impaled on the upraised bayonets when they slipped down in exhaustion'.[37] The majority of Europeans were interned in camps

---

[31] Akashi Yoji, 'Japanese Policy towards the Malayan Chinese 1941-1945', *JSEAS*, 1, 2 (September 1970), p. 68.

[32] Chen Su Lan, *Remember Pompong and Oxley Rise*, Singapore: Chen Su Lan Trust, 1969, p. 189.

[33] Turnbull, *History of Singapore*, pp. 193-4.

[34] q. Akashi, 'Japanese Policy', p. 69.

[35] Chin Kee Onn, *Malaya Upside Down*, p. 120.

[36] Reece, *Masa Jepun*, p. 46.

[37] Ibid., p. 49.

at Batu Lintang and elsewhere. Australian and British military prisoners were taken from Singapore to Sandakan in 1942 and 1943 to work on airfield and other construction projects.

'The very sight of a KP man was enough to make the more nervous of us tremble in our shoes,' as the *Sarawak Tribune* was to put it in January 1946.[38] The initial target of the *kempeitai* in Sarawak was the organisers of the China Relief Committee in Kuching, Sibu and Jesselton. Most were released after beatings and torture. The emphasis was less on punishment than in Singapore, and more on securing cooperation. Massive reprisals, however, followed Albert Kwok's uprising late in 1943. In addition some of the Australians at the Sandakan camp were tried and executed.

The Allied air raids that began in March 1945 prompted vindictive treatment of the Batu Lintang prisoners. 'I got all my bashings because I was an American,' said Harry S. Stone, USN, who had been captured in Java in 1942. 'Every time the planes – American – came over they would come and give you rifle butts.'[39] The Allied landings intensified KP activity. Lists of those who might help the Allies were drawn up. There were last-minute executions in Miri. Punjabi prisoners were executed en masse at Kuala Belait on 14 June. A mass grave of Brunei dignitaries was later found by the Australians. As they approached, the Japanese had prepared to retreat into the interior. The Batu Lintang prisoners, it transpired, were to act as fatigue parties for the retreat. On arrival up-country, 'those who had not fallen out and been bayoneted on the way were to have been liquidated on the spot'.[40] The surrender averted that.

Those on the Death Marches from the Sandakan camps were less fortunate. 'Altogether, of the more than 2,000 British and Australian prisoners who had set out from Sandakan, only six were still alive at the end of the war.'[41] The Japanese were as violent in the desperation of defeat as in the euphoria of victory, if not more so, but not merely to the Europeans.

The occupation brought an end to the raj and the company, which the British did not restore. The Japanese had not, however, won support among the peoples of Borunai Kita, whatever their

[38] q. ibid., p. 79.

[39] q. ibid., p. 169.

[40] q. ibid., p. 178.

[41] Ibid., p. 179. Cf. Tanaka Yuki, *Hidden Horrors: Japanese War Crimes in World War II*, Boulder, CO: Westview Press, 1996, ch. 2.

treatment of the *orang puteh*. Writing in 1946, an officer of the raj, the fair-minded K.H. Digby, accepted that a military administration could not be compared with a civil administration in normal conditions. Even so, Japanese conduct towards those they ruled had been self-defeating.

The Japanese had ... plenty of sticks with which to beat the authorities they had supplanted, but they ruined their whole cause by far exceeding those authorities in the severity and cruelty of their administration. What use was it for an officer to make a speech on the iniquities of the British, when, on the same day, a sentry assaulted a Mohammedan woman for failing to bow to him?[42]

Netherlands India

The treatment of the imprisoned Dutch seemed all the worse because the end of the war did not bring their immediate release. Instead their fate became caught up in the struggle of the republicans against the Allied forces and against the returning Dutch. Again cruelty was added to starvation and hard labour.

Dieuwke Wendelaar Bonga has described the regime at Muntilan, a camp on the slopes of Merapi, one of several in which she was interned as an adolescent. The women grew vegetables but were not allowed to harvest them. A girl discovered trying to smuggle vegetables back into the camp was severely punished.

At the gate house we all had to stand opposite each other and then we were ordered to beat each other up. This sounds funny, but it was not. If we giggled or did not beat hard enough, the screaming soldiers of the [Indonesian?] guards would do it for us, so we beat. Just in case it would happen again we prepared each other not to beat so hard, but just to pretend. That did not always work, as some girls panicked and really hit hard. It was horrifying.[43]

One girl received a birthday postcard from her mother, a Javanese, who was not in the camp. What was the meaning of the date on it? She tried to explain to the Japanese, but was 'beaten and questioned over and over again. ... Then they had hammered bamboo pins under her nails to make her confess. To what?'[44]

---

[42] q. Reece, *Masa Jepun*, p. 238.
[43] Diuwke Wendelaar Bonga, *Eight Prison Camps*, Athens: Univ. of Ohio Press, 1996, p. 114.
[44] Ibid., p. 123.

Dieuwke's father, a school teacher, was interned in Java, then transferred to Sumatra in May 1944. There he was to take part in buil-ding the trans-Sumatra railway, 'the death railroad of Pakan Baru'.

The Romushas were completely left to fend for themselves and after long, cruel labored workdays they had to find their own food in the jungle. ... The Dutch and British prisoners were strictly forbidden to associate them-selves with these poor men. They were threatened with beatings or worse. ... within a year over twenty-three thousand men died in this hell hole, most of whom were Romushas.[45]

The policies General Imamura adopted towards the Europeans at the outset of the occupation had been declared 'far too lax and magnanimous'. By April most Dutch officials had been interned. Other civilians had to register and were divided into three cate-gories: 'persons of ardent hostility', 'of restricted residence' and 'of designated residence'. In 1943 those in the third category were themselves restricted by the construction of barbed wire fences. Few Japanese officers were available, and Korean 'working troops' and Indonesian youths were used as guards. Dutch women were also used as comfort-women. The postwar Dutch tribunal, dealing with war criminals, did not take account of Asian women forced into prostitution. Nor, however, did it try Indonesian troop supplements for war crimes. And it tried Japanese officers for mur-der and mistreatment of troop supplements.[46] 'For three and a half years', read the political manifesto issued over Hatta's signature in November 1945,

our people have suffered from the oppression and cruelty of the Japanese, unprecedented in the previous decades of Dutch colonial rule. Our entire population has been treated like the cheapest goods to be wasted in the war effort. ... Yet in this period there has developed among our people a new consciousness, a fiercer national feeling than ever before.[47]

The Philippines

Elsewhere in the Sphere, similar patterns appeared: violent treat-ment not only of the Western prisoners, civilian and military, but

[45] Ibid., pp. 179, 180-1.
[46] Utsumi Aiko, 'Japanese Army Internment Policies for Enemy Civilians During the Asia-Pacific War' in D. Denoon *et al.*, eds, *Multicultural Japan*, Cambridge Univ. Press, 1996, pp. 186-7, 189, 194-5, 198-9, 208n.
[47] q. Anderson, *Java*, p. 181.

also of the local population. In the Philippines 11,000 American soldiers and 62,000 Filipinos who surrendered at Bataan had to undergo the infamous 120km. death march. Perhaps 10,000 Filipinos and 650 Americans died on the way to Tarlac. At least 15,000 died in the camp. The Japanese began releasing them in July 1942, by which time the death rate was 334 a day.[48] The treatment of the civilian American prisoners interned at the University of Santo Tomas, never good, worsened as the war went on. The Japanese medical officer objected, however, to the use of the words 'starvation' and 'malnutrition' on the death certificates.[49]

The level of violence and atrocity in the Philippines was increased by the presence of guerrilla war. Streets, blocks and towns were subjected to 'zonification', the population being paraded in front of a masked spy who singled out supposed guerrillas for execution.[50]

The practice ... of slapping Filipinos in the face, of tying them to posts or making them kneel in public, at times in the heat of the sun, or beating them – this upon the slightest fault, mistake or provocation, or without any other reason than failure to understand each other's language – is certain to create resentment, [Claro Recto told Wachi in June 1944] ... Even more serious is the practice of inflicting cruel, unusual and excessive punishments upon persons arrested on mere suspicion, during their investigation and before their guilt has been established.

And yet independence had been announced. The great principles that had been proclaimed had 'not percolated to the rank and file of the Japanese soldiers and civilians in the Philippines'.[51]

The final struggle for Manila was accompanied by massacres and atrocities for which Yamashita was to be held responsible and hanged.[52]

The Japanese knew that all the Filipinos were against them and that many of the younger men secretly belonged to various guerrilla units. They probably believed that if they did not fill the civilian population of the city with terror they would have to fight the civilians as well as the Americans. The rest was fiendish cruelty.[53]

[48] Jose, *Japanese Occupation*, p. 53.
[49] Hartendorp, *Japanese Occupation*, II, 508.
[50] Syjuco, *The Kempei Tai*, pp. 43-5.
[51] q. Agoncillo, *The Fateful Years*, pp. 113, 122.
[52] Finn, *Winners in Peace*, p. 81.
[53] Hartendorp, *Japanese Occupation*, II, 556.

Burma

Burma, like the Philippines, was twice fought over. There was, however, no Burman equivalent to the guerrilla warfare of the Philippines, and Rangoon was evacuated rather than fought over in 1945. The *kempeitai* were, however, true to form. Ba Than wrote:

When the British were here, the British did things at least with some semblance of law and justice. But the Japanese knew no law. ... The Thakins used to say that the British were sucking our blood. But soon they realised that the Japanese were here to suck the marrow out of our bones.[54]

Even Ba Maw, explaining tensions between the Japanese and the Burmese, found one cause 'to which nothing can give even the appearance of being rational ... the arrogance and brutality of the Japanese soldier ... so senseless and self-defeating'.[55]

Thailand

The nature of the relationship with the Thai government checked the excesses of the Japanese there. The Ban Pong incident was touched off when a Japanese sentry struck a Thai monk, and it concluded a year in which the Japanese, despite the alliance the Thais had made, failed to create the harmonious relations the Sphere rhetoric suggested.[56] The use of violence was, however, contained.

Although the *kempeitai* had, as Reynolds puts it, 'a well-earned reputation for ruthlessness, and in most areas of the Japanese empire was a law unto itself, the Thai government's success in maintaining control of domestic affairs under the alliance did restrict its activities in Thailand to a considerable degree'. *Kempeitai* men sometimes abused Thais suspected of anti-Japanese crimes, 'but Police General Adun guarded his turf with particular jealousy and was known to make preemptive arrests to keep Thai suspects out of Japanese hands'.[57]

Vietnam

In Vietnam the relationship with the Japanese was even more ambiguous. Their power impressed: by contrast to the Japanese,

---

[54] q. Yoon, 'Japan's Occupation', p. 194.
[55] Ba Maw, *Breakthrough in Burma*, p. 276.
[56] Reynolds, *Southern Advance*, pp. 138-9.
[57] Ibid., p. 180.

'the French colonial army seemed flabby and ill-disciplined', as Marr writes.

Stories circulated of Japanese siding with Vietnamese in street arguments with *colons*, even to the point of slapping the Frenchmen. Although such incidents must have been very rare, French officials in the countryside as well as the cities noted uncomfortably how any mention of Japanese victories over Europeans produced expressions of satisfaction among Vietnamese.

Yet at the same time the Vietnamese could note that the Japanese did not dislodge the French as they had the British, the Americans and the Dutch.

Gradually other, more sinister stories began to spread, about Japanese brutality to Vietnamese, detention of individuals by the Kenpeitai, torture, and beheadings. Some Vietnamese wondered if the Japanese might prove to be more oppressive than the French.[58]

The presence of both, it may be argued, checked the day-to-day oppression of either. Violence and atrocity, in Vietnam's case, were deferred to a later war.

The treatment the Japanese afforded civilian and military prisoners of war was not forgotten, though in the aftermath of the peace treaty signed during the Cold War governments accepted only a limited compensation. The treatment they afforded local people is less often remembered in Western literature, but it has not been forgotten either. Yet it may be argued that the local elites, though for the most part remarkably successful in securing political independence for their countries out of the chaos and dislocation the Japanese had created, and thus making a reality of the idealism that the Japanese themselves had only half-heartedly put forward, were far less successful in meeting the hopes that had been aroused among the masses. There, too, the Japanese legacy was of little help.

The Japanese, Elsbree concluded, 'fumbled' their opportunity to link their fortunes with the national movements. Like the colonial powers, they gave ground 'grudgingly'.[59] They also failed to

---

[58] Marr, *Vietnam 1945*, pp. 90-2.
[59] Willard H. Elsbree, *Japan's Role in Southeast Asian Nationalist Movements 1940-45*, Cambridge, MA: Harvard Univ. Press, 1953, pp. 164-5.

give the nationalist leaders any real experience of government. 'The farce of Japanese independence did not teach responsible handling of problems.'[60] Their political legacy was of mass mobilisation. The patterns of the wartime Indies were renewed in Sukarno's Indonesia, and his political romanticism was 'born out of, or ... strongly stimulated by, the experience of Japanese rule'.[61] His successor's New Order bore the stamp of his wartime military training and experience, in both its political and economic policies. The same was true of Ne Win, the dominant figure of postwar Burma. The rhetoric of Marcos's New Society irresistibly recalls the sickly style of Vargas. In the war the Japanese had trained a number of Southeast Asians in the homeland, such as Pengiran Muhammad Yusof of Brunei, and Ungku Aziz, planner of Malaysia's Look East policy. Their main lessons were delivered on the spot, and they had to do with the style of politics.

---

[60] Guyot, 'Political Impact', p. 246.
[61] Anderson in Silverstein, *Southeast Asia*, p. 25.

BIBLIOGRAPHY

Agawa Hiroyuki. *The Reluctant Admiral. Yamamoto and the Imperial Navy*, Tokyo, New York: Kodansha, 1979.

Agoncillo, T. A. *The Fateful Years*, Quezon City: Garcia, 1965.

Akashi Yoji. 'Japanese Policy towards the Malayan Chinese 1941-45', *JSEAS*, 1, 2 (September 1970), pp. 61-89.

Aldrich, Richard J. *The Key to the South*, Kuala Lumpur: Oxford Univ. Press, 1993.

Allen, Louis. *Singapore 1941-42*, London: Davis-Poynter, 1977.

Anderson, Benedict R.O'G. *Some Aspects of Indonesian Politics under the Japanese Occupation: 1944-45*, Ithaca, NY: Cornell Univ. Press, 1961.

——*Java in a Time of Revolution*, Ithaca, NY Cornell Univ. Press, 1972.

Ba Maw. *Breakthrough in Burma*, New Haven, CT: Yale Univ. Press, 1968.

Ba Than. *The Roots of the Revolution*, Rangoon, 1962.

Bamadhaj, H. 'The Impact of the Japanese Occupation on Malay Society and Politics (1941-45)', MA thesis, University of Auckland, 1975.

Barnhart, M. *Japan Prepares for Total War*, Ithaca, NY: Cornell Univ. Press, 1987.

Baudouin, Paul. *The Private Diaries*, trans. C. Petrie, London: Eyre & Spottiswood, 1948.

Beasley, W.G. *Japanese Imperialism*, Oxford: Clarendon Press, 1987.

Benda, Harry J. *The Cresent and the Rising Sun*, The Hague and Bandung: Van Hoeve, 1958.

——, James K. Irikura and Kishi Koishi. *Japanese Military Administration in Indonesia. Selected Documents*, New Haven, CT: Yale Univ. Press, 1965.

—— and John Larkin, eds, *The World of Southeast Asia*, New York: Harper & Row, 1967.

Bootsma, N.A., *Buren in de koloniale tijd*, Dordrecht: Foris, 1986.

Bose, Sugata. 'Starvation amidst Plenty: The Making of Famine in Bengal, Honan, and Tonkin, 1942-45', *MAS*, 24, 4 (1990), pp. 699-727.

Boyce, Robert and E.M. Robertson, eds, *Paths to War*, Basingstoke: Macmillan, 1989.

Brailey, N.J. *Thailand and the Fall of Singapore*, Boulder, CO: Westview Press, 1986.

Bui Minh Dung. 'Japan's Role in the Vietnamese Starvation of 1944-45', *MAS*, 29, 3(1995), pp. 573-618.

269

Butow, R.C.J. *Japan's Decision to Surrender*, Stanford Univ. Press, 1954.

Callahan, Raymond. *Burma 1942-45*, London: Davis-Poynter, 1978.

Centre for East Asian Cultural Studies. *The Meiji Japan through Contemporary Sources*, Tokyo, 1969-72.

Chandler, D. 'The Kingdom of Kampuchea, March-October 1945', *JSEAS*, 17, 1 (March 1986), pp. 80-93.

Cheah Boon Kheng. 'The Japanese Occupation of Malaya, 1941-45', *Indonesia*, 28 (October 1979), pp. 85-120.

Chen Su Lan. *Remember Pompong and Oxley Rise*, Singapore: Chen Su Lan Trust, 1965.

Chin Kee Onn. *Malaya Upside Down*, Singapore, Kuala Lumpur and Hong Kong: Federal, 1976.

Christie, C.J. 'Marxism and the History of the Nationalist Movements in Laos', *JSEAS*, 10, 1 (March 1979), pp. 146-55.

Churchill, W.S. *The Hinge of Fate*, London: Cassell, 1951.

Cole, Allen B. ed. *Conflict in Indo-China and International Repercussions*, Ithaca, NY: Cornell Univ. Press, 1956.

Collier, Basil. *The War in the Far East: A Military History*, London: Heinemann, 1969.

Conroy, H. and H. Wray, *Pearl Harbor Reexamined*, Honolulu: Univ. of Hawaii Press, 1990.

Coox, Alvin. *Nomonhan*, Stanford Univ. Press, 1985.

Crowley, J.B. *Japan's Quest for Autonomy*, Washington, DC: Public Affairs Press, 1966.

Denoon, D. *et al.*, eds, *Multicultural Japan*, Cambridge Univ. Press, 1996.

Detwiler, Donald S. and Charles B. Burdick, comps, *War in Asia and the Pacific*, New York: Garland, 1980.

Dick, Howard. 'Japan's Economic Expansion in the Netherlands Indies Between the First and Second World Wars', *JSEAS*, 20, 2 (September 1989), pp. 244-72.

Dockrill. S., ed., *From Pearl Harbor to Hiroshima*, Basingstoke: Macmillan, 1994.

Dower, John W. *Empire and Aftermath*, Cambridge, MA: Harvard University Press, 1979.

—— *War without Mercy*, New York: Pantheon, 1986.

Ducoroy, Maurice. *Ma trahison en Indochine*, Paris: Editions Internationales, 1949.

Duus, P. *Party Rivalry and Political Change in Taisho Japan*, Cambridge, MA: Harvard Univ. Press, 1968.

—— *et al.*, eds. *The Japanese Wartime Empire*, Princeton Univ. Press, 1996.

Elsbree, Willard H. *Japan's Role in Southeast Asian Nationalist Movements 1940 to 1945*, Cambridge, MA: Harvard Univ. Press, 1953.

Eng, Pierre van der. *Food Supply in Java during War and Decolonisation, 1940-1950*, Hull: Centre for South-East Asian Studies, 1994.

Evans, Stephen R. *Sabah (North Borneo) under the Rising Sun Government*, Singapore: printed by Tropical Press, 1991.

Fay, Peter Ward. *The Forgotten Army. India's Armed Struggle for Independence 1942-1945*, Ann Arbor: Univ. of Michigan Press, 1993.

Hood, E. Th. 'Japan's Relations with Thailand: 1928-1941', Ph.D. thesis, Univ. of Washington, 1967.

—— 'The 1940 Franco-Thai Border Dispute and Phibuun Songkhraam's Commitment to Japan', *JSEAH*, 10, 2 (September 1969), pp. 304-25.

Fraser, T.G. and P. Lowe, eds, *Conflict and Amity in East Asia*, Basingstoke: Macmillan, 1992.

Friend, Theodore. *Between Two Empires*, New Haven, CT: Yale Univ. Press, 1965.

Fujiwara Iwaichi. *F. Kikan*, trans. Akashi Yoji, Hong Kong, Singapore and Kuala Lumpur: Heinemann, 1983.

Garcia, M., ed., *Documents on the Japanese Occupation of the Philippines*, Manila: Philippine Historical Association, 1965.

Goodman, Grant K. *Four Aspects of Philippine-Japanese Relations, 1930-1940*, New Haven, CT: Yale Univ. Press, 1967.

——, comp., *Imperial Japan and Asia*, New York: Columbia Univ. Press, 1967.

—— 'Consistency is the Hobgoblin', *JSEAS*, 14, 1 (March 1983), pp. 79-94.

—— 'The Japanese Occupation of the Philippines: Commonwealth Sustained', *Philippine Studies*, 36 (1988), pp. 98-104.

——*Japanese Cultural Policies in Southeast Asia during World War II*, Basingstoke: Macmillan, 1991.

Gopinath, A. *Manuel L. Quezon: The Tutelary Democrat*, Quezon City: New Day, 1987.

Goto Ken'ichi. 'Indonesia under the Greater East Asia Co-Prosperity Sphere' in Denoon, *Multicultural Japan*, pp. 160-73.

—— '*Returning to Asia': Japan-Indonesia Relations, 1930s-1942*, Tokyo: Ryukei Shyosha, 1997.

Guyot, D. 'The Political Impact of the Japanese Occupation of Burma', Ph.D. thesis, Yale Univ., 1966.

Hartendorp, A.V.H. *The Japanese Occupation of the Philippines*, Manila: Bookmark, 1967.

Hicks, George. *Japan's War Memories*, Aldershot: Ashgate, 1997, 1998.

Huynh Kim Khanh. 'The Vietnamese August Revolution Reinterpreted', *JAS*, 30, 4 (August 1971), pp. 761-82.

Ichizawa Kenjiro. 'Anti-Japanese Resistance Movement in Thailand 1941-1945', in K.M. de Silva *et al.*, eds, *Asian Panorama*, New Delhi: Vikas, 1990, pp. 54-69.

Ienaga Saburo. *Japan's Last War*, Oxford: Blackwell, 1979.

Ike Nobutake, ed., *Japan's Decision for War*, Stanford Univ. Press, 1967.

Iritani Toshio. *Group Psychology of the Japanese in Wartime*, London, New York: Kegan International, 1991.

Iriye Akira. *Pacific Estrangement*, Cambridge, MA: Harvard Univ. Press, 1972.

—— *Power and Culture: The Japanese-American War 1941-1945*, Cambridge, MA: Harvard Univ. Press, 1981.

Itagaki Yoichi. 'Some Aspects of the Japanese Policy for Malaya' in K.G. Tregonning, ed., *Papers on Malayan History, Singapore*: JSEAH, 1962, pp. 256-67.

Izumiya Tatsuro. *The Minami Organ*, trans. Tun Aung Chain, Rangoon: Higher Education Dept. 1981.

Jones, F.C. *Japan's New Order in East Asia*, London: Oxford Univ. Press, 1954.

José, Ricardo T. *The Japanese Occupation*, vol. 7 of *Kasaysayan: The Story of the Filipino People*, Manila: Asia Publishing Co., 1998.

Kahin, George McT. *Nationalism and Revolution in Indonesia*, Ithaca, NY: Cornell Univ. Press, 1952.

Kanahele, George S. 'The Japanese Occupation of Indonesia: Prelude to Independence', Ph.D. thesis, Cornell Univ. 1967.

Kennedy, Joseph. *British Civilians and the Japanese War in Malaya and Singapore, 1941-45*, Basingstoke: Macmillan, 1987.

Chaivat Khamchoo and E. B. Reynolds, eds, *Thai-Japanese Relations in Historical Perspective*, Bangkok: Innomedia, 1988.

Kirby, S. W. *Singapore: The Chain of Disaster*, London: Cassell, 1971.

—— et al., *The War against Japan*, 5 vols, London: HMSO, 1957-69.

Kratoska, P. 'Banana Money: Consequences of the Demonetization of Wartime Japanese Currency in British Malaya', *JSEAS*, 23, 2 (September 1992), pp. 322-45.

—— *The Japanese Occupation of Malaya*, London: Hurst; Sydney: Allen & Unwin, 1998.

——, ed. *Malaya and Singapore during the Japanese Occupation*, Singapore: JSEAS, 1995.

——, ed. *Food Supplies and the Japanese Occupation in South-East Asia*, Basingstoke: Macmillan, 1998.

Kurasawa Aiko. 'Mobilization and Control: A Study of Social Change in Rural Java', Ph.D. thesis, Cornell Univ. 1988.

Laffey, John F. 'French Far Eastern Policy in the 1930s', *MAS*, 23, 1 (1989), pp. 117-49.

Lathrop, Alan K. 'The Employment of Chinese Nationalist Troops in the First Burma Campaign', *JSEAS*, 12, 2 (September 1981), pp. 403-22.

Lebra, Joyce C. *Japan's Greater East Asia Co-Prosperity Sphere in World War II*, Kuala Lumpur: Oxford Univ. Press, 1975.

—— *Japanese-trained Armies in Southeast Asia*, New York: Columbia Univ. Press, 1977.

Legge, John. *Sukarno*, Harmondsworth: Penguin, 1973.

Lensen, G.A. *The Strange Neutrality; Soviet-Japanese Relations during the Second World War, 1941-1945*, Tallahassee: Diplomatic Press, 1972.

Leong, Stephen. 'The Malayan Overseas Chinese and the Sino-Japanese War, 1937-1941', *JSEAS*, 10, 2 (September 1979), pp. 293-320.

Li Yuk-wai. 'The Chinese Resistance Movement in the Philippines during the Japanese Occupation', *JSEAS*, 23, 2 (September 1992), pp. 308-21.

Lockhart, Bruce M. *The End of the Vietnamese Monarchy*, New Haven, CT: Yale Univ. Press, 1993.

Lone, S. *Japan's First Modern War*, Basingstoke: Macmillan, 1994.

Lowe, P. and H. Moeshart, eds, *Western Interactions with Japan: Expansion, the Armed Forces and Readjustment 1859-1956*, Folkestone: Japan Library, 1990.

Lu, David J. *From the Marco Polo Bridge to Pearl Harbor*, Washington, DC: Public Affairs Press, 1961.

Lucas, Anton, ed., *Local Opposition and Underground Resistance to the Japanese in Java 1942-1945*, Monash Univ., 1986.

Mackie, J.A.C. *The Chinese in Indonesia*, Honolulu: Univ. of Hawaii Press, 1976.

Mahajani, Usha. *The Role of Indian Minorities in Burma and Malaya*, Bombay: Vora, 1960.

—— *Philippine Nationalism*, St Lucia: Univ. of Queensland Press, 1971.

Malay, A.J. *Occupied Philippines: The Role of Jorge B. Vargas*, Manila: Filipiniana Book Guild, 1967.

Marder, A. J. *Old Friends, New Enemies*, Oxford: Clarendon Press, 1981, (with others) 1990.

Marr, David G. *Vietnam 1945: The Quest for Power*, Berkeley: Univ. of California Press, 1995.

Martin, Bernd. *Japan and Germany in the Modern World*, Oxford: Berg, 1995.

Maxwell. G., comp. *The Civil Defence of Malaya*, London: Hutchinson, 1943.

McCoy, A., ed. *Southeast Asia under the Japanese Occupation*, New Haven, CT: Yale Univ. Press, 1980.

Meo, L.D. *Japan's Radio War on Australia 1941-1945*, Melbourne Univ. Press, 1968.

Middlebrook, M. and Patrick Mahony. *Battleship. The Loss of the 'Prince of Wales' and the 'Repulse'*, London: Allen Lane, 1977.

Miner, Deborah N. 'United States Policy toward Japan 1941: The Assumption that Southeast Asia was vital to the British War Effort', Ph.D. thesis, Columbia Univ., 1976.

Montgomery, B. *Shenton of Singapore*, London: Leo Cooper, 1984.

Morley, James W., ed. *Dilemmas of Growth in Prewar Japan*, Princeton Univ. Press, 1971.

——, ed., *Japan's Foreign Policy 1868-1941*, New York: Columbia Univ. Press, 1974.

—— *The Fateful Choice. Japan's Advance into Southeast Asia 1939-1941*, New York: Columbia Univ. Press, 1980.

Murakami Sachiko. 'Japan's Thrust into French Indochina 1940-1945', Ph.D. theis, New York Univ., 1981.

Myers, Ramon H. and Mark R. Peattie, eds, *The Japanese Colonial Empire, 1895-1945*, Princeton Univ. Press, 1984.

Nakamura Mitsuo. 'General Imamura and the Early Period of Japanese Occupation', *Indonesia*, 10 (1970), pp. 1-26.

Newell, William H., ed., *Japan in Asia, 1942-1945*, Singapore Univ. Press, 1981.

Nish, Ian, ed. *Indonesian Experience: The Role of Japan and Britain, 1943-1948*, London School of Economics, 1980.

——, ed. *Anglo-Japanese Alienation 1919-1952*, Cambridge Univ. Press, 1982.

Nitz, Kiyoko Kurusu. 'Japanese Military Policy towards French Indochina during the Second World War', *JSEAS*, 14, 2 (September 1983), pp. 328-50.

—— 'Independence without Nationalists? The Japanese and Vietnamese Nationalism during the Japanese Period, 1940-1945', *JSEAS*, 15, 1 (March 1984), pp. 108-33.

Nu. *Burma under the Japanese*, trans. and ed. J.S. Furnivall, London: Macmillan, 1954.

Numnonda, Thamsook. *Thailand and the Japanese Presence, 1941-45*, Singapore: ISEAS, 1977.

Oba Sadao. *The 'Japanese' War*, trans. Anne Kareko, Sandgate: Japan Library, 1995.

Onorato, M.P., ed. *Origins of the Philippine Republic*, Ithaca, NY: Cornell Univ. Press, 1974.

Ooi Keat Gin. *Rising Sun Over Borneo*, Basingstoke: Macmillan, 1999.

——, ed. *Japanese Empire in the Tropics*, Athens: Univ. of Ohio Press, 1998.

Osman, Sabibah. 'Japanese Economic Activities in Sabah from the 1890s until 1941', *JSEAS*, 29, 1 (March 1998), pp. 24-43.

Owen, N.G., ed. *The Philippines and the United States. Studies in Past and Present Interactions*, Ann Arbor: Univ. of Michigan Press, 1983.

Percival, A.E. *The War in Malaya*, London: Eyre & Spottiswood, 1949.

Petillo, Carol M. 'Douglas MacArthur: the Philippine Years', Ph.D. thesis, Rutgers Univ., 1979.

Phillips, Richard T. 'The Japanese Occupation of Hainan', *MAS*, 14, 1 (1980), pp. 93-109.

Post, Peter. 'Japan and the Integration of the Netherlands East Indies into the World Economy, 1868-1940', *Review of Indonesian and Malaysian Affairs*, 27, 1-2 (1993), pp. 134-65.

—— and Elly Touwen-Bouwsma, eds, *Japan, Indonesia and the War*, Leiden: KITLV P, 1997.

Prasad, B., ed. *Official History of the Indian Armed Forces in the Second World War 1939-45: Campaigns in South-East Asia 1941-1942*, Combined Inter-Services Historical Section India and Pakistan, 1960.

Quezon, Manuel L. *The Good Fight*, New York: Appleton-Century, 1946.

Reece, R.H.W. *Masa Jepun*, Kuching: Sarawak Literary Society, 1998.

Reid, A., and Oki Akira, eds, *The Japanese Experience in Indonesia*, Athens: Univ. of Ohio Press, 1986.

Reynolds, E.B. 'Aftermath of Alliance: The Wartime Legacy in Thai-Japanese Relations', *JSEAS*, 21, 1 (March 1990), pp. 66-87.

——, *Thailand and Japan's Southern Advance 1940-1945*, New York: St Martin's Press, 1994.

Rose, Mavis. *Indonesia Free*, Ithaca, NY: Cornell Univ. Press, 1987.

Salim, Leon. *Prisoners at Kota Cane*, ed. Audrey Kahin, Ithaca: Cornell Univ. Press, 1986.

Sandhu, K.S. and Paul Wheatley, eds, *Melaka: The Transformation of a Malay Capital*, Kuala Lumpur: Oxford Univ. Press, 1983.

Saniel, J.M. *Japan and the Philippines*, Quezon City: Univ. of the Philippines Press, 1962.

Santaputra, Charivat. 'Thai Foreign Policy 1932-1946', Ph.D. thesis, Univ. of Southampton, 1982.

Sareen, T.R. *Japan and the Indian National Army*, Delhi: Agam Prakashan, 1986.

——, ed. *Select Documents on the Indian National Army*, Delhi: Agam Prakashan, 1988.

Sato Shigeru. *War, Nationalism and Peasants*, Sydney: Allen & Unwin, 1994.

Seguin, Paul B. 'The Deteriorating Strategic Position of Japan: 1853-1945', Ph.D. thesis, Univ. of Minnesota, 1972.

Setchachuay, Vivat. 'United States-Thailand Relations During World War II', Ph.D. thesis, Brigham Young Univ., 1977.

Shigemitsu Mamoru. *Japan and her Destiny*, trans. D. White, London: Hutchinson, 1958.

Shillony, B.-A. *Politics in Wartime Japan*, Oxford: Clarendon Press, 1981.

Shimizu Hajime. 'Southeast Asia in Modern Japanese Thought: The Development and Transformation of "Nanshin Ron"', thesis, RSPacS, Australian National Univ., 1980.

—— ' "Nanshin-ron": its Turning Point in World War I', *The Developing Economies*, 25, 4 (December 1987), pp. 386-402.

Shiraishi Saya and Takashi, eds, *The Japanese in Colonial Southeast Asia*, Ithaca, NY: Cornell Univ. Press, 1993.

Shiraishi Takashi and Motoo Furuta, eds, *Indochina in the 1940s and 1950s*, Ithaca, NY: Cornell Univ. Press, 1992.

Silberman, Bernard S. and H.D. Harootunian, eds, *Japan in Crisis*, Princeton Univ. Press, 1974.

Silverstein, Josef. *Southeast Asia in World War II: Four Essays*, New Haven, CT: Yale Univ. Press, 1966.

Slim, W. *Defeat into Victory*, London: Cassell, 1956.

Smethurst, R.J. *A Social Basis for Prewar Japanese Militarism*, Berkeley: Univ. of California Press, 1974.

Smith, Ralph. 'The Japanese Period in Indochina and the Coup of 9 March 1945', *JSEAS*, 9, 2 (September 1978), pp. 268-301.

Smyth, John. *Percival and the Tragedy of Singapore*, London: Macdonald, 1971.

Soriano, Rafaelita H. 'Japanese Occupation of the Philippines, with special reference to Japanese propaganda 1941-1945', Ph.D. thesis, Univ. of Michigan, 1948.

Steinberg, David J. *Philippine Collaboration in World War II*, Ann Arbor: Univ. of Michigan Press, 1967.

Stenson, M.R. *Class, Race and Colonialism in West Malaysia*, St Lucia: Univ. of Queensland Press, 1980.

Storry, R. *The Double Patriots*, London: Chatto & Windus, 1957.

Stowe, J. *Siam Becomes Thailand*, London: Hurst, 1991.

Sudo Sueo. *The Fukuda Doctrine and ASEAN*, Singapore: ISEAS, 1992.

Suwannathat-Pian, K. *Thailand's Durable Premier*, Kuala Lumpur: Oxford Univ. Press, 1995.

Swan, William L. 'Thai-Japanese Monetary Relations at the Start of the Pacific War', *MAS*, 23, 2 (May 1989), pp. 313-47.

—— 'Japan's Intentions for its Greater East Asia Co-Prosperity Sphere', *JSEAS*, 27, 1 (March 1996), pp. 139-49.

Syjuco, Ma. Felisa A. *The Kempei Tai in the Philippines*, Quezon City: New Day, 1988.

Tanaka Yuki. *Hidden Horrors. Japanese War Crimes in World War II*, Boulder, CO: Westview Press, 1996.

Tarling, N. 'Atonement before Absolution: British Policy towards Thailand during World War II', *Journal of the Siam Society*, 66, 1 (January 1978), pp. 22-65.

—— 'Rice and Reconciliation: The Anglo-Thai Peace Negotiations of 1945', *Journal of the Siam Society*, 66, 2 (July 1978), pp. 59-111.

—— '"A Vital British Interest": Britain, Japan, and the Security of Netherlands India during the Inter-War Period', *JSEAS*, 9, 2 (September 1978), pp. 180-218.

—— *The Fourth Anglo-Burmese War*, Gaya: Centre for South East Asian Studies, 1987.

—— 'The British and the First Japanese Move into Indo-China', *JSEAS*, 21, 1 (March 1990), pp. 35-65.

—— *Britain, Southeast Asia and the Onset of the Pacific War*, Cambridge Univ. Press, 1996.

Taylor, Robert H. 'Politics in Late Colonial Burma', *MAS*, 10, 2 (1976), pp. 161-93.

—— *Marxism and Resistance in Burma*, Athens: Univ. of Ohio Press, 1984.

Terami-Wada, M. 'A Japanese Educator in the Philippines: The Case of Shigenobu Mochizuki and the New Philippines Cultural Institute 1942-1945', *Kabar Seberang*, 21 (1991), pp. 69 81.

Thomas, Martin. 'Free France, the British Government and the Future of French Indo-China', *JSEAS*, 28, 1 (March 1997), pp. 137-60.

Thorne, C. *Allies of a Kind. The United States, Britain and the War against Japan*, London: Hamilton, 1978.

—— *The Far Eastern War*, London: Geo. Allen & Unwin, 1986.

Tinker, H. 'A Forgotten Long March ...', *JSEAS*, 6, 1 (March 1975), pp. 1-15.

Togo Shigenori. *The Cause of Japan*, New York: Simon & Schuster, 1956.

Tonnesson, Stein. *The Vietnamese Revolution of 1945*, Oslo: IPRI; London: Sage, 1991.

Toye, Hugh. 'The First Indian National Army, 1941-42', *JSEAS*, 15, 2 (September 1984), pp. 365-81.

Trager, Frank, ed. *Burma: Japanese Military Administration, Selected Documents, 1941-1945*, trans. Won Zoon Yoon, Philadelphia: Univ. of Pennsylvania Press, 1971.

Tran My-Van. 'Japanese through Vietnamese Eyes (1905-1945)', *JSEAS*, 30, 1 (March 1999), pp. 126-46.

Tsuji Masanobu. *Singapore. The Japanese Version*, trans. Margaret E. Lake, London, 1962.

Tsunoda Ryusaku, Wm T. de Bary and Donald Keene, compilers, *Sources of Japanese Tradition*, New York: Columbia Univ. Press, 1958.

Turnbull, C.M. *A History of Singapore*, Kuala Lumpur: Oxford Univ. Press, 1977.

Twang Peck Yang. *The Chinese Business Elite in Indonesia and the Transition to Independence 1940-1950*, Kuala Lumpur: Oxford Univ. Press, 1998.

Ugaki Matome. *Fading Victory*, Univ. of Pittsburgh Press, 1991.

Utsumi Aiko. 'Japanese Army Internment Policies for Enemy Civilians during the Asia-Pacific War', in Denoon, *Multicultural Japan*, pp. 174-209.

Van Mook, H.J. *The Netherlands Indies and Japan*, London: Geo. Allen & Unwin, 1944.

Walker, J. Samuel. *Prompt and Utter Destruction*, Chapel Hill: Univ. of North Carolina Press, 1997.

White, James W., Umegaki Michio and Thomas R. Havens, eds, *The Ambivalence of Nationalism. Modern Japan between East and West*, Lanham MD: Univ. Press of America, 1990.

Willoughby, Charles A., comp., *The Guerrilla Resistance Movement in the Philippines: 1941-1945*, New York: Vantage, 1972.

Wong Kwok Chu. 'The Jones Bills 1912-16', *JSEAS*, 13, 2 (September 1982), pp. 252-69.

Yoon Won Zoon. 'Japan's Occupation of Burma, 1941-1945', Ph.D. thesis, New York Univ., 1971.

—— *Japan's Scheme for the Liberation of Burma: The Role of the Minami Kikan and the 'Thirty Comrades'*, Athens: Univ. of Ohio Press, 1973.

—— 'Military Expediency: A Determining Factor in the Japanese Policy Regarding Burmese Independence', *JSEAS*, 9, 2 (September 1978), pp. 248-67.

Young, Louise. *Japan's Total Empire*, Berkeley: Univ. of California Press, 1998.

Yu-Jose, Lydia N. *Japan Views the Philippines 1900-1944*, Manila: Ateneo de Manila, 1992.

Yuen Choy Leng. 'Japanese Rubber and Iron Investments in Malaya, 1900-1941', *JSEAS*, 5, 1 (March 1974), pp. 18-36.

—— 'The Japanese Community in Malaya before the Pacific War', *JSEAS*, 9, 2 (September 1978), pp. 163-79.

INDEX